Software Engineering
with Reusable Components

T0280299

Springer
Berlin
Heidelberg
New York
Barcelona
Budapest
Hong Kong
London
Milan
Paris
Santa Clara
Singapore
Tokyo

J. Sametinger

Software Engineering with Reusable Components

With 55 Figures and 26 Tables

 Springer

Dr. Johannes Sametinger
Institut für Wirtschaftsinformatik
Johannes-Kepler-Universität Linz
Altenberger Straße 69
A-4040 Linz, Austria

ISBN 978-3-642-08299-3

Cataloging-in-Publication Data applied for
Die Deutsche Bibliothek - CIP-Einheitsaufnahme
Sametinger, Johannes:
Software engineering with reusable components/J. Sametinger.-
Berlin; Heidelberg; New York; Barcelona; Budapest; Hong Kong;
London; Milan; Paris; Santa Clara; Singapore; Tokyo: Springer,
1997

© Springer-Verlag Berlin Heidelberg 2010
Printed in Germany

Cover Design: Künkel + Lopka Werbeagentur, Heidelberg

Preface

Software is rarely built completely from scratch. To a great extent, existing software documents (source code, design documents, etc.) are copied and adapted to fit new requirements. Yet we are far from the goal of making reuse the standard approach to software development.

Software reuse is the process of creating software systems from existing software rather than building them from scratch. Software reuse is still an emerging discipline. It appears in many different forms from ad-hoc reuse to systematic reuse, and from white-box reuse to black-box reuse. Many different products for reuse range from ideas and algorithms to any documents that are created during the software life cycle. Source code is most commonly reused; thus many people misconceive software reuse as the reuse of source code alone. Recently source code and design reuse have become popular with (object-oriented) class libraries, application frameworks, and design patterns.

Software components provide a vehicle for planned and systematic reuse. The software community does not yet agree on what a software component is exactly. Nowadays, the term component is used as a synonym for object most of the time, but it also stands for module or function. Recently the term *component-based* or *component-oriented software development* has become popular. In this context components are defined as *objects plus something*. What *something* is exactly, or has to be for effective software development, remains yet to be seen. However, systems and models are emerging to support that notion.

Systematic software reuse and the reuse of components influence almost the whole software engineering process (independent of what a component is). Software process models were developed to provide guidance in the creation of high-quality software systems by teams at predictable costs. The original models were based on the (mis)conception that systems are built from scratch according to stable requirements. Software process models have been adapted since based on experience, and several changes and improvements have been suggested since the classic *waterfall model*. With increasing reuse of software, new models for software engineering are emerging. New models are based on systematic reuse of well-defined components that have been developed in various projects.

Developing software with reuse requires planning for reuse, developing *for* reuse and *with* reuse, and providing documentation for reuse. The priority of documentation in software projects has traditionally been low. However, proper documentation is a necessity for the systematic reuse of components. If we continue to neglect documentation we will not be able to increase productivity through the reuse of components. Detailed information about components is indispensable.

Software Engineering with Reusable Components is divided into four main parts. They cover the topics software reuse, software components, software engineering and software documentation. These four parts are complemented by an introductory and a concluding chapter. The introductory chapter introduces the notions of *software reuse* and *software component*. The concluding chapter summarizes the subject matter and provides concluding remarks on the limits of component reuse and its prospects. In the following synopsis we briefly sketch the contents of the four main parts.

Part I: Software Reuse

Even though software reuse has been practiced in one form or another over many years, it is still an emerging discipline. In the first part of the book we give a comprehensive overview of the subject, describing benefits and obstacles to software reuse as well as various aspects like reuse techniques and reuse products. Nontechnical aspects like legal, economic, measurement and organizational issues are covered as well. The main focus of the book is on technical aspects of software reuse, especially reuse of software components. However, this part also contains information about other forms of reuse and distinguishes them.

This part of the book provides the reader with a clear understanding of what software reuse is, where the problems are, what benefits we can expect, the activities it encompasses, and which different forms of software reuse exist.

Part II: Software Components

In the second part of the book we give an extensive introduction to software components. We provide a classification of components and composition techniques. This classification goes beyond source code components and also covers aspects from the area of distributed computing and emphasizes the importance of open systems and standards. There is more to software components than functions and classes. Like software reuse, software components go beyond source code. Components cover a broader range than frameworks and patterns do. We give examples of successful component reuse and evaluate them by using the suggested classification scheme.

This part of the book gives the reader an overview of software components, the different kinds of components and their compositions, a taxonomy for components and compositions, and examples of successful component reuse.

Part III: Software Engineering

Software engineering covers activities that are necessary to develop a software system. The reuse of software components has consequences for the way we develop systems. Software life cycles have been influenced by many new developments that resulted in modified models like the risk-based spiral model. Software reuse introduces new activities, like domain analysis, and changes existing ones, e.g., design activities. Developing *with* reuse and developing *for* reuse are the new challenges as compared to developing systems from scratch to meet certain requirements.

This part of the book gives the reader an introduction to software engineering and software process models. Chapters on domain engineering, component engineering and application engineering depict consequences of and influences from the systematic reuse of software components.

Part IV: Software Documentation

Software documentation fulfills the vital function of retaining and transferring knowledge about various aspects of software systems. We cover the part of the documentation that is affected by the reuse of software components, i.e., system documentation. On the one hand, system documentation has to consider the information needs of software reusers. On the other hand, the reuse of software components suggests the reuse of documentation as well.

This part of the book gives the reader an introduction to software documentation in general and details consequences for system documentation that result from the reuse of software components.

Software Engineering with Reusable Components is intended for readers at universities as well as in industry. Any readers who are interested in software reuse in general and in component reuse and component-oriented software engineering in particular will find useful information in this book. Readers can expect to gain a comprehensive overview of software reuse and software components and their influences on software engineering and software documentation.

Acknowledgement. Many people have contributed to the creation of this book. It is impossible to mention them all, but the following persons and organizations have particularly contributed to this work.

- *Prof. Gustav Pomberger* has been a source of support and encouragement throughout the whole project.
- *Prof. Bart Childs* and *Prof. William Lively* made it possible for me to visit Texas A&M University in 1995. During this research visit we had discussions on many aspects of software engineering.
- *Prof. Bart Childs* has been especially generous with his support. We worked together on several aspects of documentation and literate programming that are described in this book. Bart Childs also introduced me to LATEX, which I am glad I used for the creation of this manuscript.
- *Prof. Steve Reiss* enabled my research visit at Brown University in 1996. He was very helpful in providing a productive environment and in considering and integrating documentation features into his programming environment.
- *Prof. Peter Wegner* has been available for discussions at Brown University. He made me rethink several aspects, especially about software components.
- *Reinhold Plösch*, one of my colleagues at the Johannes Kepler University of Linz, has influenced my work by careful reading of the manuscript and by making numerous comments and suggestions for improvements.
- *Anonymous reviewers* have carefully read early manuscripts and made numerous suggestions for improvements.
- *Bob Bach* made many improvements to the style of this book and polished my English. He also made helpful suggestions for improvements to the contents of the book.
- The Austrian *Fonds zur Förderung der wissenschaftlichen Forschung* has enabled the research visits at Texas A&M University and at Brown University with their grants J01063-MAT and J01236-MAT (*Erwin-Schrödinger-Auslandsstipendium*).
- The *Ch. Doppler Laboratory for Software Engineering* in Linz has been funding visits to conferences, workshops and universities. This has been important for the exchange of thoughts and ideas in the research community.
- Many other colleagues at Texas A&M University, at Brown University and at Johannes Kepler University of Linz have been supportive during the project of writing this book.

I want to thank them all for their help and cooperation.

Johannes Sametinger
Linz, Austria
March 1997

Table of Contents

List of Figures

III Software Engineering

IV Software Documentation

List of Tables

IV Software Documentation

1. Introduction

Contents

In the early days of computing software production started with simple programs by implementing algorithms. The problem domain that could be supported with software constantly grew. The systems to be built also became constantly more complex, and the teams to work on a single software system continued growing. Before long the term *software crisis* was coined.

Reuse of software components is becoming more and more important in a variety of aspects of software engineering. Recognition of the fact that many software systems contain many similar or even identical components that are developed from scratch over and over again has led to efforts to reuse existing components. Structuring a system into largely independent components has several advantages. It is easy to distribute the components among various engineers to allow parallel development. Maintenance is easier when clean interfaces have been designed for the components, because changes can be made locally without having unknown effects on the whole system. And, if components' interrelations are clearly documented and kept to a minimum, it becomes easier to exchange components and incorporate new ones into a system.

Software reuse and software components have a major influence on the structure of software systems as well as on the way we build them. Yet, many questions are still unanswered. What are software components? What are their properties that support reuse and adaptability? What are the requirements for building evolving systems? What are the implications for the software life cycle? What are the legal, economic and organizational consequences? In this book we will provide answers to these important questions.

In the rest of this chapter we briefly give an introduction to what we mean by *software component* (Section 1.1) and *software reuse* (Section 1.2). Section 1.3 provides an overview of the structure of the book.

1.1 Software Components

We can reuse many things, for example, algorithms, designs, requirements specifications, procedures, modules, applications, ideas, design patterns, architectures. Where do we draw the line between software components and other things, and why do we draw that line and concentrate on the reuse of components only?

Components are artefacts that we clearly identify in our software systems. They have an interface, encapsulate internal details and are documented separately. Recently *component-based software development* has become a buzz word. In this context it is required that components be easily combined with each other, especially without knowing from each other's existence. Many considerations about the reuse of components are independent of what a component is exactly. However, in Part II on *Software Components* we will describe various forms of components. Subsequently, we will make some general conisiderations on components, like questions of whether algorithms, designs, or design patterns are components.

The primary intention in reusing components is that we can take a component and integrate it into a software system. For example, we can take a procedure and use it for some computations. We can also reuse an algorithm that is described in a book on algorithms, like in the book on fundamental algorithms by Knuth [Knu73a]. But we cannot simply take the algorithm and integrate it into a system. We have to implement it first. Thus we reuse the idea that is described in some pseudocode and tells us how we can solve the problem. But we have to solve the problem ourselves using a specific programming language and dealing with the special characteristics of this language. If the algorithm were given already in a language that we can use in a system, then we would have a component to reuse. In this context it does not really matter whether we have the component given in the book only and we have to type it in, or if it is available in digital form already. Reusing an algorithm suffers from another drawback. The algorithm's documentation is given in the book and not available in electronic form. This prohibits its incorporation into the documentation of the whole system (unless someone undergoes the tedious effort of typing the information from the book, which might be even prohibited by copyright rules).

A software design is not a software component. We can reuse a design by reusing a set of components, for example an application framework. The framework is not one component as a whole, but consists of many components that can be modified and extended individually. But the whole group reflects a certain design which we reuse by integrating all these components into a system. Design patterns have recently become popular. Are they reusable components? They certainly can be reused, but they are not software components. We cannot take a design pattern component and integrate it into a system. However, we can take existing components and arrange them as described by a design pattern. Or we might reuse a set of components that realize a certain pattern. Design patterns describe how we can solve certain problems by arranging components (usually classes) in a certain way. In this sense they are like algorithms. They describe ideas, i.e., solutions to certain problems that can be implemented in a specific way.

This book focuses on component reuse because components are a field that promises a rich harvest in productivity through reuse. The reader might argue that the reuse of software designs is more effective. Whether this is true depends on what a component is. Reusing software designs might be more effective if we restrict ourselves to the reuse of source code components. However, in order to increase productivity, we have to see software components in a broader perspective. By reusing a component we may well reuse design. Many things can be encapsulated in components, which we strongly recommend, because it facilitates their reuse. All the algorithms described in various books on that topic can be realized as components. Object-oriented technology provides the possibility to build generic components that are, for example, capable of sorting whatever we want. There is no need to implement an algorithm every time we need to sort, and there is also no need to customize these algorithms to whatever data structures we need to sort. Components have yet another advantage; they can be documented and maintained. By using a component in various projects, we benefit from the fact that it has to be maintained only once. Bugs need not be fixed redundantly; documentation has to be written only once; and we avoid any inconsistency problems that arise when we have *similar* code spread over many locations. If we implement the same algorithm for various software systems, maybe for slightly different data structures, we also have to invest redundant effort to maintain their code, even though we successfully reused the algorithm.

Another important aspect of software components is that they must have an interface. Simply copying some source code lines and pasting them into the system to be built does not satisfy our conception of software components. There must be some kind of abstraction, and reuse should be possible without knowing the internals of the component. This is called *black-box reuse* (in contrast to *white-box reuse*). In order to increase software productivity and to ease software maintenance, black-box reuse should be the goal. Sometimes performance considerations may require to know and modify the internals of components, but this should be the exception rather than the rule.

Documentation is a necessity for reuse. Today reuse is still done by grabbing some pieces of code, studying and trying to understand them and then modifying and integrating them. The term *code scavenging* applies to this scenario. The abstraction level of reusable components has to rise in order to considerably improve productivity. The reuse of plain source code should be the exception. The more complex the components get, the more difficult or impossible it becomes to reuse them. We want components that have the proper information for retrieval and all the descriptions that are necessary for adaptation and integration. This requires extensive documentation, and we have to develop techniques and tools to support these efforts. Therefore, we also cover documentation aspects in this book.

1.2 Software Reuse

Software components and software reuse complement each other perfectly. Using software components to build software systems almost automatically leads to software reuse. (But the use of software components is not sufficient for software reuse.) And trying to reuse software almost automatically evolves in the composition of software out of components. Even though, as is also shown in this book, software reuse can be done without the involvement of any components as well.

Reusing software has a much broader influence on software engineering than one might initially think. Not only does it influence the construction process, it fundamentally affects organizational structures and project structures, and it influences legal and economic issues of software engineering. For software reuse to become a matter of fact, software life cycles have to be adapted accordingly; important new activities like domain analysis come onto the scene.

The reuse of legacy code poses new challenges. Maintaining it is hard enough, reusing it and incorporating it into new systems is even more challenging, although it can boost productivity in building new software systems. Requirements on software systems change constantly. Rebuilding new systems every time requirements change considerably is neither feasible nor economical. We must be able to incorporate old components of systems, split them into useful artefacts, and combine them with new developments. It is the wrong approach to build gigantic monolithic systems that nobody fully understands and that are hard if not impossible to adapt to new environments and situations.

Consider the US air traffic control system as an example. There have been reports that the system is overdue for replacement by a new, modern system [Joc95, Smo96]. The current system uses software from the 1970s and runs on a vacuum-tube IBM 9020e mainframe dating back even a decade earlier. The *Federal Aviation Administration* (FAA) has been working for more than 10 years to replace the antiquated system, but without success. The new system has more than a million lines of code but is riddled with bugs. Due to the lack of reliability of the new system, the old system is still in operation and continues to deteriorate. The old system cannot be adapted to today's requirements. Meanwhile the new one's monolithic structure not only makes it hard or impossible to put it into operation, but even if it did do its job as required, it also will be hard to bring it up-to-date again with ever-changing requirements.

We have to build evolving systems that are geared for change. This is the only chance to keep pace with ever changing and increasing requirements on software systems. We have been struggling with the software crisis for decades. We should get ready to do a better job. Software systems must be composed of components that can be reused and replaced. Instead of replacing a whole system every twenty years, we have to continually add, remove and replace components to adapt a system to changing requirements. After twenty years everything in the system may be different, but this will have happened gradually with small changes that are manageable.

It has been found that black-box reuse of source code components is inflexible and restrictive [Pri94]. Freeman points out that the reuse of source components implicitly involves the reuse of analysis and design, and so misses the opportunity of explicitly reusing this information [Fre87a]. While this is certainly true, we must not conclude that software components per se are worthless. On the contrary, we have to find and use higher abstractions for components than pure source code and, above all, solve the incompatibility problems. This book promotes the idea of reusing components and demonstrates various forms and levels of components and interconnections. Software reuse and/or software components will not solve all problems we encounter in software engineering, but they will contribute to an important step towards more flexible software systems that are constantly evolving and adapting. We have to educate software managers to think further than the deadlines of individual projects. Reusable, adaptable software components rather than large, monolithic applications are the key assets of successful software companies.

1.3 Structure of Book

The book is divided into four main parts: Part I on *Software Reuse*, Part II on *Software Components*, Part III on *Software Engineering*, and Part IV on *Software Documentation*. The parts are independent of each other and can be read in any order. The four parts are complemented by this introduction and a conclusion in Chapter 21 (the only chapter in Part V).

– *Part I: Software Reuse*
  Chapter 2 gives an introduction to software reuse and describes benefits of and obstacles to software reuse. Technical aspects of software reuse are described in Chapter 3. Nontechnical aspects like legal and organizational issues follow in Chapter 4. Finally, Chapter 5 explains how to install systematic reuse in a company.

– *Part II: Software Components*
  In Chapter 6 component definitions, component interfaces, and component platforms are discussed. Chapter 7 describes forms of component composition and interoperation. Attributes of components are discussed in Chapter 8. Chapter 9 discusses existing component taxonomies and proposes a new classification based on the contents of the previous chapters. In

Chapter 10 samples of successful component reuse are given and classified according to our proposed classification.

- *Part III: Software Engineering*
  Chapter 11 provides a general introduction to software engineering. Chapter 12 covers software process models. Domain engineering, an important activity for software reuse, is depicted in Chapter 13. Chapter 14 contains aspects of component engineering (development for reuse). Finally, in Chapter 15 application engineering (development with reuse) is described.

- *Part IV: Software Documentation*
  The fourth part focuses on documentation aspects. In Chapter 16 we give a general introduction to software documentation. Documentation for the purpose of reuse is described in Chapter 17. Literate programming, an important concept for consistent and complete documentation is described in Chapter 18. In Chapter 19 we present a case study that has been done to demonstrates the importance of reuse in documentation. In Chapter 20 a method to systematically reuse documentation is depicted.

Chapter 21, the conclusion, discusses paradigm shifts and describes limits and prospects of component reuse.

Part I

Software Reuse

2. Software Reuse

Contents

The term *software crisis* was coined in the late sixties to describe the increasing burden and frustration of software development and maintenance. Programmers have been reusing code, subroutines and algorithms since the early days of programming. But all this has been done informally. McIlroy introduced the concept of formal reuse through the *software factory* concept. Academia got attracted to reuse in the late 1970s. In the 1980s large-scale reuse programs were done. Several advances were made, including repositories, classification techniques, creation and distribution of reusable components, reuse support environments and corporate reuse programs. More recent work has addressed nontechnical factors: management, economics, culture and law [PF93].

In this chapter we give an introduction to and motivation for software reuse (Section 2.1) and describe its benefits (Section 2.2) and obstacles (Section 2.3). A summary follows in Section 2.4.

2.1 Introduction and Motivation

Code scavenging, using source code generators, or reusing knowledge can contribute to increased productivity in software development. The reuse of life cycle objects, primarily code, is often done in an informal and haphazard way. If done systematically, software reuse has many benefits.

In the subsequent two subsections we discuss definitions and motivations for software reuse.

2.1.1 Reuse Definitions

Many different viewpoints exist of what software reuse is. We give a few examples from the literature.

For Freeman reuse is the use of any information which a developer may need in the software creation process [Fre87a]. Similarly Basili and Rombach see software reuse as the use of everything associated with a software project, including knowledge [BR88]. For Tracz reuse is the use of software that was designed for reuse [Tra95]. Braun defines reuse as the use of existing software components in a new context, either elsewhere in the same system or in another system [Bra94d].

An important aspect is whether software to be reused may be modified. Cooper defines software reuse as the capability of a previously developed software component to be used again or used repeatedly, in part or in its entirety, with or without modification [Coo94]. Lim mentions *work products* (i.e., products or by-products of the software development process, e.g., code, design, test plans) that are to be used in the development of other software without modification [Lim94]. We adopt Krueger's general view of software reuse [Kru92]:

> *Software reuse is the process of creating software systems from existing software rather than building them from scratch.*

Additionally, we affirm McIlroy's vision of reuse: the goal is the use of off-the-shelf components as building blocks in new systems with modifications occurring in a controlled way.

It is not always possible to simply reuse components. Development of components and/or systems is still necessary. Other than compositional reuse, e.g., generative reuse, is useful as well. But when we succeed in defining standards for component composition, this kind of reuse will increase software productivity considerably.

Research work in software reuse includes the development of new technology, but also the extraction of reusable parts from existing, possibly old systems. Prieto-Díaz has documented a historical overview of software reuse and described the evolution of a definition [Pri94].

2.1.2 Motivation

Hardware engineers have succeeded in developing increasingly complex and powerful systems. Of course, hardware engineering cannot simply be compared with software engineering. But software engineers, too, are faced with a growing demand for complex and powerful software systems. New products have to appear more rapidly and product cycles seem to decrease to almost nothing. Advances in software engineering have contributed to increased productivity. Examples include high-level programming languages, object-oriented technology, prototyping-oriented software development, and computer-aided software engineering.

Studies on reuse have shown that 40% to 60% of code is reusable from one application to another, 60% of design and code are reusable in business applications, 75% of program functions are common to more than one program, and only 15% of the code found in most systems is unique and novel to a specific application [Tra88a]. According to Mili et al. [MMM95] rates of actual and potential reuse range from 15% to 85%.

Maximizing the reuse of tested (if not verified or certified) source code and minimizing the need to develop new code alone can bring improvements in cost, time and quality, and reusing source code is only the (low-level) beginning of reuse. Practicing reuse systematically requires additional effort, e.g., managerial and organizational changes.

Although systematic software reuse is not the concept to solve all problems, it promises to have positive impacts on development costs, productivity, functionality, quality, reliability, portability, efficiency and maintainability of software. This is discussed in more detail in the next section.

2.2 Benefits of Software Reuse

Software reuse has a positive impact on software quality, as well as on software costs, and productivity. Reuse benefits have been treated in the literature many times, for example, in the Encyclopedia of Software Engineering [Bra94d], in the NATO Standards for Software Reuse [Bra94a, Bra94b, Bra94c], in Ph.D. dissertations [Tai93], and in various overviews of software reuse, i.e., in journals [MMM95], in reuse books [Kar95, SPM94], and in software engineering books [Som92].

In the following we elaborate on quality improvements and effort reduction in more detail. Examples from industry that demonstrate such benefits are mentioned at the end of this section.

2.2.1 Quality Improvements

Software reuse results in improvements in quality, productivity, performance, reliability and interoperability.

- *Quality*
  Error fixes accumulate from reuse to reuse. This yields higher quality for a reused component than would be the case for a component that is developed and used only once. However, this requires the administration and maintenance of components and is not achieved by simply reusing.

– *Productivity*
A productivity gain is achieved due to less code that has to be developed. This results in less testing efforts and also saves analysis and design labor, yielding overall savings in cost. When reuse is being installed, productivity may decrease shortly due to increased learning effort and the need to develop reusable components. This temporary decrease in productivity should easily be compensated by a long-term increase.

– *Performance*
Extensive reuse can be worth the effort invested in optimizations. This may yield better performance of a reused component than might be practical for a component that is developed and used only once. However, generalizations that make components more reusable can have a negative influence on overall performance. For example, Bardo et al. have reported an estimated 15 to 25 percent penalty in load module size with minimal overhead in execution for avionics simulator software [BEK⁺96].

– *Reliability*
Using well-tested components increases the reliability of a software system. Furthermore, the use of a component in several systems increases the chance of errors to be detected and strengthens confidence in that component.

– *Interoperability*
Various systems can work better together if their interfaces are implemented consistently. This is the case when they use the same components for these interfaces. Even though written standards improve interoperability, different implementations might differently interpret parts of these standards.

Bauer provides an example of improved quality due to software reuse [Bau93]. The quality of reused components (numbers of errors per lines of code) was about 9 times better during component test and about 4.5 times better during system test. In another project there were even no errors found in reused components during the entire life cycle of the project. The components reused in these projects were macros implementing abstract data types. Unfortunately, there is no information given on the amount of reuse.

2.2.2 Effort Reduction

Software reuse provides a reduction in redundant work and thus development time, which yields to a shorter time to market. This is especially important considering the importance of good timing, i.e., early availability for software systems. Additionally, documentation and costs as well as team sizes can be reduced.

– *Redundant work, development time*
Developing every system from scratch means redundant development of

many parts like user interfaces, communication, basic algorithms, etc. This can be avoided when these parts are available as reusable components and can be shared, resulting in less development and less associated time and costs.

— *Time to market*
The success or failure of a software product is very often determined by its time to market. Using reusable components will result in a reduction of that time. As much as a 42% reduction has been reported on a specific project [Lim95].

— *Documentation*
Even though documentation is very important for the maintenance of a system, it is often neglected. Reusing software components reduces the amount of documentation to be written but compounds the importance of what is written. Only the overall structure of the software system and the newly developed components have to be documented. The documentation of reusable components can be shared among many software systems.

— *Maintenance costs*
Fewer defects can be expected to occur when proven components have been used, and less of the software system must be maintained. The reusable components are maintained by a separate group rather than separately in each software system.

— *Training costs*
Over time, software engineers become familiar with the reusable components available for their development efforts. So they have a good working knowledge of many components of these systems when they are starting to design and develop new systems.

— *Team size*
Large development teams suffer from a communication overload. Doubling the size of a development team does not result in doubled productivity. If many components can be reused, then software systems can be developed with smaller teams, leading to better communication and increased productivity.

2.2.3 Other Benefits

The support of rapid prototyping and expertise sharing are amongst additional benefits of software reuse.

— *Rapid prototyping support*
Reusable components can provide an effective basis for quickly building a prototype of a software system. This provides the opportunity to get customer feedback early in the life cycle, thus supporting the conception of the requirements. This can also help to uncover hidden requirements.

- *Expertise sharing*
  Good designs can only be learned from good designers. It is important that software engineers study the designs of excellent peers in order to improve their design skills. Software reuse supports this very naturally. This does not mean that we should study the implementation details of all the components we reuse; the interfaces alone can reveal important information about how a component and its interoperability have been designed.

Reuse benefits are not completely independent from each other, but rather influence each other.

2.2.4 Industry Examples

Reuse benefits have been reported in various industrial settings.

- An empirical study from a NASA software production environment has shown that modules reused without modifications (revisions) had less interaction with other modules, simpler interfaces, less interaction with human users, and higher ratios of commentary compared to newly developed or modified (revised) modules [Sel89]. In this study 25 software projects (ranging from 3,000 to 112,000 source code lines) were considered. An average of 32% of software had been reused or modified from previous systems.
- At Motorola software reuse is considered a candidate technology for initiatives and goals to improve productivity and quality [Joo94].
- At Hewlett-Packard a reuse assessment of two reuse programs has indicated higher quality (reduction in defect density ranging from 24% to 76%) and a 40% to 57% increase in productivity [Lim94].
- IBM has formed the *Reuse Technology Support Center*, involving close to 30 of their sites worldwide. Their best programs report savings in the millions of dollars, with reuse accounting for 20% to 30% of the software [TG93].

Other industry examples are cited by Braun [Bra94d]:

- Raytheon Missile Systems has reported an average of 60% reuse and a 50% increase in net productivity in new developments (1979).
- NEC Software Engineering Laboratory has reported a 6.7 to 1 productivity improvement and a 2.8 to 1 quality improvement (1987).
- Fujitsu has experienced an improvement from 20% of projects on schedule to 70% on schedule (1987).
- GTE has reported 14% reuse and savings of $1.5 million, with projected figures of 50% reuse and savings of $10 million (1987).
- SofTech, Inc. has reported an increase in productivity to 10 to 20 times the industry average (1987).
- Universal Defense Systems has reported 60% reuse in a system of 700,000 lines of Ada code (1991).

– Celsius Technology has experienced a 250% increase in productivity, projecting an additional increase of about 300% (1992).

Experience reports cited by Mili et al. also document increases in productivity and quality [MMM95].

2.3 Obstacles to Software Reuse

Despite the benefits of software reuse, it is not as widely practiced as one might assume. There are many factors that directly or indirectly influence the success or failure of reuse. These factors can be of conceptual, technical, managerial, organizational, psychological, economic or legal nature. In this section we list examples of such obstacles and divide them into various groups, even though sometimes an assignment to one of these groups is ambiguous.

In the literature obstacles to software reuse have been described by various authors, e.g., Braun [Bra94d], Griss [Gri93], Horner [Hor93], Jones [Jon94] and Prieto-Díaz [Pri93a].

The subsequent sections describe managerial, organizational, economic and technical obstacles to software reuse.

2.3.1 Managerial and Organizational Obstacles

Reuse is not just a technical problem that has to be solved by software engineers. Management support and adequate organizational structures are equally important. Common reuse obstacles are:

– *Lack of management support*
  Since software reuse causes up-front costs, it cannot be widely achieved in an organization without support of top-level management. Managers have to be informed about initial costs and have to be convinced about expected savings.

– *Project management*
  Managing traditional projects is not an easy task. We have even less experience with projects exploiting reuse. Making the step to large-scale software reuse has an impact on the whole software life cycle.

– *Lack of explicit procedures*
  Software development is a complex process involving many activities. Successful software reuse has effects on the whole software life cycle, design methods, project planning and estimating. Models for such processes are used to determine various steps to be accomplished in a certain order. If these models do not explicitly consider software reuse, it is likely that it will not happen in practice.

- *Inadequate organizational structures*
  Organizational structures must consider different needs that arise when explicit, large-scale reuse is being adopted. For example, a separate team may be installed for gathering, maintaining and providing reusable components.

- *Not invented here*
  People may feel hindered in their creativity and independence by reusing someone else's software. They want to develop their own new software rather than maintaining software from someone else. They may also be biased against someone else's software through a lack of trust. This is called the *not-invented-here* syndrome.

- *Legal issues*
  The more widespread software reuse becomes, the more legal and business issues have to be addressed, e.g. liabilities and data rights. Increased use of third-party software increases the significance of these issues.

- *Lack of management incentives*
  Lack of incentives prohibit managers from letting their developers spend time in making components of a system reusable. Their success is often measured only in the time needed for completing a project. Doing any work beyond that, although beneficial for the company as a whole, diminishes their success. Even when components are reused by accessing software repositories, the gained benefits are only a fraction of what could be achieved by explicit, planned and organized reuse. It is not sufficient to simply access components in a repository. Well-designed components have to be systematically developed and used following a careful reuse-based process [Gri93].

Nontechnical issues around software reuse are discussed in Chapter 4. For example, more details on legal issues are given in Section 4.1 on page 38. More details on organizational aspects can be found in Section 4.3 on page 40.

2.3.2 Economic Obstacles

Reuse can save money in the long run, but it is not for free. Costs associated with reuse are [Tra94]:

- costs of making something reusable,
- costs of reusing it, and
- costs of defining and implementing a reuse process (installing reuse).

Reuse requires up-front investments in infrastructure, methodology, training, tools and archives, with payoffs being realized only years later. Developing components for reuse is more expensive than developing them for single use only. Higher levels of quality, reliability, portability, maintainability, generality and more extensive documentation are necessary. Such increased costs are not justified when a component is used only once. Constructing a set of reusable components is not possible without long-term support from upper management.

2.3.3 Conceptual and Technical Obstacles

Most research is being done on technical support for software reuse. Object-oriented programming is an example of technological support for reuse. However, just using object-oriented technology is by far insufficient for effective reuse.

- *Difficulty of finding reusable software*
  Software cannot be reused unless it can be found. Reuse is unlikely to happen when a repository does not have sufficient information about components or when the components are poorly classified. Suppose we know that someone has written a software component that exactly matches our needs. Finding it is impossible unless we have a well-organized repository containing that particular component with some means of accessing it.

- *Nonreusability of found software*
  Easy access to existing software does not necessarily increase software reuse. Unintentionally, software is seldom written in a way so that others can reuse it. Modifying and adapting someone else's software can become even more expensive than programming the needed functionality from scratch.

- *Legacy components not suitable for reuse*
  Reusing components is hard or impossible unless they have been designed and developed for reuse. Simply gathering existing components from various legacy software systems and trying to reuse them for new developments is not sufficient for systematic reuse. Re-engineering can help in extracting reusable components from legacy systems. However, the efforts needed for the extraction and transformation to useful components might be considerable.

- *Object-oriented technology*
  It is widely believed that object-oriented technology has a positive influence on software reuse. Unfortunately and wrongly, many also believe that reuse depends on this technology or that adopting object-oriented technology suffices for software reuse.

- *Modification*
  Components will not always be exactly the way we want them. If modifications are necessary, we should be able to determine their effects on the component and its previous verification results.

- *Integration*
  Sometimes components are available with the functionality that is needed for a new software system. Still if it is not possible to integrate components

into the system, they are of no use. Unfortunately most components are ill-equipped to cope with integration requirements. Software components must be constructed in a way that subsequent reuse can be efficient and straightforward.

– *Garbage reuse*
Certifying reusable components to certain quality levels helps in minimizing possible defects. Poor quality control is one of the major barriers to reuse. A reusable component has to perform its claimed functions. We need some means of judging whether the required functions match the functions that are provided by a component.

More basic technical difficulties with software reuse have been addressed by Taivalsaari [Tai93] and include:

– agreeing on what a reusable component constitutes,
– understanding what a component does and how to use it,
– understanding how to interface reusable components to the rest of a design,
– designing reusable components so that they are easy to adapt and modify (in a controlled way), and
– organizing a repository so that programmers can find and use what they need.

Risks of software reuse include the unavailability of technology and resources, lack of management support, sluggishness of people to change and the instability of domains [GFW94]. Additionally, risks can evolve from legal aspects, e.g., liability issues or repository agreements [Hub94].

Software risk analysis [Boe91], legal advice and incremental introduction of reuse programs (see Chapter 5) help in avoiding or reducing these risks.

2.4 Summary

Software reuse is the process of creating software systems from existing software rather than building them from scratch [Kru92]. In this chapter we have provided several other definitions of software reuse, various benefits, and obstacles to reuse.

The most common benefits of software reuse are quality improvement and effort reduction. Obstacles to reuse are of managerial, organizational, economic and technical nature.

Card and Comer point out two fundamental mistakes that contribute to failure in software reuse [CC94]. First, organizations treat reuse as a technology-acquisition problem rather than a technology-transition problem. Second, they fail to approach reuse as a business strategy. It is sufficient neither to buy some sort of reuse technology nor to tackle technical problems only.

The *not-invented-here* syndrome and a general resistance to change can hinder successful software reuse. Software developers like to be creative and feel pride in their own software. Managers feel more comfortable when their project's success is completely controlled by themselves, and they do not depend on outside resources [Bra94d]. The only way to overcome these obstacles is to systematically install a reuse program (see Chapter 5).

3. Technical Aspects of Software Reuse

Contents

Software reuse has many technical and nontechnical aspects, for example, ad-hoc reuse, institutionalized reuse, black-box reuse, white-box reuse, source code reuse, design reuse.

In this chapter we describe various technical aspects of software reuse. Nontechnical aspects follow in Chapter 4. Section 3.1 covers reuse facets and provides an overview of various aspects of reuse. Reuse substances, reuse scopes, reuse techniques, reuse intentions, and reuse products are described in Sections 3.2 to 3.6. A summary follows in Section 3.7.

Table 3.1. Facets of software reuse

Facet	Examples
Substance	ideas, concepts, artifacts, components, procedures, skills
Scope	vertical, domain-specific, horizontal, general-purpose, internal, external, small-scale, large-scale
Mode	planned, systematic, institutionalized, ad-hoc, opportunistic, individual
Technique	compositional, generative
Intention	black-box, white-box, glass-box, as-is, by adaptation, modified
Product	specification, design, source code, architectures, documentation, text

3.1 Reuse Facets

Prieto-Díaz identified six perspectives from which to view software reuse. The resulting facets are [Pri93b]:

– *Substance* defines the essence of reused items.

– *Scope* defines the form and extent of reuse.

– *Mode* defines how reuse is conducted.

– *Technique* defines the approach that is used to implement reuse.

– *Intention* defines how elements will be used.

– *Product* defines what is reused.

Table 3.1 shows these facets with examples. Reuse substances, reuse scopes, reuse techniques, reuse intentions, and reuse products are described in subsequent sections. Reuse modes are affected by nontechnical aspects and, therefore, are described in Chapter 4 (Section 4.3.1 on page 41).

3.2 Reuse Substances

The essence of reused items is manifold. For example, we mentioned earlier that ideas and concepts are often taken (and reused) from books about algorithms. Ideas and concepts can also be 'retrieved' from experienced software engineers who had been asked for advice. Information about procedures and skills can be represented in expert systems, but is also often reused on an ad-hoc and individual basis.

Concentrating on the reuse of components does not mean excluding the reuse of ideas and concepts. The reuse of a component automatically means the reuse of ideas and concepts that are built into the component. The advantage is that reusers do not have to worry about them. They do not have to understand the concepts involved in the development of the components, yet they implicitly reuse them through the component. For example, reusing the *idea* for hash tables requires a thorough understanding of the concepts required in order to implement them. If a component already provides the functionality of hash tables and exports a clean interface, we can simply reuse the underlying ideas and concepts.

Freeman argues that with source code alone we miss the opportunity of explicitly reusing analysis and design information [Fre87a]. We have to consider higher levels of components that cover more than pure source code. Naturally, not everything can be packed into components. Thus reusing components does not cover all aspects of software reuse. For example, it is difficult to reuse procedures and skills by means of components because they cover some kind of meta-information. However, the reuse of components provides prerequisites for planned and systematic reuse.

3.3 Reuse Scopes

The amount of possible software reuse depends on the degree of commonalty among applications that share software. A domain is an area of activity or knowledge containing applications that share a set of common capabilities and data [STA93]. Domains are described in more detail in Chapter 13.

If the majority of applications are in a specific domain, a higher degree of reuse is probable than among applications across a broad range of different applications. Domain-specific reuse and general-purpose reuse are often called vertical and horizontal reuse, respectively.

Another possible differentiation of scope is distinguishing between internal and external reuse. Internal reuse means the multiple use of a component within a software system for which it was originally written. External reuse is the use of a component originally written for another software system.

Small-scale reuse is reusing small code components like subroutines, functions, modules, and classes. Compared to the efforts needed to build large software systems, the net win is marginal. Unfortunately, small-scale software reuse is an everyday occurrence, whereas large-scale software reuse too often remains an elusive and unrealized goal. Large-scale reuse requires the consideration of many nontechnical issues, as described in Chapter 4.

3.4 Reuse Techniques

Various techniques or approaches can be used in order to achieve software reuse. *Compositional reuse* supports bottom-up development of systems from a repository of available lower-level components; classification and retrieval is important in this context. *Generative reuse* is often domain-specific, adopting standard system structures (reference architectures or generic architectures) and standard interfaces for components. A combined approach is also possible.

3.4.1 Abstraction

Abstraction is essential in any software reuse technique. As Wegner states, abstraction and reusability are two sides of the same coin [Weg83]. Krueger states that "without abstraction developers would be forced to sift through a collection of reusable artifacts trying to figure out what each artifact did, when it could be reused, and how to reuse it." [Kru92].

Raising abstraction levels is a major challenge in software engineering. The relation between abstraction and reuse gives a first hint about the difficulties we face in software reuse.

Every software abstraction has two levels: specification (what is done by the abstraction) and realization (how is it done). The realization of one level of abstraction is the specification of the next lower level of abstraction. Every abstraction contains a hidden part (not visible in the specification), a fixed part, and a variable part. The variable part maps into the collection of possible realizations. The creator of an abstraction can decide in which part to put certain information, e.g., the size of a stack could be variable, fixed or hidden. The specification must contain all the information needed by the reuse of its realization.

Finding concise abstractions for components is a difficult task. The best-known successes are in application domains with application-specific, one-word abstractions, e.g.: sine, matrix (in numerical analysis), stack, list (in abstract data types).

3.4.2 Compositional Reuse

Compositional reuse is based on the idea of reusable components that (ideally) remain unmodified in their reuse. Higher-level or more complex components are built by combining lower-level or simpler components. Only if needed components are not available and cannot be created by modification of existing components are they built from scratch or constructed from lower-level components. The components suitable for reuse are collected in repositories.

Compositional reuse is based on component repositories (e.g., function libraries) or on principles of organization and composition, like pipe architectures or the object-oriented construction of software systems.

Component repositories. Successful reuse requires having a wide variety of high-quality components, proper classification and retrieval mechanisms, sufficient and proper documentation of components, a flexible means for combining components, and a means of adapting components to specific needs. In an ideal scenario reused components are largely atomic and remain unmodified. However, often this ideal cannot be achieved and the components have to modified and changed in order to fit the reusers' special needs. During composition components are regarded as passive elements that are combined by predefined principles which are crucial for systems being built from existing components.

Today, the nature of a reusable component technology strongly depends on the programming languages used. Components can be reusable functions, e.g., statistics libraries, numerical libraries, or packages, modules, subsystems and classes. The latter can include data-centered artifacts like abstract datatypes.

Challenges in the context of repositories are techniques to locate components efficiently, e.g., classification schemes, retrieval techniques, and to integrate them in software systems. This leads to the next aspect of compositional reuse, component composition. Chapter 14 provides more details on repositories and classification schemes.

Component composition. Software components exist in many different forms. They cannot be arbitrarily assembled and expected to communicate and cooperate. In order to enable the combination of components they must rely on the same kind of composition technique.

Module interconnection languages and the Unix pipe mechanism are examples of possible composition of reusable components. The Unix pipe mechanism is one of the well-known examples of a simple, yet powerful composition and integration technique where complex programs can be built out of simpler ones. The alliance of components is accomplished by connecting the output of one component to the input of another [Ker84].

Incompatibilities of components are among the main hindrances of successful component reuse. In Chapter 7 we deal with different forms of composition and interoperation and describe composition mismatches.

Code and design scavenging. Scavenging fragments from existing software systems and using them as part of new software development is an ad-hoc and unsystematic, although effective approach to reusing software system designs and source code [Kru92]. In this scenario reused components are fragments taken from various locations of other systems rather than self-contained, tested and documented components from a repository. Nevertheless, it is a kind of composition, and experienced programmers can gain high productivity increases. We distinguish between code and design scavenging:

– *Code scavenging*
   Blocks of source code are copied from an existing system.

- *Design scavenging*
  Large blocks of code are copied. Many of the internal details are deleted.
  The global template of the design is retained.

There is no abstraction involved in scavenging. The developer is forced to become closely involved with implementation details of the reused fragments.

3.4.3 Generative Reuse

Generative reuse is based on the reuse of a generation process rather than the reuse of components. Large frame structures are used as invariants, i.e., reused without change. Variant functionality must be added to customize the invariant parts. The components that are reused are not concrete and self-contained as in the compositional approach. The parts to be reused are incorporated into a program that generates reusable patterns.

Typical examples of this kind of reuse are generators for lexical analyzers, parsers, and compilers (e.g., lex and yacc on the Unix platform), conventional application generators (e.g., fourth-generation languages), expert system generators, and structure-oriented editor generators.

Generators that synthesize software from reuse libraries to construct systems for a target domain compose prefabricated, interchangeable components and thus contain compositional aspects also (see Batory et al. [BST$^+$94]). Subsequently, we distinguish between application generators, language-based generators, and transformation systems. Programming languages can be seen as low level specification languages. This is briefly sketched at the end of this section.

Application generators. Application generators reuse complete software system designs. They are appropriate in application domains where [Kru92]:

- many similar software systems are written,
- one software system is modified or rewritten many times during its lifetime, and/or
- many prototypes of a system are necessary to converge on a usable product.

Application generators allow inexperienced people to generate customized applications. In application generators, reusable patterns exist in the generator itself in the form of source code. Application generators currently provide only small coverage for software development. But the focus on narrow domains is also an advantage. Highly productive creation of quality commercial software with application generators has been reported [Lev86]. A survey of application generators is given by Horowitz et al. [HKN85].

Language-based generators. Language-based generators provide a specification language that represents the problem domain and simultaneously hides implementation details from the reuser. Specification languages allow developers to create software systems using constructs that are considered high-level relative to programming languages [Kru92]. They are also known as executable specification languages.

Specification languages help in reusing implementation patterns of programming languages, similar to programming languages that help in reusing assembler patterns. These languages typically have mathematical abstractions that are not widely used in the conventional software life cycle. Specification languages are used to describe abstract specifications, from which executable programs are automatically generated. Language-based generators differ from application generators mainly in that they use general-purpose, application-independent abstractions rather than application-specific ones. The primary concern is development and modification efficiency rather than high execution speed. This may eliminate them as development vehicles for various of today's production systems, but they can be used as a basis for rapid prototyping and validation of software systems.

The Setl optimizer is an example of this kind of generation [DFSS89]. It is based on representing computations as operations on mathematical sets.

Transformation systems. With transformation systems, software is developed in two phases: describing the semantic behavior of a software system and applying transformations to the high-level specifications. For example, abstract programs are transformed into their concrete counterparts in an approach described by Cheatham [Che89].

Martin distinguishes the subcategories skeleton approach, kitchen sink approach, parameterized approach, and stepwise refinement approach [Mar90]:

– *Skeleton approach*
  In the skeleton approach, the reuser starts with a generic application skeleton and fills in details and missing parts. The generic part may cover many aspects of an application, e.g., user interface details or event handling.

– *Kitchen sink approach*
  The kitchen sink approach works the other way around. The reuser starts with a detailed and extensive framework and prunes parts away that are not needed for the current application.

– *Parameterized approach*
  The parameterized approach provides certain parameters to modify the resulting software.

– *Stepwise refinement approach*
  In the stepwise refinement approach, reusers refine the software's behavior in incremental steps.

The Draco system generates applications from domain-oriented specifications [Nei89]. It can be regarded as application generator and as transformation system that use patterns within transformation rules.

Programming languages. Programming languages such as C, C++ and Ada are usually not treated as examples of software reuse. But their goals and achievements have strong parallels to the current-day aspirations of software reuse researchers [Kru92].

In the same way as we regard language-based generators, application generators, and transformation systems in the context of software reuse, with programming languages we do not reuse software itself, but rather we reuse language patterns. The artifacts to be reused are assembly language patterns. Of course, these languages provide only a relatively low level of abstraction. However, they provide a factor of 5 speedup in writing source code [Bro75].

As with generators, programmers use variant and invariant parts of the abstraction and do not have to worry about all the assembly language details that are actually reused. The compiler provides the transformation from the specification (programming language) to the implementation (assembly or machine language).

3.4.4 Generation vs. Composition

Generation-based systems have the advantage that the reused patterns can be designed and implemented carefully by experienced programmers. But they are applicable only to a certain domain and are typically restricted to the reuse of source code. Also, they cannot be applied easily in all situations. Often they are too general or to specific for applications under consideration.

Components are applicable to a wider variety of applications. Additionally, they are more modular and self-contained and thus maintainable. Their disadvantage is that they are seldom perfect or general enough. This might lead to many modifications, which reduces productivity gains and can lead to immense numbers of components in repositories.

Table 3.2 summarizes the comparison of compositional and generative reuse (see Biggerstaff and Richter [BR89]). Compositional reuse provides the more general approach. The generative approach is useful in specific domains and can be built on top of components.

3.5 Reuse Intentions

Depending on whether the internals of a software component are visible to reusers we speak of *black-box* or *white-box* reuse. If a component is a black box we cannot modify its internals: we use it as is. White-box components are usually modified, even though this is not necessarily the case. They offer both as-is reuse and reuse by adaptation. The term *glass-box reuse* means white-box visibility but black-box reuse.

Table 3.2. Compositional reuse vs. generative reuse

Reuse technique	Composition	Generation
Reused component	building blocks	patterns
Nature of component	atomic and immutable, passive	diffuse and malleable, active
Emphasis	component repositories, composition principles, (code/design scavenging)	application generators, language based generators, transformation systems
Examples	function/class libraries, Unix filters	parser generators, 4th generation languages

3.5.1 Black-Box Reuse

Reusing a component as a black box means using it without seeing, knowing or modifying any of its internals. The component provides an interface that contains all the information necessary for its utilization. The implementation is hidden and cannot be modified by the reuser. Thus reusers get the information about what a component is doing, but they do not have to worry about how this is achieved. The implementation can be changed without any effects on reusers.

Usually a black box is reused as-is. Object-oriented techniques allow modifications of black boxes by making modifications and extensions to a component without knowing its internals. This is one of the major contributions of object-oriented programming to software reuse. However, components have to be designed so that such modifications become viable.

3.5.2 White-Box Reuse

White-box reuse is the typical case in the unplanned ad-hoc reuse that is still widespread today. It means reuse of components of which internals are changed for the purpose of reuse. White boxes are typically not reused as is, but by adaptation. They create more opportunities for reusers due to the ease of making arbitrary changes. On the negative side of white-box reuse, it requires additional testing and costlier maintenance. Unlike black boxes, a new component derived by modifications to an existing component must be regarded as a new component and thoroughly tested. Additionally, the new component requires separate maintenance. If many copies of a component exist with slight modifications, it becomes burdensome to fix errors that affect all of them. If the changes made to a component are only minor, e.g., a few variable renamings or changes in procedure calls, the term *grey-box* reuse is also used.

3.5.3 Glass-Box Reuse

The term glass-box reuse is used when components are used as-is like black boxes, but their internals can be seen from outside (see Goldberg and Rubin [GR95]). This gives the reuser information about how the component works without the ability to change it. But this information may be crucial for understanding how certain tasks are carried out. It may also give the reuser some confidence from being able to see inside the component and capture how it works. Additionally, getting internal information provides some kind of knowledge transfer and, for example, can help in building new components.

Glass-box reuse has its negative sides. It may lead to dependencies on certain implementation details which become fatal when the internals of the component are changed. Unfortunately, giving reusers detailed information about a component's internals often serves as compensation of nonexistent or insufficient documentation.

3.5.4 Generative Reuse

Generative reuse is itself a reuse technique, but it can be seen as kind of black-box reuse [GR95]. Instead of picking one of several existing black boxes, a component's specification is created and its implementation automatically generated by a program generator. The program generator is a black box; its internals are of no interest to the reuser. Also, the generated implementation will not be modified. If changes are necessary, they will be made in the specification and the implementation is recreated. (In practice, however, modifications to the generated implementation are sometimes made due to shortcomings in the generator.)

3.5.5 Black-Box vs. White-Box Reuse

Black box reuse is more difficult to achieve than white-box reuse but promises higher quality and reliability of the resulting software system. The potential of customizing black-box components can increase their reuse potential but has to be carefully considered and designed. Black-box components have the advantage of possible verification and certification. Even though we are far from having a market of verified and certified components, such attributes will become essential in the future.

3.6 Reuse Products

There are many work products that can be reused, e.g., source code, documentation, designs, specifications, objects, text and architectures. Source code is the most common reuse product. However, higher increases in productivity will result from reusing higher levels of abstraction. This can mean that source code is generated automatically from higher levels of abstractions. The abstraction level of the source code also plays a major role in the benefit of the reuse process. For example, object-oriented programming techniques allow the construction of application frameworks that facilitate not only source code reuse but also design reuse. Design patterns have recently emerged and help to reuse the knowledge of experienced designers of object-oriented software systems. In the context of source code reuse, documentation reuse also becomes important. This affects not only system documentation for the source code but also specifications as well as user documentation and project documentation.

Different categorizations for reuse products have been proposed, most of them relying on one or more of the following factors [MMM95]:

- the stage of development at which the knowledge is produced and/or used, e.g., design vs. implementation,
- the level of abstraction, e.g., source code vs. tools, and
- the nature of knowledge, e.g., artifacts vs. skills.

Without systematic planning, reuse seldom goes beyond the implementation stage and the source code level. Types of reusable artifacts can comprise data reuse (e.g., standardization of data formats), architecture reuse (e.g., standardization of design and programming conventions), design reuse (e.g., for common applications like GUI), and program reuse (e.g., executable code) [Jon84].

In this section we give examples of what can be reused for software development. The most prominent examples of today's reuse include algorithms, function libraries, class libraries, application frameworks and design patterns. Other examples include project plans, cost estimates, requirements, designs, architectures, user documents and test cases. Components per se are discussed in detail in Chapter 6.

3.6.1 Algorithms

Algorithms have a long tradition of successful reuse. Numerous books contain a variety of useful algorithms. A prominent example is Knuth's "The Art of Computer Programming" [Knu73a, Knu73b, Knu73c]. Many of these books contain algorithms and data structures in certain programming languages. They allow the reuse of these algorithms with only minor modifications. Often they are depicted in some sort of pseudocode and have to be translated to a specific programming language. As-is reuse is rarely possible. Often adaptations and modifications have to be made, especially concerning the data structure to be processed by a certain algorithm. For example, an algorithm in a book may depict sorting algorithms by sorting integer values. If customer records have to be sorted, then slight modifications of the algorithms will be necessary.

Advances in programming languages have made the need to adapt and modify less painful. Generic implementations and templates make algorithms work with different data structures without explicit modification. Concepts of object-oriented programming allow the most elegant kind of algorithm reuse. By inheritance, implemented algorithms can be made to work with objects not foreseen at the time these algorithms were implemented. This evolution in programming languages has brought a rise in the abstraction level from the reuse of concepts and ideas to the reuse of source code without the need for modifications (but still reusing the concepts and ideas).

3.6.2 Function Libraries

Functions are the most common form of reusable components. For many programming languages, standard libraries have been defined, for example, for input/output or mathematical functions.

A few decades ago languages had much functionality defined in the language itself, e.g., PL/I. Later on, the trend was towards lean languages with standard libraries for various functionalities, e.g., Modula-2.

There are many example of function libraries, from collections of standard routines (e.g., the C standard libraries) to domain-specific libraries (e.g., for statistics or numerical purposes).

3.6.3 Class Libraries

Class libraries are the object-oriented version of function libraries. Classes provide better abstraction mechanisms, better modifiability and adaptability than functions do. Reusability has greatly benefited from concepts like inheritance, polymorphism and dynamic binding. In many class libraries there are classes devoted to generic data structures like lists, trees and queues.

The major problem with class libraries is that they consist of families of related components. Thus members of different families have incompatible interfaces. Often several families implement the same basic abstraction but have different interfaces. This makes libraries hard to use and makes interchanging components difficult. Also, most class libraries are not scalable [BST+94].

3.6.4 Software Architectures and Designs

A software architecture is the global structure of a software system with its major subsystems, including the specifications of these subsystems and their interrelationships. It includes the collection of components and their interactions. A description of a software system's architecture usually contains the collection of its components at the highest level of abstraction. For example, if the system consists of independent processes, then the description of the architecture contains these processes with a description of their functionality and the interactions among them. If a software system runs as a single process, then its subsystems are considered as being the architecture. These can be modules and classes or subsystems containing several such modules and/or classes. The next lower level is generally considered as being part of the software design.

A series of common patterns for the global structure of software systems has been successful and reused repeatedly. Such patterns include communicating processes, hierarchical layers, pipes and filters, clients and servers, and interpreters [SG94]. The reuse of software architectures is possible through generic architectures for certain application domains. A high-level generic design for a family of applications can be defined to meet requirements within the domain.

Software design incorporates the activities of creating the software architecture of a system plus decomposing software components. This is repeated until the level of detail allows the coding of the specified components. The steps involved include the design of the architecture of the whole system or subsystems, component interfaces, component implementations, data structures and algorithms. Software design is a matter of practice and experience. It is learned not from reading a book but from studying existing, well-designed systems. Reuse of software design is mainly reuse of knowledge. However, with application frameworks it is possible to reuse not only source code but also the design (see below). Thus components are capable of supporting the reuse of software design.

Software architectures and software designs complement each other in that behind most design methods are preferred architectural styles. Design methods can also evolve from a specific architectural style [Gar95].

3.6.5 Framework Classes

For large-scale reuse, isolated classes are small-scale primitives that are too fine-grained. To boost productivity, systems have to be built out of large-scale composites. Thus we have to focus on sets of classes that collaborate to carry out a common set of responsibilities, rather than on individual classes. Frameworks are flexible collections of abstract and concrete classes designed to be extended and refined for reuse [Tai93]. Components of class libraries can serve as discrete, stand-alone, context-independent parts of a solution to a large range of different applications, e.g., collection classes. Components of frameworks are not intended to work alone; their correct operation requires the presence of and collaboration with other members of the framework components [Tai93]. Reusers of framework classes "inherit" the overall design of an application made by experienced software engineers and can concentrate on the application's functionality. They do not have to worry about user interfaces, window systems, event handling, refreshing, etc.

The major advantage of framework classes over library classes is that frameworks are concerned with conventions of communication between the components [LI93]. Today the combination of components from different class libraries is the exception rather than the rule. This is because there is some implicit understanding of how components work together. High cohesion and low coupling increase the reusability of components. But unless the component does have extensive functionality, it is required to cooperate and communicate with many others. In a framework this interaction is built in and eases interaction of its components.

3.6.6 Design Patterns

Software design patterns capture the intent behind the design of a software system. They standardize piecework to larger units. For example, many times there exists a special arrangement of classes and/or objects in order to avoid reuse errors.

A subsystem is a set of classes with high cohesion among themselves and low coupling to classes outside the subsystem. Design patterns can correspond to subsystems, but often they have a finer level of granularity. Design patterns have been identified to avoid dependence on classes when creating objects, on particular operations, on specific representation or implementation, on particular algorithms, and on inheritance as the extension mechanism. Design patterns have been described by various authors, e.g., Coad [Coa92], Gamma [Ge93], Gamma et al. [GHJV95] and Pree [Pre95].

Research work on design patterns is still going on, and it is not yet clear which patterns will become widely accepted. Gamma et al. have presented an extensive collection of design patterns [GHJV95]. These patterns promise to be one further step in increasing the abstraction level in software development. They can help both in improving the development process and in recapturing design decisions behind the structure of certain parts in a system.

We see design patterns as a means of transferring design knowledge. Thus design patterns provide an efficient means of studying and later reusing the designs of experienced software engineers. Patterns can help to improve productivity by shortening the learning curve for novice and intermediate programmers and by yielding simpler, more resilient systems [DS94]. In contrast to methodologies that tell us how to do something, design patterns show us how to do it. They are standard techniques for software development similar to algorithms, which operate on a lower level.

3.6.7 Applications

Entire applications can be thought of as components that provide well-defined services. They can reference or embed other applications and invoke services by sending messages. Besides production gains, reusing applications offers the flexibility to customize environments and let users stick to their preferred tools, e.g., the Emacs text editor. Applications are reused as black boxes. They have to provide an interface to allow other applications to interact with them, e.g., to send commands.

Increasing capabilities of applications to interoperate are providing alternatives to large monolithic applications. Composing applications from fine-grained applications rather than building one big closed system provides many possibilities for reuse.

3.6.8 Documentation

Documentation is an important part of a software system. We distinguish between product documentation and process documentation [Som92]. Product documentation describes how to use a system (e.g., user interface description, functional description, reference manual) and how it is implemented (e.g., system architecture, design, component implementations). Process documentation describes the process of creation (e.g., plans, estimates, schedules).

Documentation is hard to reuse in a systematic way. The usual case is copying a document and editing it. The reuse of components should involve the reuse of their documentation as well. If components are integrated into a software system, so should be their documentation. Chapter 20 describes how this can be accomplished.

3.7 Summary

In this chapter we have described different views to reuse, including substances, scopes, modes, techniques, intentions and products. Technical aspects have been described in detail. Nontechnical aspects follow in Chapter 4.

The essence of reuse comprises ideas, artifacts, and skills. By reusing components, which are artifacts, we cannot reuse any skills. But we are able to reuse ideas and concepts, which, to some degree, can be incorporated into components. The form and extent of reuse, defined by reuse scope, is strongly dependent on nontechnical measures that are taken. The same holds for reuse modes, e.g., individual and systematic reuse.

Reuse techniques include generative and compositional reuse. Reuse intentions define how components are to be reused, i.e., as black boxes, grey boxes, glass boxes or white boxes. The reuse products we mentioned contained various products of the software life cycle like algorithms and class libraries. Software components have not been explicitly described as reuse products. This is done in detail in Part II on *Software Components*.

4. Nontechnical Aspects of Software Reuse

Contents

Many nontechnical aspects have to be considered in order to improve systematic software reuse and to make it the normal way of software creation. Technical aspects are important prerequisites for successful reuse. However, they do not suffice to make software reuse happen. Systematic reuse requires long-term, top-down management support because [FI94]:

- years of investment may be required before it pays off,
- legal issues may have to be considered, and
- changes in organizational funding and management structures may be necessary.

In this chapter we outline various nontechnical aspects that influence the software reuse process, including legal, economic, organizational and measurement issues. These aspects are covered in Sections 4.1, 4.2, 4.3, and 4.4, respectively. A summary follows in Section 4.5.

4.1 Legal Issues

Many legal issues in the context of software reuse are still diffuse. For example, what exactly are the rights and responsibilities of providers and consumers of reusable components? What happens if a reused component fails in a critical application? Such issues are not so important for reuse within companies or organizations, but may be a hindrance for reuse across such boundaries [FI94].

Software is legally protected as intellectual property. Laws for this protection may differ among various countries. The following types of protection are usually provided for software: *trade secret protection, copyright protection* and *patent protection* [Yoc89]. They are all legal concepts and apply to different aspects of software.

4.1.1 Trade Secret Protection

Trade secret protection is for the "know-how" that is embodied in software. Know-how in this context is substantial and secret information that is proprietary and leads to a commercial advantage. This becomes a problem when software is transferred to others, as is the case with intercorporation reuse. In this case the reuser is obliged to sign a nondisclosure agreement before the components to be reused are delivered. If, despite signing a nondisclosure agreement, the reuser does not keep the information confidential, damages may be claimed. However, others cannot be prevented from using the knowledge unless a patent protection is in effect [Kar95].

4.1.2 Patent Protection

Patents are granted for technical inventions that are new and involve inventive steps. The decision whether something is patentable is often difficult and requires legal advice. For example, patents are granted for processes or methods which describe how products work. A computer is a product and an algorithm is such a process [Kar95].

4.1.3 Copyright Protection

Copyright protection is the most common form of protection for software. It covers the software itself but not any underlying ideas and principles, which may be protected by patents. Copyright owners hold the right to reproduce their software, to reuse, maintain and adapt it, to reverse engineer it, to make backup copies, and to authorize third parties to perform such activities. Buyers of copyright protected software are allowed to make backup copies and to study the software, especially to get information about interoperability, unless this is provided by other means [Kar95].

4.1.4 Responsibilities and Liabilities

In the context of software reuse, questions about responsibilities and liabilities have to be addressed. Especially for reuse across company boundaries, questions about a guarantee that the software works become important. Who will fix it in case it does not work? Who is liable in case the reused component malfunctions? So far, software is usually reused at one's own risk. This is especially true if the reused software is in the public domain. It is the responsibility of the reuser to check whether reused components fulfill quality standards and meet specifications. Careful testing of software before it is reused may also be important in this context. If software to be reused is purchased, such issues should be addressed in the purchase agreement [Bra94d].

Cooper states that the risks of liability deserve serious management attention but do not appear to offer a significant impediment to software reuse [Coo94]. A main distinction has to be made whether reused software has been modified in a new system. In case of modifications by the reuser, the reuser bears the primary liability. This is similar to the situation when vendor-supplied hardware components are integrated into one's system.

4.2 Economic Issues

Costs associated with software reuse must be justified by the expected benefits; i.e., there must be sufficient return on investment. The following questions have to be answered [Coo94]:

- How can the expected benefits be measured and priced?
- How are the various abstract levels of software reuse measured?
- What is the potential extent of reuse for a particular software component?
- What is the projected shelf-life for that component?
- How frequently will the requirements of that component change?

The reuse process is an economic model of supply and demand. The model includes producers, consumers and a distribution mechanism. How much producers are able to transfer depends on how well their products match what the consumers need. The following factors affect this [CC94]:

- the quality and reusability of the producer's software
- the skill and knowledge of the consumer about reuse and the reusable software
- the degree of congruence between the producer's and consumer's project requirements

Costs incurred by a project creating reusable components must be recovered from the reusers of those components [FI94].

4.2.1 Initial Investments

Initial investments are needed in order to install a reuse program. These investments include costs that do not directly support the completion of a company's primary development goals. Instead, money is invested to make components of this development effort more reusable. The completion of maintenance investments is the starting point of reuse investments [BB91].

Separating these costs may be difficult. Making software maintainable is often an integral part of the development process, whereas making its components reusable is not. However, maintenance will also benefit from money being spent for software reuse. The reuse benefit can be calculated by comparing costs for activities done with reuse and those done without reuse, e.g., comparing the costs for developing a software system from scratch to the costs of developing this software system utilizing reusable components from a repository. Reuse investments are cost effective when they are smaller than the sum of all reuse benefits [BB91]. The benefits can only be estimated at the time the investments have to be made. If early estimations indicate that benefits will be small, then only limited investments should be made.

4.2.2 Reuse Effectiveness

Making reuse cost-effective can be accomplished by increasing the level of reuse, by reducing the average cost of reuse, and by reducing investments to achieve reuse benefits [BB91]. Early in the development phase the merit of investing in certain components must be identified and their reuse potential must be determined. Buying components from the commercial software market may be taken into consideration. Even if the initial cost is higher, it might turn out that in the long run a commercial product might prove more effective if it is well documented, generalized and of high quality.

Reuse effectiveness can be improved by reducing reuse costs and reuse investments (without reducing reuse). Reuse costs can be reduced by making components easy to find, adapt and integrate into new systems. Investments can be reduced by accurately predicting future needs. The measurement of reuse effectiveness is covered in Section 4.4.

4.3 Organizational Issues

Organizational factors can greatly affect the implementation of reuse programs. Findings indicate that organizational changes will be required before the full potential of software reuse can be realized [BKZ93]. Project managers want their projects to succeed, probably even at the expense of other groups in the same company. In fact, this enhances their career opportunities because it makes them more successful than their direct competitors. In such a corporate culture, development groups are not encouraged to build generalized software components that may be reused not only in their own future projects but also in projects of other groups. Building generalized components for the sake of reusability decreases productivity of their current project and increases productivity in projects where these components can be reused, i.e., possibly in other groups.

In this section we describe different reuse modes, organizational models, producer and consumer models, and reuse maturity models.

4.3.1 Reuse Modes

Different modes of performing software reuse comprise planned, systematic and institutionalized reuse versus ad-hoc, opportunistic and individual reuse.

The most common form of reuse is informal and ad-hoc, where no methods for reuse are defined. It is the responsibility of the individual software developer to possibly identify and locate reusable components. The productivity increase is only marginal.

Systematic reuse requires up-front efforts to define guidelines and procedures, and to measure reuse performance. It means a change of software development methods. Establishing a reuse program is a long-term process and is not easy. Systematic software reuse requires appropriate organizational structures. The Reuse Adoption Process of the Software Productivity Consortium focuses on the transfer of reuse technologies like processes, methods, and tools into an organization.

Navarro has described the Flexible Software Factory (FSF) Adoption Strategy, which is used to initiate and guide the transformation of a software engineering organization to a state where software reuse is instrumental to the production process [Nav93]. The goal is to have an organization that aligns work, objectives, intentions and any resources to support software reuse. This strategy consists of various phases and activities. The purpose is to understand the software engineering organization, determine needed changes, and finally to effectively incorporate reuse into the production process. For more details see Navarro [Nav92, Nav93].

4.3.2 Organizational Models

Large-scale reuse in an organization cannot be adopted without organizational changes. Technology is an important prerequisite for reuse, but people make it work. Reuse in an organization can only be achieved when people cooperate [GR95]. Producing valuable and reusable software components is not enough. We must ensure their transfer to the consumers.

Various models for organizations that support software reuse exist. These models influence development practices and are an indicator of reuse maturity in a software company. In practice, a company might reflect some combination

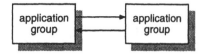

Fig. 4.1. Ad-hoc reuse

of these models. We distinguish four different models which are described subsequently (see Goldberg/Rubin [GR95] and Karlsson [Kar95]):

1. Ad-hoc reuse among application groups
2. Repository-based reuse among application groups
3. Centralized reuse with a component group
4. Domain-based reuse

Ad-hoc reuse among application groups. Frequently companies use organizations based on projects. If there is no explicit commitment to reuse then reuse can happen in an informal and haphazard way at best. Most of the reuse, if any, will occur within projects (see Fig. 4.1).

The reuse of components from different projects may occur but is the exception. Goldberg and Rubin call this "reuse in the hallway" and describe the situation with the following short story [GR95]:

> An engineer is pacing around his office late at night—mumbling to himself—until a colleague bumps into him:
> "What are you doing?" she asks.
> "Thinking," he says.
> "What about?" she asks.
> He explains his problem. She smiles. She has solved a similar problem.
> "Come along," she urges. "I will show you my solution."
> And together they go to her office to find the solution.

Repository-based reuse among application groups. The situation slightly improves when a component repository is used and can be accessed by various application groups (see Fig. 4.2). However, no explicit mechanism exists for putting components into the repository and no one is responsible for the quality of the components in this repository. This can lead to many problems and hamper software reuse.

The repository-based reuse approach is based on quantity because any components can be put into the repository and there is no control over their

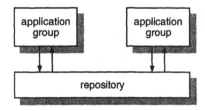

Fig. 4.2. Repository-based reuse

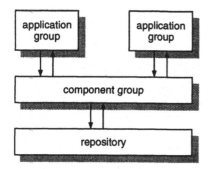

Fig. 4.3. Centralized reuse

quality and usefulness. If no effort had been made to make the components reusable, then reusers must be cautious. And as there is no control over the input and no maintenance of the components, reusers have to be cautious even when the components had been prepared with high quality and reusability in mind.

Goldberg and Rubin distinguish between the *ad-hoc model* and the *supply and demand model* [GR95]. In the former there is no control over what goes into and out of the repository. In the latter, components are encouraged to enter the repository and compete for attention. Components that are not reused by others are removed from the repository.

The reuse of a central repository may yield to a large number of available components. Unfortunately, reusers cannot trust these components since no quality control is in effect.

Centralized reuse with a component group. In this scenario a *component group* is explicitly responsible for the repository (see Fig. 4.3). The group determines which components are to be stored in the repository, ensures the quality of these components and the availability of necessary documentation, and helps in retrieving suitable components in a particular reuse scenario. This amounts to centralized production and management of reusable software components. Application groups are separated from the component group, which acts as a kind of subcontractor to each application group. An objective of the component group is to minimize redundancy.

In the *expert services model* members of the component group (called *reuse team* by Goldberg and Rubin) work on specific projects also [GR95]. Especially during start-up of a new project, the knowledge of members of this group about the availability of reusable components is invaluable. The component group can also gain knowledge about components in the project that are possible candidates for inclusion in the repository. They also gain first-hand information about problems and possible improvements of existing components.

Another form of the component group is the *product center model* [GR95]. In this model members of the component group are not loaned to projects; the group is responsible for the administration of the central repository, but does

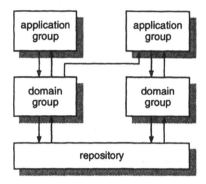

Fig. 4.4. Domain-based reuse

not give support in retrieving and reusing them. In this case reuse is viewed as a standard part of software development. It is a matter of course that application groups use the existing repository and do not need any explicit help in doing so.

Having a central component group raises the question of who pays for it. The organization can regard the group as some kind of overhead or investment and pay for it; or the costs can be covered by projects that benefit from that group by reusing components.

Domain-based reuse. The specialization of component groups amounts to domain-based reuse, as depicted in Fig. 4.4. Each domain group is responsible for components in its domain, e.g., network components, user interface components, database components.

Application groups may build their applications by integrating components from different domains. This organization yields to the acquisition of specific skills and knowledge of specific software domains. One possible drawback may be an overhead in communication between project and domain groups.

Résumé. As software companies increase their commitment to reuse, they will pass from ad-hoc reuse with application groups only through domain-based reuse with domain groups and application groups. Adopting domain-based reuse requires sufficient company size to maintain specialized groups. Component groups are responsible for developing reusable components. Domain groups are also responsible for the development of reusable components; in addition, they have to gain knowledge about their specific domain. Application groups are obligated to develop applications by using components created by these specialized groups. These subareas, component engineering (design for reuse), application engineering (design with reuse) and domain engineering (design for reuse in a certain domain) are described in Chapters 13, 14 and 15.

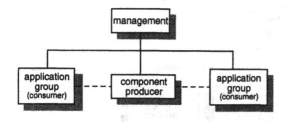

Fig. 4.5. Lone producer

4.3.3 Producers and Consumers

Having one or several groups for component administration creates a distinction between producers and consumers of components. Producers (component groups) design and develop reusable components. Consumers (application groups) design and develop products with reusable components. The relationship between consumers and producers is essential. Producer groups can be located at different organizational levels. Four models of these producer/consumer relationships have been identified at Hewlett-Packard and are depicted by Fafchamps [Faf94]:

1. *Lone producer*
   A single individual handles the reuse needs of several application groups (see Fig. 4.5). The lone producer's primary role is to design, develop and/or maintain reusable components. Maintenance is typically done by newly hired programmers, whereas design and development activities are performed mostly by experienced programmers. Lone producers face the problems of informal change requests, work overload, isolation and communication overload.

2. *Nested producer*
   Each application group has an individual who provides reuse services and expertise. Nested producers are members of the application group and contribute to the development of this product (see Fig. 4.6). However, their reuse position may be at risk when managers of the application

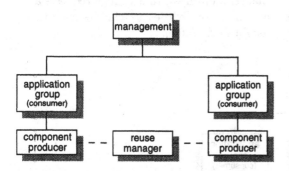

Fig. 4.6. Nested producer

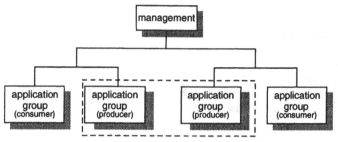

Fig. 4.7. Pool producer

group face critical phases in product development and divert reuse efforts toward product needs.

3. *Pool producer*
   Two or more groups collaborate to produce and share components (see Fig. 4.7). Pool producers belong to a stable and identifiable organizational group. The communication overhead may be high in this model, because the groups may be at geographically different locations. Communication increases with the number of groups and product lines.

4. *Team producer*
   Groups of producers interact with groups of consumers. Consumer groups develop products; they are inwardly oriented. A producer group interacts with the consumer groups; they are outwardly oriented. Producer groups have a dedicated manager, their own budget and a typical group structure (see Fig. 4.8).

These consumer/producer models have various advantages and disadvantages. For example, Fafchamps reports that the *nested producer model* did not work well at Hewlett-Packard. This is most likely due to "double management" in this model. The most important thing for all these models is that the right people are selected for the producer groups (i.e., highly skilled and experienced in software techniques, in the application domains, and also in communication and interpersonal relationships), that change requests are managed properly, that ownership and responsibilities are clarified, and that conflict-resolution strategies are established [Faf94].

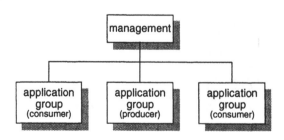

Fig. 4.8. Team producer

Prieto-Díaz has also identified specific roles that are crucial in a reuse infrastructure: librarians, asset managers and reuse managers [Pri90]:

− *Librarian*
The librarian is responsible for the promotion of reuse by making components easily available to potential reusers.

− *Asset manager*
The asset manager controls compliance with quality standards of reusable components.

− *Reuse manager*
The reuse manager coordinates the overall reuse effort and supports the collection of relevant data needed as feedback for domain analysis.

Librarians and asset managers are members of the component group and/or the domain group. Reuse managers are responsible for one or more such groups.

These roles complement the tasks of the domain analyst, domain expert and domain engineer, who are members of a domain group. They are described in Chapter 13.

4.3.4 Reuse Maturity

Reuse maturity is a measure of the effectiveness of an organization's reuse activities. The evaluation of reuse maturity can be an incentive to take steps for increasing it. The presence or absence of adequate organizational structures is a good indicator for reuse maturity in organizations. Assigning an organization to one of the models described in the previous sections gives a first clue about the maturity reached.

A five-level maturity model has been proposed by Koltun and Hudson [KH91]. In this model the five levels are distinguished by motivation, planning for reuse, breadth of reuse involvement, responsibility for making reuse happen, process by which reuse is leveraged, reuse inventory, classification activity, technology support, metrics, and legal/accounting considerations. The five levels are *initial/chaotic, monitored, coordinated, planned* and *ingrained.* Table 4.1 gives an overview of the characteristics of the various levels of this maturity model.

Similar models have been developed by other authors and/or organizations, for example, a five-stage maturity model by the Software Productivity Consortium. The proposed stages are *ad-hoc reuse, repeatable reuse, portable reuse, architectural reuse,* and *systematic reuse.* An overview of various models is given by Griss et al. [GFW94].

Table 4.1. Characteristics of reuse maturity levels

Level	Characteristics
1. *Initial/chaotic*	short-term thinking reuse costs are feared resistance to reuse reuse is individualized, uncoordinated, unmonitored
2. *Monitored*	managerial awareness little active promotion of reuse reuse costs are known individual achievements
3. *Coordinated*	organizational responsibility domain analyses for product line reuse tactics payoff of reuse is known component standardization,
4. *Planned*	life cycle view of reuse reports of reuse costs and savings reuse is supported and encouraged reuse across all functional areas
5. *Ingrained*	corporation wide view reuse is regular business domain analyses across all product lines corporation wide definitions, guidelines, standards

4.4 Measurement Issues

It is often said that we cannot manage what we cannot measure. Software reuse is no exception to the rule. Reuse spans multiple projects and has an influence even on organizational structures of companies. To manage such enterprise-wide activities requires some kind of monitoring. Software metrics can be used to estimate costs, cost savings, and the value of software practices [Pou92].

In the following subsections we describe various measures that are useful in the context of software reuse.

4.4.1 Reuse Level

The amount of software reuse (the *reuse level*) in a certain software system can be determined by the ratio of reused components (or their lines of code) to the total components of the system (or total amount of code lines). This measure does not consider more subtle aspects like adaptation costs, but it is objective.

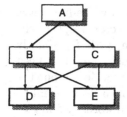

Fig. 4.9. Sample system with five components

$$\text{reuse level} = \frac{\text{number of reused components}}{\text{total number of components}}$$

A proposal that reuse be measured as the number of lines of code incorporated in a system without modification, divided by the total number of lines of code in the system has also been made by the Software Productivity Metrics Working Group of the IEEE [BKZ93]. We can further distinguish between external and internal reuse and determine these levels. The internal and external reuse levels consider components that have been developed for the system or outside the system, respectively [FI94].

Example. A small system consists of five components, say A, B, C, D and E (see Fig. 4.9). Component A calls components B and C; both B and C call D and E. If D and E are reused and the other three components have been developed from scratch, we get a reuse level of $\frac{2}{5}$ or 0.4.

Object-oriented systems. Object-oriented software development allows the simple modification and extension of components through inheritance. In this case a new component reuses a fraction of the component it inherits from. Different ways of calculating reuse levels are possible. We can simply regard the components as either new or reused or do a more subtle distinction by considering how often a component is reused through inheritance, or even how often and how many of its functions are called.

4.4.2 Line and Word Runs

A reuse measurement based on lines and words for a low-level determination of white-box reuse has been proposed by Childs and Sametinger [CS96b].

The number of lines that are identical in file **a** and file **b** as opposed to the total number of lines (of file **a**) gives an indication of how much of file **a** has been reused in file **b**.

$$\text{line reuse percentage} = \frac{\text{number of identical lines}}{\text{total number of lines}} \times 100$$

This formula can be used in both directions, i.e., to determine how much of file **a** is being reused in file **b** and to determine how much of file **b** originates from file **a** (by using the total number of lines of file **b**).

Comparing lines and words gives a good indication about white-box reuse. Let R_l and R_w denote the reuse percentage of lines and words, respectively. As it turns out, usually R_l and R_w do not differ much, with R_w slightly higher than R_l. If both R_l and R_w are high, then obviously reuse had been achieved. If R_l is low, but R_w is high, then reuse had been achieved, but the reused text had been modified on a more local basis, which leads to many different lines (and a lower R_l), but still leaves many equal words (leading to a higher R_w). Finally, if both R_l and R_w are low, then apparently there is only little reuse.

If several consecutive lines are identical in two files, it is likely that they were reused. If there is a solitary identical line, it might have been reused, but it also might have nothing to do with reuse at all. For example, consider lines in C and cplusplus source code containing closing braces ('}'). In some cases such lines may be regarded as being reused in a certain context, i.e., when the surrounding lines are reused as well.

We obtain a modified reuse percentage by only considering lines (or words) when they are part of a run of certain length. For more details see Chapter 19, where we describe a case study with line and word runs.

4.4.3 Return on Investment

Henderson-Sellers suggests metrics based on reuse savings and generalization costs [HS93]. The return-on-investment metric is defined as follows:

$$\text{return on investment} = \frac{\text{reuse savings}}{\text{generalization costs}}$$

It is important that long-term generalization costs not exceed long-term reuse savings; otherwise reuse is not recommended. Reuse savings can be determined by estimating the costs for developing all components anew and subtracting the costs necessary for partly new development plus costs for finding reusable components and for their modification (if needed). Generalization costs are difficult to assess, but will somehow depend on the size of components. Regarding a single project only would suggest that components from a repository are reused without providing components for the repository, thus minimizing generalization costs. Therefore, return on investment has to be assessed over a number of projects.

It is also important to consider the whole spectrum of life cycle costs, e.g., costs for testing, verification and maintenance. On the one hand, these costs will hopefully be reduced by reusing a component. On the other hand, despite cost reductions during development, the integration of a component may have an impact on the overall system design and a negative impact on software maintenance [MR90].

low reuse maturity:

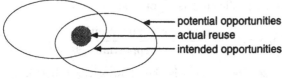

potential opportunities
actual reuse
intended opportunities

high reuse maturity:

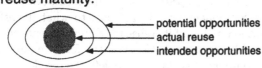

potential opportunities
actual reuse
intended opportunities

Fig. 4.10. Reuse maturity

4.4.4 Reuse Maturity

Section 4.3.4 on page 47 described reuse maturity levels. It is difficult to quantify these levels. Organizations often measure their reuse efforts by the ratio of reused source code lines to the total number of source code lines. This is not sufficient for the measurement of reuse maturity because it does not reflect how many reuse opportunities had been missed [DW92].

Reuse maturity can be seen as the range of expected results in *reuse efficiency, reuse proficiency* and *reuse effectiveness* that can be achieved in an organization by following a reuse process [DW92]. But even though we give formulas below, it is difficult to determine the results unless high reuse maturity has been achieved by an organization. Otherwise the input parameters are not readily available and have to be based on estimated numbers.

Fig. 4.10 shows two examples of low and high reuse maturity [DW92]. In the upper example potential and intended opportunities do not match each other well. Thus actual reuse is limited from the start. In the lower example these opportunities match better, facilitating higher actual reuse.

It is crucial for organizations to recognize existing reuse opportunities and to exploit them systematically. Failing to recognize them leads to fruitless efforts.

Reuse efficiency. Reuse efficiency measures how much of the intended reuse opportunities have actually been exploited by an organization. It is determined by the ratio of the percentage of exploited reuse opportunities to the percentage of intended reuse opportunities. If the intended reuse is 50% (i.e., the organization aims at exploiting 50% of the reuse opportunities) and the actual reuse is 25%, then the reuse efficiency is $\frac{25}{50}$ or 0.5.

$$\text{reuse efficiency} = \frac{\text{exploited reuse opportunities}}{\text{intended reuse opportunities}}$$

Reuse proficiency. Reuse proficiency is the ratio of actual reuse to potential reuse, i.e., the ratio of the percentage of exploited reuse opportunities to the percentage of potential reuse opportunities. If the potential reuse is 75% and actual reuse is 25%, reuse proficiency is $\frac{25}{75}$ or 0.33.

$$\text{reuse proficiency} = \frac{\text{exploited reuse opportunities}}{\text{potential reuse opportunities}}$$

Reuse effectiveness. Reuse effectiveness is the ratio of reuse benefits to reuse costs. It can be measured by the ratio of the difference between what the development of a new component would have cost to what it costs to reuse the component times the number of its reuse to the investments costs to acquire or develop the reusable component. Consider the following example: the development of a new component costs USD 10,000; the development to make it reusable costs USD 13,000; to reuse the component costs USD 1,000. If the component is used twice, then the reuse effectiveness is $2 \times \frac{10,000-1,000}{13,000}$ or 1.38.

$$\text{reuse effectiveness} = \text{no. of reuses} \, \frac{\text{cost of development} - \text{cost of reuse}}{\text{cost of acquisition or development}}$$

4.4.5 Industrial Example

Significant and largely positive effects of software reuse on software development have been found in two reuse programs at Hewlett-Packard [Lim94]. Metrics were collected in these programs and demonstrated that reuse can provide a substantial return on investment. Findings indicated that software reuse positively influenced quality, productivity and development time. Returns on investment (savings/costs) were 216 and 410 percent with gross savings of 5.6 and 4.1 million US dollars, respectively. The relative cost of creating reusable code components was about twice as high as creating these components without supporting their reuse. The relative cost to reuse these components, i.e., integrate them into new systems, was only about a quarter to a fifth of the costs to develop them anew.

The FAGQM (Framework Assisted Goal Question Metric) model is presented and illustrated by Vaishnavi and Bandi [VB96]. It suggests metrics for the perspective of development for reuse and development with reuse. A framework for setting up a software measurement program is described by Goldberg and Rubin [GR95].

4.5 Summary

In this chapter we have described legal, economic, organizational and measurement aspects of software reuse. This chapter is intended to give an introduction rather than to provide detailed information on the subject.

Readers who are interested in more details on nontechnical aspects of reuse are referred to further literature. Griss, Favaro and Walton give a good overview of the subject [GFW94]. Nontechnical issues are also covered in the books by Karlsson [Kar95] and Goldberg/Rubin [GR95]. Zand and Samadzadeh have edited a special issue of the *Journal of Systems and Software* on software reuse; this issue covers many nontechnical issues [ZS95]. Producers and consumers at Hewlett-Packard are described by Fafchamps [Faf94].

5. Installing a Reuse Program

Contents

The benefits of reuse are quite apparent. So the question is not whether to install a reuse program but rather how to install it. Some of the benefits of reuse can certainly be realized by casual approaches. However, adopting large-scale, institutionalized reuse requires many steps and is not trivial at all [Bra94d]. Reuse programs should start small and gain experience through pilot projects in order to be successful and effective. A common misconception is that object-oriented programming will bring software reuse for free.

In this chapter we describe how to install a reuse program. Steps that have to be undertaken to install a reuse program are depicted in Section 5.1. Selling the idea to management is discussed in Section 5.2. In Section 5.3 we consider how to motivate reuse, and in Section 5.4 we cover third-party components and component markets. A summary follows in Section 5.5.

5.1 Steps to Install a Reuse Program

Software reuse must be explicitly installed. It requires start-up costs and has effects not only on technical aspects. A reuse program should be installed in progressive steps, where each step sets the basis for the following steps. This enables starting a reuse program and learning from it. Advantages for this incremental approach are [Pri91c]:

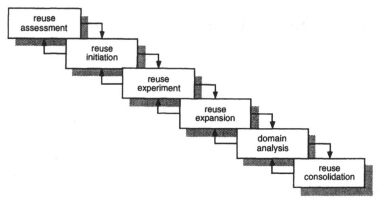

Fig. 5.1. Steps to install a reuse program

- immediate return on investment,
- confidence within the organization,
- ease of management,
- possibility to tune and refine the reuse program, and
- possibility to monitor and evaluate reuse.

Additionally, the process should be systematic and formal, i.e., consistent, repeatable and decomposable into well-defined steps [Pri91c]. These steps may be carried out repeatedly, increasing the scope of reuse in case its adoption has been successful so far. The steps for adding the practice of reuse to an organization are described in the subsequent sections. An overview of these steps is depicted in Fig. 5.1.

Various reuse benefits were described in Section 2.2 on page 11. Reuse programs can be tuned to benefits that fit the business objectives of an organization. The objectives should be clearly defined, e.g., productivity/quality improvements, time to market [GFW94].

Several authors have described how to set up reuse programs, e.g., Braun [Bra94d], Goldberg and Rubin [GR95], Griss [Gri93], Griss et al. [GFW94], Joos [Joo94], Mili et al. [MMM95] and Prieto-Díaz [Pri91c].

5.1.1 Reuse Assessment

Despite of the apparent benefits of reuse, its potential in a certain organization have to be understood and should be assessed before a reuse program is installed. The potential payoff/cost to the organization have to be analyzed. The following questions should be addressed during this phase:

- *Is software reuse feasible in our organization?*
  Is software production large enough to justify a reuse program? Will management support a reuse program? Are there enough (human and financial) resources for a reuse program? Can we afford a reuse program? How many

similar systems will be produced? Are reusable assets already available? What do we want to reuse?

- *Is our domain suitable for reuse?*
  How broad/complex is the domain? Is the domain mature and well understood? Is it stable or rapidly changing?

- *How is the cost/benefit relation?*
  What is the desired level of reuse? How much will the reuse program cost? Is it economically justified?

- *How will we implement reuse?*
  What are the steps to implement the reuse program?

In case an organization is developing software in more than one domain, it is recommended to identify those which are well understood, have applications with similar requirements, and are important for the organization. Initial reuse installment can be restricted to only one or several of these domains.

5.1.2 Reuse Initiation

Existing software has to be analyzed in order to find, evaluate and select potentially reusable software components. The components may need to be generalized and/or complemented with specific reuse documentation. Then they need to be stored in a repository to serve as the base of reusable components in the organization. The effort needed for performing these tasks will vary depending on the scope of the reuse program to be installed. This may range from a part-time individual at almost no cost to the installment of a separate organizational unit. Especially in the latter case, support from top management is essential because initial costs face a slow return on investment [Pri91c] (see also Section 4.3 on page 40 on organizational issues).

Not every component that is reusable will be considered in this initiation step. Thus categories of reusable components should be identified and prioritized. It is important to acquire components that are important for the business. Assigning components to different levels of generality can be useful in this context. Examples of such levels are: components of interest to any business, components of interest to any company within the industry, and components specific to the company [GR95].

5.1.3 Reuse Experiment

Risks and costs are reduced by starting with a reuse experiment. This will facilitate learning about technical and organizational issues that impede the reuse program. The experiment can be done with an ongoing project as well as with a new one that is to be approached with reuse.

It is important that success criteria be defined and measurements be taken for the experiment. The project should not be too long, so that results are not delayed too long. Depending on the results, the reuse program should be extended (positive results) or reworked (unsatisfactory results).

5.1.4 Reuse Expansion

If the reuse experiment has been successful, a commitment to change has to be institutionalized. Other applications have to be integrated into the reuse efforts and the repository of reusable components has to be extended and consolidated. Incentives to support the program should be provided until reuse becomes part of the culture [Joo94].

Other domains can be considered for reuse either by doing an experiment in that domain also, or, in case reuse benefits are convincing enough, by developing the needed resources right away.

5.1.5 Domain Analysis

Domain analysis is necessary in order to institute systematic reuse. It comprises activities to identify needs that are common to multiple projects in a certain domain. Chapter 13 covers the topic in depth.

5.1.6 Reuse Consolidation

Institutionalized reuse requires adjustments of organizational structures and additional activities like domain analysis and administrating the component repository. Software development processes have to be adapted. Reuse training for engineers as well as tool support for reuse has to be established [Joo94].

Steps for installing reuse may be rerun even if reuse has been installed successfully already. For example, the abstraction level of reused components should be as high as possible. In a first step the reuse of function libraries may be considered. In a next installation cycle, object-oriented technology may be considered as well. Depending on the maturity of component technology, further component types should be included in the reuse program.

5.2 Management Commitment

Installing a software reuse program cannot be accomplished successfully without the commitment of management. Substantial effort may be necessary to convince managers of the necessity of a reuse program. Without their support reuse installmation is doomed to fail.

Griss et al. provide some guidelines on how to sell reuse to management [GFW94]. Important topics are:

- benefits and costs,
- extent of required changes,
- degree of (managerial and technical) innovation,
- amount of needed management time and effort,
- involved risks, and
- a plan for reuse introduction.

Reuse has to be presented as a concept that is sufficiently mature, where both technical and nontechnical aspects are understood well enough to be ready for exploitation.

The primary goal in installing software reuse is not to "do reuse" but to improve certain aspects in the software process, e.g., product quality. In this sense, as Ylä-Rotiala points out, software reuse is nothing more than an improvement of software engineering methodology [YR95].

5.3 Reuse Motivation

People are an important factor in the successful installation of a reuse program. Components will only be used if people are willing to do so. On page 16 we mentioned the *not-invented-here* syndrome. As long as software reuse is not a matter of fact, people have to be motivated to overcome their negative attitudes.

Discomfort with reuse is often expressed by statements like: "We don't want to do extra work to benefit someone else," "We can do this better," "We won't use it if it's built by someone else" [GR95], or "Reusable code is too slow," "Reusable code is too hard to understand," "It is quicker to write this on our own" [GFW94]. Competition within organizations can be a hindrance in this respect.

Under pressure to complete a software project as quickly as possible software, engineers do not have time to design, implement and document with reuse in mind. Short-term needs of individual projects have to be balanced with long-term needs for building a collection of reusable components. Developers and project managers have to be encouraged to build reusable components and to incorporate existing components into their systems. Examples of incentive programs have been described by Poulin [Pou95] (see also [Joo94]).

There are several possibilities to increase the motivation for software reuse, but not every attempt will lead to successful reuse when responses to symptoms of reuse obstacles are misaligned with reuse goals. For example, a bonus for placing a component into the repository does not necessarily lead to a collection of useful components [Mal93]. Problems with various motivations are depicted by Goldberg and Rubin [GR95]:

- *Royalty payments*
  One form of propagating reuse is to pay royalties to the creators of soft-

ware components every time their component is reused in a different context. This model is widely used in the book domain. Books are reusable components, too. Goldberg and Rubin point out that this model may lead developers to prefer reusing their own components or those of their friends. Also it is difficult to determine the degree of ownership of object-oriented components, where inheritance may yield to more than one owner. This problem gets even worse with components at higher levels of abstraction, where many developers have contributed to a component.

– *Reuse bribes*

Instead of paying the authors of components, we can motivate reuse by rewarding those who reuse the components. But in this case, developers may tend to reuse as much as possible, even though it may not be justified at all.

Other motivating activities include punishments for not reusing and rewards for appropriate reuse. Reuse incentives are important to encourage reuse, but reuse incentives alone are not a key to successful software reuse. For example, Poulin and Wasmund have reported that reuse incentives helped to create reuse awareness and did not cost much, but did not change much either [Pou95, Was94]. But there have also been positive reports, e.g., monetary rewards at GTE [Pri91b].

Developing software the way it has always been developed and providing motivation for software reuse in some form described above does not necessarily change much. Software developers do not need extra payments or bribes to make a design before starting to implement, because this is the way we develop software systems. In this sense we have to change the culture so that reusing existing software components and making new components reusable is the way we do software engineering. And we have to keep in mind, as stated by Goldberg and Rubin [GR95], that it is not the goal to reuse software components, but by doing so we hopefully increase software productivity and design better software systems from the viewpoint of adaptability, modifiability and maintainability.

We should reward software engineers for meeting their goals and objectives. However, these goals and objectives are not primarily to reuse components. They are to build reliable, high-quality software systems in a certain amount of time. Software engineers must objectively judge whether it is better to reuse a component or to develop a new one. "Reuse is not the goal; it is the means to a goal" [GR95].

Achieving these goals requires changes and incentives not at the software engineering level but at the project and upper management level. Building reusable components is in contradiction to the goal of building a single software system with minimal cost. Therefore, it is necessary to distinguish between producers and consumers of components and have both application groups and component groups (see Section 4.3 on page 40).

Education and training is another important contribution for the success of software reuse. A series of courses has been proposed by Griss et al. [GFW94]: *introduction to reuse*, *"consumer" course*, *"producer" course*, *domain analysis*, *advanced programming*, and *librarian and maintainer training*. Reuse lexicons help in agreeing on basic definitions. Additionally, handbooks and guidebooks can be helpful.

5.4 Third-Party Components

Reuse activities incorporate systematic creation and reuse of components. However, components considered for reuse may also be developed by others (outside the company). In this case several points have to be taken into consideration [Pit93]:

– *Quality*
  Quality of third-party components is usually the major concern of managers and developers. Unfortunately, validation and verification of (complex) components is not viable in practice. A list of known defects and reference sites may give a first indication of a component's quality. The concept of programming by contract offered in the Eiffel programming language is an example of ensuring a certain behavior of components [Mey88].
  The quality of a purchased component will usually be higher than the quality that could be achieved by developing for a comparable price. Quality concerns may sometimes simply express the *not-invented-here* syndrome.

– *Costs and benefits*
  Using third-party components may reduce a product's time to market, but it also means increased dependence on component suppliers. Costs are avoided by not having to develop and maintain certain components. Potential costs lie in the possibility of having to adapt and modify them.

– *Ease of modification/adaptation*
  Many components are difficult to adapt and modify or have only limited capabilities in this respect. It is important to know one's own requirements for third-party components and, in case they do not completely fulfill them, to determine whether it is possible and how difficult and time-consuming it is to make needed modifications.

– *Risk analysis*
  Commitment to the reuse of third-party components always involves certain risks. One way of managing these risks is by using conventional risk management, e.g., Boehm's spiral model [Boe91] (see Section 12.4 on page 156). For example, the component vendor may be required to

Table 5.1. Software reuse at various levels

Level	Criterion
3. Intl./national level	existence of a component market
2. Corporate level	institutionalized reuse culture
1. Project level	reuse-driven development

provide support in fixing bugs and/or making certain enhancements. Especially when using components from small vendors it is advisable to take precautions in case the vendor files bankruptcy.

– *Legal issues*
Legal issues have to be considered as well (see Section 4.1 on page 38).

The scenario of composing software systems out of components will not be achieved unless we manage to install a *market* of reusable components. Limited markets do exist in the form of software repositories. For example, class libraries and function libraries are commercially available, and collections of reusable assets are also used within companies to increase software productivity. However, we do not yet build software by using commercially available components like building blocks ("legos"). The primary challenge for *software component markets* is the integration of the components. Even if we pick components with the needed functionality, we will not be able to build the application by simply integrating these components because too many integration mechanisms exist which often cannot be combined.

In the context of software component markets, Morrison has suggested various success levels for software reuse [Mor91]. The goal is to achieve higher-quality products with lower costs for the customer. At the project level, development and maintenance have to be done with reuse in mind; i.e., components have to be designed and developed for reuse, and applications have to be designed and developed with reuse. At the company level it is important that a reuse culture be institutionalized, that reusable components be maintained and made accessible. At the national and international level, markets of reusable components must exist to avoid redundant developments in many companies (see Table 5.1).

Software component markets raise many nontechnical questions, as addressed in Chapter 4.

5.5 Summary

Systematic software reuse can only be achieved with careful planning. It requires much effort to be successful. We have described steps to install a reuse program. These steps will vary slightly depending on a company's or department's size and the extent of reuse to be accomplished.

Reuse maturity models can also be taken as a guideline to install reuse. Actions have to be taken to make the transition from one maturity level to the next.

The market for software components is not extensive yet, but third-party components are available and provide alternatives to custom development. In order to increase the availability of third-party components and to extend the flexibility of software, component technology has to be advanced. This is the topic of Part II.

Part II

Software Components

6. Software Components

Contents

We envision an ideal scenario of software engineering as building applications by assembling high-level components. If any required components are not available, they have to be built out of lower-level components. Finally, when even low-level components are not available, they have to be implemented in some programming language. Thus components are created either by composition or by programming.

The idea of this scenario is not new. In 1969 McIlroy envisioned an industry of reusable software components [McI76]. In 1982 Wasserman and Gutz saw the programmer of the future working with "standard components, programming in the large with a decreased need for programming in the small" [WG82]. These visions were based on the conception of source code components. We see a much broader definition of components.

In this chapter we discuss definitions of software components in Section 6.1, various forms of component interfaces in Section 6.2, and component platforms in Section 6.3. A summary follows in Section 6.4.

6.1 Component Definition

Several definitions of components and reusable components have been provided in the literature. We distinguish two different approaches. Components can be seen as some part of a software system that is identifiable and reusable. Functions and classes are examples of such components. Components can also be seen as the next level of abstraction after functions, modules and classes. The term *component-oriented programming* (as a successor to *object-oriented programming*) is often used in this context.

We propose a component definition and discuss related work in Sections 6.1.1 and 6.1.2, respectively.

6.1.1 Definition

In the introduction in Section 1.1 on page 2 we already previewed what we mean by software components in the context of reuse. We said that software components are any artefacts that we can integrate into and clearly identify in software systems. They have an interface, encapsulate internal details, and are documented separately. Now we give a more precise definition:

> *Reusable software components are self-contained, clearly identifiable artefacts that describe and/or perform specific functions and have clear interfaces, appropriate documentation and a defined reuse status.*

We clearly take the (conservative) approach of defining existing abstractions as components. If we want reuse to become a matter of fact, we have to start with existing components rather than to wait for new abstractions on the horizon. However, should a new technological breakthrough bring new kinds of components into being, our definition will (most probably) nicely cover them as well.

According to the definition given above, a component has to be self-contained, clearly identifiable, etc. We will elaborate the elements of our definition in more detail.

– *Self-containedness*
 Components should be *self-contained*, i.e., reusable without the need to include other components for reuse. In this sense, a function is regarded as a component if it can be reused on its own, i.e., without the need of any other functions. If other functions are needed as well, then the whole set of functions must be seen as reusable component, with one of the components serving as the interface to the whole group. For this reason, programming languages have introduced the concept of *modules* and *packages*. Function libraries are a set of functions that are reused. Not a single function but the whole library serves as reusable component with many different interfaces and functionalities. The same holds for higher-level components. One

module can serve as the interface for a set of modules which are the entity for reuse, i.e., the component to be reused. One process can serve as the interface for a set of processes which can even run on different machines. Classes of application frameworks typically cannot be reused stand-alone, but the whole collection of classes has to be reused (and thus is the reusable component).

It may not always be practical to integrate all parts with a component in order to make it self-contained, but the dependencies have to be clearly documented (see Section 6.3.2 on page 78 on such dependencies).

– *Identification*
Components have to be *clearly identifiable*, e.g., contained in a file rather than being spread over many locations and intermixed with other artefacts of software or documentation.
We use the term *artefact* in our definition to indicate that components can have a variety of different forms, e.g., source code, documentation, executable code.

– *Functionality*
Components describe and/or perform specific functions; i.e., components have a clearly specified functionality which they perform or describe (see *Documentation* below). We use the formulation *and/or* in the definition to indicate that components may also be descriptions of functionality without performing functions themselves. Thus we can regard software life cycle documents (e.g., specifications, design documents) as components although they do not harbor programatic functionality.

– *Interfaces*
Components have to have clear *interfaces* and hide details that are not needed for reuse. Details on interfaces are given in Section 6.2 on page 71.

– *Documentation*
Documentation is indispensable for reuse. The most useful component is rendered useless for reuse purposes when appropriate documentation is not available. Appropriateness depends on the kind of component and its complexity. Enough information must be provided to retrieve a component from a repository, evaluate its suitability for a certain reuse context, make adaptations, and integrate the component into its new environment. We deal with documentation in detail in Part IV.

– *Reuse status*
Components must be maintained to support systematic reuse. The *reuse status* contains information about who is the owner of a component, who maintains it, who can be contacted in case problems arise, and what is the quality status of the component. The reuse status or parts thereof may be known implicitly when reuse is limited to certain departments or small

companies. However, it becomes crucial information once reuse extends beyond company boundaries.

We have provided a broad and general definition of reusable software components. According to this definition we can have a variety of components like functions, classes, applications, subsystems, design documents, distributed processes, Ada packages, Omega prototypes, etc. However, we cannot simply reuse any of these components in a certain reuse context. A classification is important to assign components to specific categories and limit component retrieval to categories appropriate in a certain context. We provide a component taxonomy in Chapter 9.

6.1.2 Related Work

Here we discuss several existing definitions of components. We start with simple definitions and proceed to more sophisticated ones.

- Holibaugh et al. define a component vaguely as a "logical part of a system or program" [HP88]. This is an example of a general definition without explicit consideration of reuse aspects.

- Booch defines a *reusable software component* more specifically (at the source code level) as "a logically cohesive, loosely coupled module that denotes a single abstraction" [Boo87]. As such, these components provide vehicles to formally express algorithms and data structures; support software engineering principles like abstraction, information hiding, modularity, and locality; exploit facilities of programming languages (Ada in this case); and offer mechanisms for reuse.

- McGregor et al. use a more general definition. They write: "A component is any unit that provides a relatively independent piece that is used in combination with a number of components in different configurations" [MDK96].

- Hooper and Chester use the term *software component* "to mean any type of software resource that may be reused (e.g., code modules, designs, requirements specifications, domain knowledge, development experience, or documentation)" [HC91].

- Nierstrasz and Dami define *software components* as "static abstractions with plugs" [ND95]. By 'static' they mean that components can be stored in repositories. By 'abstraction' they mean that internal details are hidden and an interface to the component describes its (possibly complex) functionality. Finally, 'plugs' are well-defined ways of interaction and communication with the component and can have a variety of forms, e.g., parameters, ports, messages. This definition suggests that components are "static entities that are needed at system build-time" [Nie95].

- In the context of OpenDoc, a component software architecture, the following definition is given [Met94]: "Software components are defined as prefabricated, pretested, self-contained, reusable software modules—bundles of data and procedures—that perform specific functions."

- The NATO Standard for the Development of Reusable Software Components offers the following definition: A reusable software component is "a software entity intended for reuse." It "may be design, code, or other product of the software development process" [Bra94a, Bra94b, Bra94c]. Similarly, Kain defines a component as "a product of the development process that exhibits certain qualities of usability and separability" [Kai96]. These definitions are general and comprise more than just source code. Anything may be a reusable software component as long as it is intended for reuse and/or separable from its original context.

- Wegner sees component-based programming as the next (evolutionary) step after procedure-oriented programming and object-oriented programming [Weg93]. Components are "a generalization of objects that extends the primitives for realizing interaction to include distributed components, graphical user interfaces, databases, robots, and virtual reality." Interaction is a key characteristic of components. In procedure-oriented programming, software systems are sequences of actions. In object-oriented programming software systems are already collections of interacting entities. Components provide a more general model of computation by including distributed components, graphical user interfaces, etc.

- Szyperski sees component-oriented programming as a refined variation on object-oriented programming [Szy95]. Without explicitly defining what a component is, he considers information hiding, polymorphism, late binding and safety as crucial aspects for component-oriented programming.

Many of these definitions see components as some form of abstraction in existing programming languages with additional requirements regarding their characteristics, like *self-contained, independent* or *tightly coupled.*

Our definition provided in the previous section can be seen as a superset of the definitions listed in this section. We intentionally want a general definition of components to provide a broad range of reuse. Systematic reuse should be started with whatever component technology is available. Once new technologies become available and mature, reuse should be extended to cover new types of components as well.

Another difference between the definitions is, again due to our emphasis on reuse, that we explicitly include appropriate documentation and a defined reuse status. This is somewhat vague as it strongly depends on the type of component. However, in Part IV we provide more information on this topic.

6.2 Component Interfaces

Components are not completely independent of other components and of their environments. Many components are implemented in a specific programming language and cannot be reused in the context of arbitrary other languages. Other components run on a certain operating system and may require a certain window system.

An interface determines how a component can be reused and interconnected with other components. It defines an operation or a set of (usually related) operations that is available for a component. Most programming languages require the explicit documentation of a component interface. Classes and modules have been designed to explicitly separate interface and implementation. Procedural interfaces do not always document the complete interface; e.g., global data can be directly accessed without being documented in the procedure heading.

Executable components often do not have an explicit interface. There is no tool that checks whether such components are compatible. The needed information is available in the documentation at best. However, abstraction is provided, implementation details are hidden. The source code need not even be available.

Interfaces of components are crucial for their composition. One component exports certain functionality; another imports functionality. Two components can be composed, i.e., put together, if the requirements of the importing component match the provided functionality of the exporting component.

Multiple interfaces. Components may have multiple interfaces. This is useful to structure complex functionality or, for example, to provide backward compatibility.

Interface types. Components have different types of interfaces. They have a *programming interface*, a *user interface*, and/or a *data interface*. For reuse all three interfaces are important, although the programming interface is certainly the most important one.

All three types of interfaces are interesting in the context of reuse because they can provide a means for reusing a component. For example, tools with command-line user interfaces can be reused by means of pseudo ttys; i.e., another program simulates the input and output medium for the tool. Data interfaces can be used to subsequently transform data until it has reached its final form. Any components that read data in the required format and produce data in whatever format is required can be used in this transformation process. Unix filters are a prominent, successful example of this approach. In subsequent sections we discuss these interface types in more detail.

6.2.1 Data Interfaces

The simpler a component's interface is, the easier it is to reuse it. Components that read input data, perform some transformations or do calculations, and write output data have proven to be highly reusable. Components do their work without requesting further input after being invoked and can easily be reused for automating tasks (like *batch processing*).

ASCII text is the most common data format and the most common denominator for many software systems. Thus systems with textual input and output have proven most successful in automation. Other data formats are possible as well, for example, using a database. However, this reduces the likeliness that two components share the same data formats and can be used together.

Reusing components in a series, one component inputting the previous component's output, has provided the basis for one of the reuse success stories. The Unix operating environment provides the pipe mechanism that eases the connection of tools with textual input/output. The tools are the components and called filters (see Section 10.3 on page 133). Unix filters are processed sequentially and on a single machine (no distribution).

Textual input/output of two tools makes composition easy. However, it does not guarantee correct and useful interoperation of components. Texts can have various structures and semantics. Components may require the text for their input to conform to a certain structure. If another component's output does not provide this structure, connecting these components is technically feasible but does not make sense.

6.2.2 Command-Line User Interfaces

Software systems that require interaction from the user are more difficult to reuse. If a system has only a command-line user interface rather than a graphical user interface, pseudo ttys can be used to embed them in other software. This mechanism has been used to endow legacy systems with modern graphical user interfaces. Instead of redeveloping or restructuring the whole software system, only the user interface has to be developed, with the original (reused) system running in the background.

An example of the interconnection of interactive programs is *expect*, a program that reads scripts that resemble the user dialog [Lib90]. Components can be any batch or interactive programs. Two components are connected by another component (*expect*) that controls them by a given script. The main advantage of using a tool like *expect* is that it can easily deal with legacy applications, as there is no adaptation or modification necessary on these applications. The supported programs are not graphical; i.e., modern graphical user interfaces are not supported.

The reuse of tools with command-line user interfaces is more complicated than the reuse of tools with simple textual input/output. It is also more flexible, but the additional effort needed has prevented such tools from being reused extensively.

6.2.3 Graphical User Interfaces

Modern software systems have graphical user interfaces. Their reuse in a new environment provides a new challenge. The most trivial mechanism for application communication is sending keystrokes to other applications; this might be supported by the operating system. This requires no special arrangements on the part of an application but enables only limited reuse potential. More successful approaches require handling communication in an application.

A first step toward the integration of applications with graphical user interfaces is *dynamic data exchange* (DDE), which enables two applications to update information by automating the manual copying and pasting of data. The two applications are said to be connected through a link, where the application sending data is called the *source* the application receiving data is called the *destination*. Two applications can either exchange data whenever the data changes in the source application or whenever the destination application requests the data. The source may also notify its destination about data changes and supply the data only on demand.

Links between two applications can either exist permanently or be established by the user. Permanent links are automatically established whenever the source application is run. User-established links provide the flexibility of integrating arbitrary data of various applications. Besides exchanging data, this mechanism can also be used for sending commands. For example, one application can force another one to open or close a file.

DDE provides limited possibilities for communication between applications. Although useful in many situations, it does not really support the reuse of applications in order to build new software systems. Program control is not transferred among applications for the purpose of editing data, and data does not appear in destination applications as it would in source applications. Displaying data can require essential programming effort, though this problem has been solved already in the other application. These drawbacks are eliminated by cooperative application components as described in Chapter 7.

6.2.4 Programming Interfaces

Some software systems are designed for reuse; they provide a means for reusing and even extending them, i.e., an *application programming interface* or API.

Depending on the API and the application itself, reuse scenarios can differ. For example, an application may have a graphical user interface but allow its reuse without displaying anything on the screen (for the reuse of certain functionality). In this case the reuser provides the user interface. If the reused application's user interface is reused (or has to be reused), it may be possible to modify or extend the interface (e.g., menu entries) and add functionality to the application.

This kind of reuse should not be confused with the *use* of an application. Users of an application may use an API to modify and/or extend the application. With *reuse* we mean the integration of an application's functionality into another, new software system.

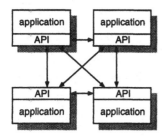

Fig. 6.1. Applications using Tcl/Tk

From the perspective of reuse, APIs are important as they allow the reuse of full-fledged applications. However, applications often bundle more functionality than may be required in certain reuse scenarios. This leads to unnecessary overhead. Additionally, two applications together may have the functionality that is needed, but they may not be reused together because each one provides its own user interface and cannot be reused in the background, or because their data formats are not compatible.

6.2.5 Command Language Interfaces

Command languages provide communication mechanisms between interactive programs and can allow reusers even to program both programs' appearance and actions. By the possibility to extend the built-in features of programs, command languages boost the power of these programs. Examples of the provision of powerful command languages are Unix shells [Ker84] and the Emacs editor [Sta86]. However, large-scale software reuse requires application-independent command languages, so that not every new program requires a new language to be developed and/or implemented. An example of a powerful application-independent command language is Tcl [Ous90, Ous94], available as a C library package. The idea is that the library implements general-purpose constructs. Individual applications make extensions for application-specific commands, which is simplified by a set of utility routines. Tcl can be used for communication purposes between applications and for programming the graphical window interfaces of applications (by configuring an application's interface actions and its interface appearance). Fig. 6.1 shows the basic structure of four communicating applications that use the command language Tcl.

As far as software reuse and software components are concerned, command languages do not offer a possibility to simply put existing applications together and build new, more powerful applications. However, they provide the possibility to integrate existing applications in new ones, e.g., to integrate an existing text editor or debugger into a programming environment. Or, a text editor and a debugger can communicate and synchronize with each other; i.e., the editor displays whatever source code line is being executed by the debugger.

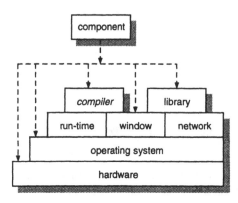

Fig. 6.2. Dependent platforms of a component

Even though command languages provide a means of communication via the possibility to easily control applications, they do not offer a way of interconnecting applications. This means that applications are still responsible for reading/inputting commands and can implement this in various ways, e.g., by reading from the console or by reading from a port. Connections between components are not standardized and depend on the implementation of a component.

6.3 Component Platforms

Even though two components may fit together perfectly by means of their interfaces, they may require different run-time systems or operating systems. Unless they can communicate across different processes, this is a hindrance for combining such components.

By *component platform* we mean any software a component is built upon. Typical platforms are operating systems, run-time systems, window systems and other libraries. Platforms are sets or collections of homogeneous components.

Fig. 6.2 shows an example with a source code component that uses routines from a library and the operating system. Its reuse requires the appropriate compiler and run-time system as well as these routines. A component's platforms have to be available in order to reuse the component. Additionally, the platforms have to be in harmony with the platforms of the software system we build. This is the topic of this section.

Generally, components are the more reusable the less platforms they depend on and the more portable these platforms are. Fig. 6.3 shows a component which depends on platforms that are not bound to a specific machine.

Table 6.1 shows some examples of components and their platforms. It is important that platforms may further restrict the reuse of components. For example, a shell script will not run on all available Unix platforms, but

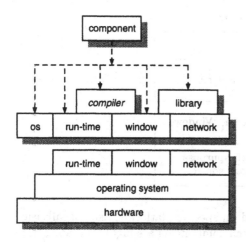

Fig. 6.3. Independent platforms of a component

only on several of them. A C++ class may need a certain compiler as different compilers generate different code for templates. Even certain versions of platforms may be necessary for the reuse of a component.

Components can be available in different forms. For example, a C++ class can be available in source code or object code (plus interface description). The source code version is more reusable as it can be transformed with different compilers to different object codes for different run-time systems. There can be limitations, however, when the definition of a programming language is not strict enough to prevent dependencies of a source code component on a certain compiler implementation.

Table 6.1. Examples of component platforms

Component	Platforms
Ada package	Ada-95, Corba, Ada math library
Shell script	Unix
Application	Unix, Tcl/Tk, X/Windows
C++ class	C++ gnu compiler, standard IO library
Smalltalk class	Smalltalk-80

Table 6.2. Examples of execution platforms

Platform	Examples
Programming system	Smalltalk, Java, VisualBasic
Operating system	Unix, Posix, Macintosh, Windows
Hardware	Intel processor, special-purpose hardware (robot/plane control)

Successful reuse stories are based on specific platforms, like VisualBasic controls or Unix pipes and filters. Such components are highly reusable, but their reuse is limited to these platforms.

6.3.1 Platform Categories

If we have components classified by their platforms we are able to determine a component's reusability in certain contexts. Based on the role a platform plays for a component, we distinguish execution and composition platforms.

Execution platforms. Execution platforms are necessary in order to execute a component. Execution platforms determine the environment on which a component, i.e., a complete running system, can be executed. Typically, a component requires a certain operating system for execution, but it may also require specific hardware or a programming system if it is being interpreted. Table 6.2 provides some examples.

Composition platforms. Composition platforms are necessary for components that do not run on their own but rather have to be integrated with other components to form an executable program. Compilers and linkers are the most prominent form of this category. Other examples are libraries for the user interface, for data storage, or for common services like sorting and searching.

Mathematical libraries might be statically linked to a software system; however, a database system might not be linked and become a direct part of another system. The database might supply an interface for a certain programming language and provide interface routines which become part of the system. The database may be accessed via interprocess communication, but this is hidden in the interface routines. Table 6.3 provides some examples of composition platforms.

6.3.2 Component and Platform Dependencies

Reuse is burdensome when the reuse has to handle dependencies among components. For example, sometimes the reuse of functions requires certain li-

Table 6.3. Examples of composition platforms

Platform	Examples
Code generation	compiler, linker, 4th generation system
Graphical user interface	window system (X/Open, Motif, Macintosh finder, Windows 95)
Data storage	file system (I/O libraries), database access
Common services	math libraries, sorting/searching, containers
Interprocess communication	remote procedure calls, sockets, TCP/IP
Interoperation	Tcl/Tk, Corba, OLE, OpenDoc

brary routines. If this is not clearly documented, reusing the functions can be frustrating. There can be dependencies on platforms as well as on single components, such as functions that have been developed for a certain software system.

If we want to use two components together, they have to share the same execution platform or have different execution platforms but a common composition platform. If they have different execution platforms it is important that they be executable. For example, a C++ class and a Smalltalk class can be used together, say, when they both use Corba for interoperation. However, both classes have to be embedded in some system in order to be executable.

The composition platform plays an important role for the reusability of a component as well. For example, two C++ classes cannot be used together when they use different application frameworks, i.e., when they are embedded in two different application frameworks. Theoretically, it may be possible to include two different application frameworks or class libraries into one system, but this leads to overhead and still limits how the two classes can be combined.

There are relationships among platforms. For example, compilers for programming languages typically exist for several different computer systems, making components implemented in these languages portable and reusable on these systems. Also, if a class is based on a specific class library, it can be used on whatever platform this class library is available. Java classes can be reused on a variety of machines because the Java platform is available on many different machines, i.e., operating system platforms.

Components that are included in their reuse context (like source code components) are more restricted by platform constraints than components that run on their own. Executable components require certain forms of interoperation, like certain protocols, but may run on different machines with different hardware and different operating systems. The World-Wide-Web provides an example of such independence of machine characteristics.

A component can be available in different forms, e.g., as source code or in binary form. The form influences the platform dependencies. If a component is available in binary form, it is more restricted in its reuse than if it is available in source code form. This is true unless the binary form is standardized, as is the case for Java components.

The portability of a component correlates with its reusability. Originally, portability referred to the ease with which a software component could be run on different hardware. Today's software components are more complex and face many dependencies on software platforms as well, e.g., operating system, window system, run-time system. The easier it is to use a component in different contexts the higher is its chance for reuse. Low coupling, as described in Section 8.3 on page 110, is important in this respect as a component is also (indirectly) dependent on platforms of components with which it interacts.

6.3.3 Open Systems

Software systems are based on several platforms. These platforms can be specific or open. Open platforms are available for several specific platforms. The less platform dependencies a component has and the more standardized/open these platforms are, the more portable and reusable is a component.

Open systems are vendor transparent platforms in which users can mix and match hardware, software and networks from various vendors [Uma93]. We eventually want to combine software components from different vendors on hardware *and* software from various vendors interoperating over networks from various vendors. Composability, portability, and integration are critical for open systems [QW93, Uma93]:

- *Composability*
  Composability means that two components can work with each other through well-defined interfaces. This is also referred to as portability of data and information.

- *Component portability*
  Component portability means that components developed on one platform should be usable on different platforms with no or minimal change. This can be achieved through developing components by using only standard interfaces that are available on different platforms.

- *User portability*
  User portability means the ease of switching among user interfaces of dif-

ferent components. User portability is important due to the high costs of user training.

– *Integration*
Integration means the ease with which a component can be used by other components.

Open systems provide high composability and portability through standardized platforms. These standardized platforms are mapped by many vendors to their specific platforms. Thus components that use the standardized (open) platform can be mapped to any of these specific platforms without additional effort.

Standards are crucial for open systems. Examples are X/Open standards, OSI standards and Posix standards. For example, a component might be executable under Unix, yet be restricted to certain Unix implementations. If Posix is the execution platform, then the component should be reusable on a larger variety of systems (all Unix systems that adhere to the Posix standards).

Open components rely on open platforms, and their reuse scope is broader than for other, more specific components.

6.3.4 Design Patterns

Design patterns were mentioned in Section 3.6.6 on page 34. We do not consider patterns themselves as software components. However, patterns can be regarded as platforms similar to class libraries or application frameworks. To be reusable in the context of a certain class library, a class has to fulfill certain requirements, e.g., provide particular methods or inherit from particular classes from this library. The same holds for design patterns. Once a set of patterns is defined, it should be documented for reuse by defining *abstract classes*. This means that every time the pattern is reused the corresponding classes implementing the pattern inherit from the abstract classes representing that pattern.

McGregor et al. have suggested associating components with design patterns and facilitating pattern-based retrieval in component repositories [MDK96]. Components can participate in many patterns and require other components in order to fully implement a pattern. Components may both be able to participate in certain patterns and be reusable stand-alone, or they may require reuse in the context of a certain design pattern.

Design patterns have to be defined for a certain platform, most likely a class library. In a certain reuse context we may require components for this class library or, more confined, components that play a certain role in a specific design pattern.

6.4 Summary

In this chapter we have discussed definitions, interfaces and platforms for components. We have defined *reusable software components* as self-contained, clearly identifiable artefacts that describe and/or perform specific functions and have clear interfaces, appropriate documentation and a defined reuse status.

Plugging software components together is often difficult if not impossible. Components have different interfaces. We distinguish user, data and programming interfaces. Programming interfaces are the primary means of software reuse, but data and user interfaces have proven to be useful for that purpose, too.

Components do not exist in a vacuum, but have many dependencies to other software, e.g., operating system, window system, compiler version. We distinguish between execution and composition platforms. These categories contain platforms that are needed for the execution of components (like operating systems) and composition (like compilers, remote procedure call facilities).

Design patterns also form a platform in that they can be the basis for the implementation of a component and restrict the component's reuse.

7. Component Composition

Contents

Terms like *composition, interconnection, interaction, communication* and *interoperation* are closely related. In the literature they sometimes have different semantics but are often used interchangeably.

In this chapter we deal with various aspects of component composition and component interoperation. Forms of composition are described in Section 7.1. Forms of interoperation follow in Section 7.2. Composition mismatches and possible remedies are described in Section 7.3. A summary follows in Section 7.4.

7.1 Forms of Composition

Nierstrasz and Dami define software composition as "the process of constructing applications by interconnecting software components through their plugs" [ND95]. Plugs are "well-defined ways to interact and communicate with the component." In the same book De Mey defines component composition as "communication between components through their composition interfaces" [dM95].

We distinguish two basic forms of software composition. On the one hand, components can be integrated into a system and become an inherent part of that system. This is the case when source code is compiled and linked to a system. We denote this with *internal composition* (internal to an executable program). On the other hand, components can act independently, i.e., run on their own. They communicate with other components by means of inter-process communication, e.g., by remote procedure calls. We denote this *external composition*. The distinction between *active* and *passive* components in [DvK87] is somewhat similar.

Nierstrasz and Dami further make a distinction among *functional composition*, *blackboard composition* and *composition by extension* [ND95] and among *macro expansion*, *high order functional composition* and *binding of communication channels* [NM95]. We base our classification thereupon. We regard blackboard composition as a form of interoperation, which is described in Section 7.2 on page 98.

7.1.1 Internal/External Composition

We speak of *internal composition* when components are included in a software system, e.g., by linking them to a system or by including their source code. They exist in the form of source code or executable code and are the typical subject of today's software reuse. Different levels of abstraction reflect the historic evolution of abstraction mechanisms provided by programming languages.

External composition means compositions running as independent programs. Often such components can be used as complete programs by themselves or as part of a software system. For many operating systems large catalogs of such components exist. For example, many separate components plus a simple mechanism (see pipes and filters; see Chapter 10) to combine them exist for the Unix operating system. The environment, e.g., the operating system, has to provide means of composing components.

7.1.2 Textual Composition

Textual composition is used for macros. Macros are not necessarily components and are often used for arbitrary textual replacements. However, they can represent reusable components that are modified according to parameters and inserted (duplicated) at the location of their reuse.

Another form of textual composition is the use of parameterizable components, i.e., templates or generics. In contrast to macros, syntactic *and* semantic checks are performed. Examples are generic packages in Ada, templates in C++, and composition in the GenVoca model [BST+94]. These parameterizable components have a higher level of abstraction than macros as they are used in combination with functions, modules or classes. Thus using such components involves textual composition and functional, modular or object composition (see next sections).

Macros. Macro expansion may, at first sight, not appear to be a composition technique. But despite its simplicity and limitations, it is. Macros are reusable components with clear interface definitions. With a macro processor, we can reuse macros. Composition in this case is done by textual replacement. This is a first step to software reuse.

Macros, as for example used in C and C++, are character- and file-oriented without any notions of scope and type. The main use of the macro processor is for including interface definitions, defining symbolic constants, commenting out code, etc. [Str94]. Macros can comprise arbitrary source text, e.g., part of an expression or function. There is no formally defined interface, but parameters are usual, and global/shared data can be used also.

Macros are often used to compensate for lacking programming language features. This is true for C and other languages like PL/S. For example, at IBM a collection of reusable macros that implement data types have been developed for PL/S [Bau93].

Possible applications of macros are constants, e.g., preprocessor-defined identifiers that were used in C programs until the language provided a feature to define constants, or simple (inline) functions, i.e., preprocessor defined "functions" that are reused by (automatic) textual insertion (and replacement of the parameters); e.g., the following is a macro for C to determine the maximum of two arbitrary values:

```
MAX(a,b) ((a)>(b)?(a):(b))
```

Macros have the lowest level of abstraction, providing only textual replacements with parameterization. It is interesting that their reuse has not been superseded by components of a higher level of abstraction. Rather, macros have kept their *raison d'être* in parallel to modern abstraction concepts like classes. The C and C++ programming languages provide examples of this coexistence.

The main disadvantage of macros is that they fail to obey scope and type rules, which are of utmost importance for software reuse. The interface of macros is not formally defined, but rather can be arbitrarily chosen by the user for each component. This increases complexity and makes proper reuse painful. Additionally, the use of macros can have side effects that may be difficult to detect.

Macros can be used for any textual replacements. Thus they can also be used for the generation of higher-level abstractions, e.g., for the generation of modules or classes.

Textual composition has disadvantages. Reused components cannot be interchanged other than by modifying and rebuilding (i.e., preprocessing, compiling, linking) the reusing component. The reused components do not physically exist as such at run-time, but are integrated into the reusing component. Components are merged.

7.1.3 Functional Composition

Functional composition is the most widespread mechanism for component composition. Components are functions that have parameters and are activated by a function call with arguments for the parameters. Most programming languages offer this composition mechanism.

Functions (and procedures, i.e., functions without a return value) were introduced to avoid repetitive statements and to divide programs into smaller units. Parameters are used to transfer data, but global variables can also be used for information interchange. In the development of software systems, the concept of functions has proven especially useful for practicing the principle of *stepwise refinement* and *top-down design*. From a reuser's perspective, functions can be regarded as low-level components that provide some output data for a certain set of input data. Some old-fashioned programming languages provide only the concept of *subroutines*, i.e., functions without the possibility to specify parameters.

Examples of collections of reusable functions include the statistics library SPSS, the numerical analysis library IMSL, and C function libraries that can be used for a variety of applications, e.g., input/output, string handling, mathematical functions.

Disadvantages of functions are that usually only functions written in the same language can be called (even though it is sometimes possible to cross language boundaries). Connections between two components are hard-wired in (one) component, and it is possible to use global variables for information exchange (e.g., C library functions), which obscures their interface.

Functions have their own scope and a defined interface with type checking. The separation between interface and implementation of functions allows their reuse without knowing the implementation. The use of global variables can diffuse a clear interface definition and complicate reuse.

Coroutines. *Coroutines* are a variation of functions that, upon invocation, do not execute from their beginning to their end. Instead, they execute from the point where execution had last been suspended to a point where execution is suspended again. Thus a function executes its entire body, whereas coroutines might only execute portions of it [DJ95]. Usually two or more coroutines are designed to work together in a specific way. Stand-alone coroutines that are designed for reuse in various contexts are not known to the author.

Remote procedure calls. The idea of *remote procedure calls* is to use the simple function call mechanism for distributed computing. In general, remote procedure calls provide the same abstraction for component composition as function calls. Due to the abstractions provided by remote procedure call mechanisms, differences to regular function calls may not be noticeable at first sight. However, they enable the composition of components from different platforms (run-time systems, operating systems, etc.).

7.1.4 Modular Composition

Modules (or packages) are simply collections of data structures and/or functions. However, they have provided an important abstraction mechanism with data encapsulation and information hiding. In order to build large systems it is necessary to minimize the interdependencies of components so that they can be developed separately and reused in different contexts.

Modules avoid implicit interfaces and require complete definition of what is exported to the reuser of a module. Additionally, modules can have internal states and change their behavior over time.

Module interconnections depend on import and export commands hard-wired in the code of a software system. This has some major problems like forced agreement in name spelling, dispersion of structural information and forced asymmetry of interaction [Sha94].

Examples of module collections include Ada Math Advantage (consisting of over a hundred frequently used mathematical and utility components, e.g., signal processing, image processing, linear algebra, interpolation, statistics, and basic math operations), NAG Ada Library (a library of reusable mathematical source code components), and N.A. Software Ada Encyclopedia (containing about 200 high-level routines and many ancillary functions and type definitions in a wide ranging numeric library).

7.1.5 Object-Oriented Composition

By means of *inheritance*, object-oriented programming enables the extension of components without losing compatibility. The composition mechanism is similar to functional composition. However, through *polymorphism* and *dynamic binding* different components can be activated via the same 'function' call.

Through the concepts of encapsulation (like modules and packages), inheritance, polymorphism and dynamic binding, object-oriented programming is advantageous for software reuse. A class may inherit the structure and behavior of another class and additionally extend and modify it. From the reuser's point of view, the main advantage is that software components, i.e., classes work together without knowing of each others existence. Thus components achieve greater independence. For example, a graphics editor can work with arbitrary objects (as long as they are presented by a subclass of a certain (abstract) base class). This spawns the concept of application frameworks, which provide the additional advantage of design reuse. Plug compatibility is achieved by a combination of mechanisms and techniques provided by object-oriented programming languages, such as interchangeable objects, uniform public interfaces, polymorphic parameters, and dynamic access of interchangeable operations [Wan94].

The possibility to specialize classes without the need to modify their source code brings several major advantages to programming [Wan94]:

- reuse of existing source code,
- adaptation of programs to work in similar but different situations,
- extraction of commonalties from different classes, and
- organization of objects into hierarchies.

Multiple inheritance allows derivation from multiple base classes and is a convenient way of defining new objects as combinations of existing types.

Examples of collections of reusable classes are the Eiffel Base Libraries (several hundred reusable classes including basic structures like arrays and strings, fundamental data structures and algorithms; libraries for lexical and syntactical analysis, for graphics and user interfaces, and for databases and persistence [Mey94]), the ET++ Class Library (an application framework with many fundamental data structures like container classes), the GNU Standard C++ Library, the GUI class library InterViews, the C++ library for molecular biosequence analysis molbio++, and the NIH Class Library.

Usually classes are not combinable over language boundaries, except sometimes to modular languages, e.g., from C++ to C. Even though the object-oriented approach enhances reusability drastically, the problems encountered in module reuse are not eliminated.

Distributed objects are the object-oriented version of remote procedure calls. Challenges for this mechanism are object identification and the transfer of objects rather than simple data structures. Objects typically have references to other objects, which makes it difficult to decide which data to pass as parameters.

Summarizing, we can say that classes are like modules. In addition to modules, they provide object-oriented mechanisms like inheritance and dynamic binding. This allows more flexibility and increases the reuse potential of existing code.

7.1.6 Subsystem Composition

Whether the abstraction level of a class or a module is higher is not always clear and depends on the programming language. If we compare modules of languages like Modula-2 and classes of languages like Smalltalk and C++, then classes definitely offer higher abstraction. However, some languages also

provide the possibility to combine classes in modules, in which case modules
have to be seen at a higher level than classes, e.g., in Oberon [RW92]. We
adhere to the historic evolution of these concepts and use the term module
as in the programming language Modula-2.

Most programming languages do not provide means of grouping modules
and/or classes to higher units of abstractions, which we call *subsystems*. Subsystems can consist of classes and functions and import and export interfaces.
An implementation of a subsystem must provide the subsystem's exported
interfaces. For composition, a subsystem's imported interfaces must be provided.

P++ is an example of a language that offers subsystem abstractions
[BO92, SB93]. It is an enhanced version of C++ and was primarily developed
to support the GenVoca model of software system construction, which is the
formalization of domain-independent principles and similarities of software
generators [BST+94]. P++ incorporates the ideas of encapsulation, abstraction and parameterization. Encapsulation is provided by a component construct for large-scale program construction with subsystems. Abstraction is
supported by standard interfaces (the *realm* construct). Finally, parameterization supports easy customization and composition of components. Components are the basic unit of software system construction. A set of functions and class declarations defines a component's interface. Components
with the same interface belong to a realm and are interchangeable. Additionally, components can extend their interfaces and still belong to a (more
general) realm. The *Predator* library is an example of a collection of components encapsulating data structures specified as hierarchical composition
components [TBSS93].

Component composition and customization is achieved by parameterization [BST+94]. This is the key mechanism for component composition,
because components allow not only simple parameterization with constants
and types but also with other components. As Batory argues, this kind of
composition produces hierarchical software systems [BO92]. P++ is being
developed and used at a research laboratory at the University of Texas in
Austin. Broader experience is necessary in order to evaluate its usefulness.
Even though subsystems provide an additional abstraction level, the components are still constrained to a certain programming paradigm and language.

7.1.7 Source Code Parameterization

In order to make source code more adaptable and thus reusable, parameterization has been introduced. Parameterization is achieved by source code skeletons with placeholders that can be filled variably, thus producing different
codes from a single skeleton. The placeholders act as formal parameters that
can take values or types as arguments. This parameterization potentiality
allows the user (programmer) to make functions, modules and classes highly

adaptable. This increases the reusability of these items, as they can easily be fitted to the actual needs and also work with new, user-defined types without the need for modification. A typical application of skeletons is the parameterization of container classes, which provide vectors, lists, sequences, etc. for various kinds of objects or types. Parameterization can also be seen as separation of algorithm specification and implementation specification [VK89], or as a separation of type-dependent and type-independent parts [CL95]. Only the essential properties of algorithms are captured, whereas types and representations of the data are left unspecified until actual reuse. There exist various ways of parameterizing source code, e.g., using macros, using pointers and using templates or generics.

Macros. Macros provide the possibilities not only to define and reuse simple source code components but also to parameterize these components in a useful way and, for example, to define generic functions or even generic classes. Macro parameters can be used for both ordinary function parameters and for generic (e.g., type) parameters.

Generic pointers. Weakly typed languages like C allow the use of pointers (`void*`) to make functions generic. The idea is that 'generic' pointers are converted to pointers of known types. This is usually accomplished through function calls (also via pointers). Such generic components are used by supplying functions with the desired type conversions. Despite its usefulness, the approach using this kind of generic functions has several drawbacks. For example, pointers have to be used even for built-in types. There is no type-checking which diminishes the reliability of such components. Additionally, functions with the desired type conversions have to be provided [Wan94].

Templates. Templates are another means for parameterizing source code. They operate at a higher level of abstraction and comply with scope and type rules. Parameterization through templates avoids the drawbacks of macros and pointers, but also has problems; e.g., it can cause duplication of similar program entities and make a software system much larger. Even though macros and pointers can increase the reusability of source code, templates are a better (and contemporary) means of parameterizing source code. Realms in P++ provide a means for parameterizing subsystems (described above).

Examples of collections of generic components are the Booch Components (consisting of several dozen domain-independent data structures and tools, each with multiple implementations so that a client can select the representation that provides the most suitable time and space characteristics), the Generic Reusable Ada Components for Engineering (GRACE) (a library of almost 300 Ada software components based on commonly used data structures such as strings, matrices, lists, stacks, queues, trees), Math Pack (containing over 350 Ada mathematical subprograms in 20 reusable generic Ada packages, including linear algebra, linear system solutions, integration, differential equations, etc.), and LEDA (a C++ library of efficient data types and algorithms, providing basic data types like lists, stacks, queues, trees, sets, etc.). The Booch components were originally written in Ada; versions in C++, Smalltalk and Eiffel are also available.

Though reusability is greatly enhanced through parameterization, existing problems as depicted in the sections about functions, modules and classes are not eliminated.

Source code parameterization is a textual composition technique because textual replacement is performed before compilation. However, in contrast to macros with arbitrary text replacement, templates and realms provide higher abstraction levels with syntactic and semantic checking by the compiler.

7.1.8 Distributed Computing

Distributed computing plays a major role for component composition. Distributed computing systems consist of multiple autonomous processors that cooperate by sending messages over a communications network or by sharing memory. Initially, distributed systems were implemented with conventional sequential programming languages, usually with the help of library routines designed for sending and receiving messages. Then languages have emerged that were designed to support the building of distributed systems. Finally, configuration languages have come forth to make distributed programming still easier, more robust and more flexible. Running applications on distributed computing systems has many advantages, e.g., [BST89]:

– *High speed*
  The turnaround times for single computations can be decreased through parallelism, e.g., determining the prime factors of large numbers.

– *High reliability and availability*
  In many application domains like airplane or power plant control, reliability and availability are crucial aspects of the software. Replication of processes and data can increase the quality of the software in this respect.

– *Functional specialization*
  Large software systems have a variety of functionality, e.g., operating systems.

– *Inherent distribution*
  Many application domains are inherently distributed and cannot be realized without distributed computing. Electronic mail and file transfer are examples of such domains.

Processes yield a level of component abstraction that is worth consideration for software reuse. Functional specialization, like providing file, print and process services of operating systems, not only yields good performance due to dedicated processors, but also increases reusability and interchangeability because various services can easily be separated from the whole system and reused in other contexts. Another advantage is that we can mix components of various programming languages and paradigms. The main drawback is performance loss. However, the severeness of this drawback depends on the granularity of a distributed system.

Executable components do not have abstractional concepts associated with them which have evolved over time (like source code abstractions). The reusability of such components is primarily influenced by the means that are offered to communicate with them. An application that can be started but provides no further interface for communication cannot be composed with other components. Some tools provide simple command-line user interfaces using standard input and output. With appropriate support from the operating system, such tools can be integrated with other components. Reusable components have to offer some sort of interface. Reusability is higher for components with standardized interfaces than with interfaces specific to some component platforms.

7.1.9 Object Models

Arbitrary software components run on different machines and platforms and are implemented in various programming languages. To allow the composition of differing components, they must have a common denominator. Object models have been developed for that reason. They are primarily used to simplify distributed computing on heterogeneous systems, but can support additional functionality, like *compound documents* (see below).

Corba. The *common object request broker architecture* (Corba) is a standard specification by an industry consortium, the *object management group* (OMG). Corba was developed in order to simplify distributed computing on heterogeneous systems. Composition is accomplished through component interfaces described by an *interface definition language* (IDL) [MZ95]. Components in this context are typically applications.

Among Corba's advantages are the use of an object-oriented paradigm and the hiding of programming languages' and operating systems' differences. The *object request broker* (ORB) plays a central role for the composition (and interoperation) of applications. Fig. 7.1 depicts how application objects communicate via the ORB with *service components* and *common facilities* (see Mowbray and Zahavi [MZ95]).

In our terminology Corba objects are components. Thus we should speak of a *component request broker* rather than an *object request broker*. However, due to the uniform use of the Corba terminology throughout the literature, we uphold the original terminology as well.

The most important aspects of Corba are the object request broker and the interface definition language. They provide the vehicle for evolving common facilities and object services, which can be supplied by various vendors. Service components provide the means for the composition of applica-

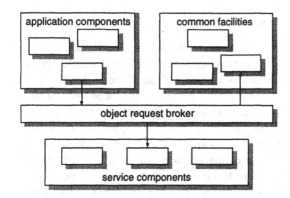

Fig. 7.1. Object management architecture

tions through standard interfaces. Common facilities include standard services (e.g., printing) as well as any other, commercially supplied services.

Object request broker. The object request broker is responsible for communication between components. Its functionality is defined in the common object request broker architecture (Corba). An ORB has to find implementations for requested operations, perform any needed preprocessing, and communicate any needed data. Communication is possible either through static interfaces or through a *dynamic invocation interface* (DII). DII is a generic facility provided by the ORB in order to retrieve interface descriptions at run-time from an interface repository. This allows clients to utilize operations that are unknown at the time of compilation.

Interface definition language. An interface definition language has been defined for Corba in order to ensure language independence. It is used to describe a component's interface and is then mapped to the programming language in which the component is implemented. For a client component, the same interface is mapped to its implementation language. The mapping is done by an IDL compiler that generates stub programs for clients and skeleton programs for the component implementation (server component).

In order to utilize an operation of a server, a client calls a local function in the generated stub. The stub performs all the necessary operations in order to communicate with the ORB, e.g., marshalling parameters for transmission. The ORB transfers the client's request to the generated skeleton on the server side. The skeleton is responsible for parameter marshalling as well, makes a local call to the requested server's operation, and returns results upon completion of the processing. Besides regular results, exception information can also be passed back to the client [MZ95].

Using IDL does not necessarily require that two components be distributed. Client and server components can also be compiled and linked as a single application.

7.1.10 Compound Documents

Many common business applications have bloated into *mega-applications*; i.e., many features have been added over time and versions. The complexity of these applications is burdensome for both users and developers. An alternative to mega-applications has emerged, which is called *compound documents*. The idea is to create lean software components that work cooperatively rather than to develop monolithic mega-applications. Thus new applications can be built by simply wiring together existing components. Such components give the end user the power of easily integrating applications bought from different vendors. The end user partly takes the role of a software developer. This will result in increased software reuse (and use) and a reduction of the need for custom software.

Components will have enough functionality and flexibility to satisfy customer needs with a combination of purchased software components when these software components are designed to be reused in various contexts. Users can concentrate on creating front-end applications, i.e., applications that handle data from different other applications, e.g., a budgeting system using components for a network storage facility, a macro language, a data entry facility, a chart organization facility, and a budget account management system. Typically, data can be either *linked* or *embedded*. Linked data use a placeholder instead of the actual data and can be accessed through various documents. Embedded data are accessible only within a single document.

The lack of communication facilities in applications requires them to incorporate functionality that is provided by other applications already. For example, window-based debuggers incorporate full text editors. Not only does this require more development effort, but users must also handle the same functionality with different tools. Having small applications with reduced functionality and communication and configuration facilities gives a bigger boost to software reuse than the isolation, storage and reuse of the source code components in monolithic applications.

With compound documents the developer's focus shifts from files and (mega-)applications to single objects. Such objects can, for example, be a certain range of spreadsheet cells or text. They are implemented as a component that can be composed with other, similar components for the creation of an application. An arbitrary programming model or language can be chosen for the implementation.

OpenDoc and OLE. There exist two competitive compound document architectures, OpenDoc and OLE [Api95, Ren94, RGM94]. OLE 2.0 is Microsoft's technology for revolutionizing the way software is built, sold and used; it provides distributed object computing for applications integration in the Windows system. OpenDoc is supported by a vendor-neutral association including members like Apple, IBM and Adobe. Examples of provided features include integrated displays, in-place-editing of components and integration of information across components.

Object models provide structures and functions for the integration of application components and are the architecture beneath compound documents. OLE and OpenDoc use different object models, the *Component Object Model* (COM) and the *System Object Model* (SOM), respectively.

COM is a general model describing how objects interact with each other. It provides the possibility to create new objects from existing ones and supports the naming, finding and linking of objects both on single machines and platforms and across networks.

The composition of compound documents is ideal for the creation of front-end applications, which can improve reusability considerably. The primary purpose is to combine the functionality of applications that allow the user to edit some kind of data.

The combined use of OpenDoc, OLE and Corba technology for inter-application communication is possible as well. For example, OpenDoc's *Component Glue* provides a wrapping mechanism to treat OLE objects as OpenDoc objects.

Like compound documents, command languages (see Section 6.2.5 on page 75) are also a 'pitfall' for monolithic mega-applications, as they enable a component's reuse in different contexts. However, they cannot provide the tight integration that is possible with compound document technology. Additionally, command languages can be provided in object models and thus be available for compound documents automatically. OpenDoc's *Open Scripting Architecture* (OSA) is an example of an automation and scripting API that supports application-independent scripting, distributed automation and work flow applications [App95].

7.1.11 Component Applications

Monolithic applications have all their functionality built in. Users can configure and adapt such applications only by predefined means. Any new functionality, e.g. support of a new protocol in a World-Wide-Web browser, has to be added by software developers and released in a new version of the system (see Fig. 7.2). All the functionality is hard-wired into the application.

If an application can be extended dynamically, then it can be adapted by adding the appropriate components. Consider a word processing system, which may consist of many components like a spell checker, hyphenation, thesaurus, equation editor, graphics editor, spreadsheets, etc. Not only can such components be added and removed to configure the application to the customers' needs, the user may also choose among various components for the same functionality or add functionality that had not been foreseen at the time the application was built (see Fig. 7.3).

The user can also combine components from different vendors and combine various functionalities in one application. We are used to having different tools and applications for different activities. Related activities may be supported by a single tool or application. We may want to configure a simple

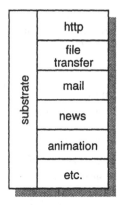

* **Fig. 7.2.** Monolithic application

application that covers everyday activities. These activities will vary among different users, and software vendors are unlikely to build packages that fit the needs of all users. One user might pick a mail tool, a news tool, and a word processor with various goodies like spell checking and graphics, while a programmer might use the same word processor for writing documentation or even source code and integrate a debugger into the environment. As these components are dynamically loaded, complex configurations do not have a negative effect on performance.

7.1.12 Integrated Environments

Software solutions for various domains have to support a variety of activities. For example, a financial framework has to retrieve real-time and historical data from financial information sources, provide various display mechanisms, include a decision support system, etc. Another well-known example is programming environments which combine tools like editors, compilers, debuggers, visualization tools and much more.

Reiss has described different approaches to provide all the required functionality of an integrated environment [Rei95a]. Two obvious and simple so-

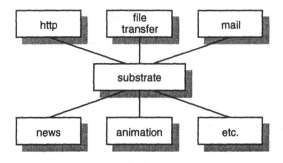

Fig. 7.3. Component application

lutions are building the environment as a single system and providing a set of independent tools.

Single systems provide a uniform user interface and, naturally, a high degree of integration. But they have the drawback of high development effort. They are closed systems and have restricted extensibility and customizability. For the user, it is difficult or impossible to add existing tools or new functionality. For the software engineer, single systems get difficult to understand and maintain because they are large and tend to grow with every new version release.

On the other hand, sets of independent tools are easier to extend and customize and require less initial development effort due to the possibility to reuse existing tools. In order to share data among these tools, they usually have text files as their primary input and output. This is an advantage for extensibility but a disadvantage for development and performance due to duplication of effort and excess file input and output. A disadvantage on the user's side is the lack of a consistent and integrated environment. Each tool may have a totally or, sometimes even worse, a slightly different user interface, an own command language. Lack of communication among the tools forces the user to do all the integration, e.g., to know which tool's output to use for another tool's input, or to locate erroneous source code by hand after reading the compiler messages.

Single systems are common on personal computers, whereas tool sets tend to dominate workstations. The Unix operating system is the classic example of an open environment that offers an enormous variety of independent tools.

An integrated environment consists of various tools plus an underlying communication and integration mechanisms. This mechanism serves as the glue among the tools and offers many advantages. For example, due to the high degree of integration the tool set appears to users to be a single, homogeneous environment. And newly developed tools can be integrated into the environment later on without too much pain and hassle.

7.1.13 Open Platform Composition

On several platforms in several domains, component composition works successfully. Examples are 4th generation languages, object-oriented application frameworks and visual programming systems. Composition becomes difficult when components of different platforms become involved.

Object models provide the next step to enable component composition and interoperation beyond programming language, operating system and machine boundaries. Object models can provide mechanisms for various integration forms, e.g., object linking, object embedding, drag-and-drop support, and clipboard support for the implementation of compound documents.

Integrated environments demonstrate how a variety of different applications can be combined in a single environment. No object models support this yet, and we do not know yet what functionality we will need to provide a generic platform for such integrations.

Components are strongly influenced by platforms. If platforms had standardized communication among each other and if platforms were assigned to layers with clear interfaces between the layers, component composition would become more flexible. Object models are first steps in this direction, but more standards at various levels will be needed to achieve what we call *open platform composition*. It is not clear yet how such a platform will look, what it will support, and what levels there will be.

7.2 Forms of Interoperation

The ability of software components to communicate and cooperate despite differences in language, interface and execution platform is called *interoperability* [Kon95, Weg95].

Successful composition of components does not necessarily imply their successful interoperation. Two components may simply pass control or send a message to each other. They can also be involved in a more complicated form of interoperation, e.g., sharing data or using the same components for data access.

Minsky clearly separates connection and interaction of components (of programs and the human brain): "First, we must know how each separate part works. Second, we must know how each part interacts with those to which it is connected. And third, we have to understand how all these local interactions combine to accomplish what that system *does*—as seen from the outside" [Min85].

The NATO Standard for the Development of Reusable Software Components specifies a taxonomy of *interface types* of reusable software components [Bra94a]: subprogram call, task invocation, memory sharing with subprogram or task, communication via shared file with or without simultaneous access, and communication via message passing or mailbox mechanism. What this standard terms *interface types* is what we see as forms of interoperation.

7.2.1 Control and Data Integration

The central aspect of integrated environments is their integration mechanism. It should be simple, inexpensive and scalable and easily allow the incorporation of new and existing tools [Rei95a]. We distinguish between *control integration* and *data integration*.

Data integration. Data integration can be accomplished by means of a database or a file system. Single-system environments typically use data structures and can utilize either a database or a file system and can also maintain temporary data structures for information interchange among the

Table 7.1. Comparison of integrated environments [Rei95a]

Type	Advantages	Disadvantages
Single system environment	high degree of integration, shared data structures, consistent interfaces	closed system, large system, lack of scalability
Loose collection of tools	open environment, wide variety of tools	duplication of effort, inconsistent interfaces, little inter-tool communication
Environment with data integration	high degree of integration, shared data structures, open environment	complex databases, modification of tools, hard to extend
Environment with control integration	wide variety of tools, open environment, inexpensive	limited data sharing, performance, possible inconsistencies

various tools. The user can invoke the tools from within an integrated user interface.

Independent tools tend to rely on the file system and usually have to be invoked separately and explicitly. Environments can use a database for integration, which makes it easier to keep the information consistent and lets new tools access the information. However, databases are complex systems, may be language-dependent and may not fulfill the requirements of future tools [Rei95a, Rei95b].

Control integration. Control integration can be used when the tools of an integrated set do not have to share large amounts of data but rather each other's services. It suffices to exchange commands and add some parameters. In addition, they may share information in files and reduce communication to commands and file names. Passing of messages is adequate for this purpose. Each tool must have the capability to send and receive messages and must offer its functionality to other tools through messages.

With control integration, the resulting environment remains a loosely coupled set of tools. New tools can be integrated without too much effort; they must be endowed with the message mechanism.

Table 7.1 summarizes advantages and disadvantages of single-system environments, loose collections of tools, environments with data integration, and environments with control integration [Rei95a].

From the viewpoint of reuse, a loose collection of tools seems to be the best scenario. Any tools that comply only with minimal standards can be included in the toolset. For the user, however, this situation is often frustrating because of the need to deal with inconsistent interfaces and to do integration work by hand. These disadvantages do not exist in single-system environments, which rarely provide any reuse opportunities, however. Environments with some kind of integration are a good compromise, adding the advantages of monolithic systems and sets of uncoupled tools. Whether data integration, control integration or a mixture is better depends on the domain. As Reiss pointed out, for programming environments control integration is the right answer [Rei95a]. A financial framework might need a higher degree of data sharing.

Unfortunately, components of an integrated environment have to be endowed with the necessary means for communication with other components. Command languages are a useful means to do this (see Section 6.2.5 on page 75).

7.2.2 Categories of Interoperation

When two components interoperate, we have a *sending* component (initiating the interoperation) and a *receiving* component. The sending component activates the receiving component and passes *control* to this component. The receiving component *reacts* to the control input; it performs some action and, depending on whether communication is synchronous or asynchronous, returns control to the sending component. Some amount of information is usually passed along with interoperation. If more extensive data exchange is needed, components may use another component for that purpose (see Fig. 7.4).

The receiving component may or may not be known to the sending component. This has a major influence on the flexibility of compositions. Interconnections can be between two components (*peer-to-peer*), to a fixed set of components (*multicast*), and to a dynamic set of components (*broadcast*). Static interconnections are peer-to-peer. Dynamic interconnections can be either peer-to-peer, multicast or broadcast. The data component also may or may not be known to both the sender and receiver.

Table 7.2 gives an overview of the categories resulting from these distinctions. We distinguish *no*, *static*, *dynamic* and *broadcast* for *control* and *data*, which leads to sixteen categories. Some forms of interoperation in this table seem somewhat exotic, like the combination *no control* and *dynamic data*. However, they do have practical applications.

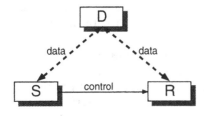

Fig. 7.4. Component interoperation

Table 7.2. Interoperability matrix

	no data	static data	dynamic data	broadcast data
no control	C C	C — D — C	C — ○ — C, D D	C — ○ — C, D D
static control	S → R	S — D — R	S — ○ — R, D D	S — ○ — R, D D
dynamic control	S → ○ → R, R	S — ○ — D — R, R	S — ○ — R, R, D D	S — ○ — R, R, D D
broadcast control	S → ○ → R, R, R	S — ○ — D — R, R, R	S — ○ — R, R, R, D D	S — ○ — R, R, R, D D

Next we describe a few examples of component interoperation and assign them to one of the proposed categories. In Chapter 10 we provide more extensive examples with categorizations of components, composition and interoperation.

– *No control*
  Components share data without directly communicating with each other. For example, two functions can access global variables, but neither of them calls the other one directly. Pipes and filters of the Unix operating system provide an interesting form of interoperation in this category. Filters do not pass control to each other. They simply read input data, do some form of processing, and create output data. Through the pipe mechanism one filter's output data can be used as input data for the next filter. Thus we have an example of *no control* and *dynamic data*.

– *Static control*
  Function calls (either local are remote) are the typical means of *static control*, i.e., the sending component has a fixed receiver attached to it.

- *Dynamic control*
  Function calls with dynamic binding are used in object-oriented software systems. This is often referred to as sending messages, since the function to be called cannot necessarily be determined at compile-time. This has many advantages for reuse because objects can be interchanged, allowing a more flexible way of composing components.

- *Broadcast control*
  Broadcast control is typical for event handling in application frameworks, visual programming systems and infrastructures for tool integration. Involved components may share separate data.

- *Broadcast data*
  Broadcast data is included for orthogonality reasons and is probably the most unusual form presented in the interoperability matrix. Forms of broadcast data may appear when the data is duplicated in, say, two databases and components (indirectly) make their updates to both presentations of the data.

It is essential for software reuse that components can be composed without to be known to each other. This allows component composition without modifying components (*dynamic control*). For example, a function calls a sort function. In order to call a function shellsort instead, the program text in the calling function has to be modified. Object-oriented programming provides more flexibility through dynamic binding. A calling object is not aware of the call's receiver. This makes this object work with a variety of other objects without being modified. Component composition is easiest and most flexible when interconnections among components are not *point-to-point*. Reusing components is easy in environments where each component can react to events generated by any other components and create new events without being aware of any recipients.

7.3 Composition Mismatches

Both software components and their interconnections have a variety of forms. Different packaging of components and different interactions between components very often prohibit successful reuse. Component composition and interoperability is sometimes compared to electrical appliances that can be plugged into wall sockets to connect them with a source of electricity. The plugs are standardized so that new appliances can be used right away. Unfortunately, standardization often ends at a country's border. Travellers know the problem that the razor they use at home is not plug-compatible in various other countries. In this situation adaptors are needed to bridge the different interfaces (for composition).

In some countries different voltages are used and prohibit compatibility even with an adaptor that fits both ends; i.e., composition is possible but interoperability is not. These situations require a transformer. Sometimes one of the components, the razor, has the capability to use two different voltages.

Unfortunately, software components and their interfaces for interoperation are more complex than electrical appliances. We have multiple standards for packaging and communication, and we have legacy code which we cannot afford to redevelop in order to comply to new standards. But even if we complied to a simple standard, e.g., ASCII text for interoperation among any components, this would guarantee that components could communicate and cooperate. It would not ensure component compatibility, however, because different assumptions can be made even about simple text streams.

Garlan et al. describe architectural mismatches that occurred while building a system from existing components [GAO95]. Various categories of assumptions were encountered about the nature of components, about the nature of connectors, about the global architectural structure, and about the construction process. Additional reasons for two components failing to successfully interoperate are different assumptions about representations, synchronization, semantics, control, etc. [Sha95].

Inappropriate composition mechanisms of today's software components are also reflected in the fact that many components exist in multiple forms in order to be used in various contexts. For example, in the Unix environment many operations are provided as system calls and as filters. Both versions have the same functionality, but cannot be used interchangeably. Shaw has listed ad-hoc tricks to connect mismatched components [Sha95].

- *Component modifications*
  Modify one of the components in order to cooperate with the other one. This is possible when the internals of the component is available. However, it is expensive and limits the component to the incorporated form of interoperation. When new requirements arise, new modifications are necessary. This is definitely not the way to go for large-scale software reuse.

- *Parallel component versions*
  We have mentioned the example of Unix operations that exist in parallel with different forms of composition. Again, parallel versions may be a short-term solution but cannot be accepted on the long run (even though having parallel components has long been practiced).

- *Adapters/wrappers*
  Wrapping components is very common in solving interoperation problems. For example, tools with textual interfaces can be wrapped and integrated in window-based environments. This solution avoids direct modification of the component and is more flexible, as new wrappers can be developed to integrate the component in other environments.

– *Components with converters*

Components can be provided with various converters. Many of today's desktop applications are capable of reading and sometimes writing several file formats. This allows the exchange of data among many applications (*by hand*).

– *Multilingual components*

Multilingual components can be executed on various platforms without any modifications. Examples are applications for the Apple Macintosh that run on Motorola's 680x0 and PowerPC processors. The *fat binaries*, as they are called, do represent an intermediate form as described above, but contain executable code for both processors. Using fat binaries allows Apple to change the processor family in its computers without sacrificing upward compatibility. The price to be paid is the overhead of roughly doubling the size of the components.

– *Intermediate forms*

Using an intermediate composition form can be useful when many different components are involved. Defining a standard for such a form may foster many components which can easily be reused in this environment (see Sections 7.3.1 and 7.3.2).

There is no generic solution for solving two components' inability to communicate and cooperate. Most of the listed tricks are helpful in many situations by either preventing or solving composition mismatches. However, they do not provide a solution to the reuse problem itself; i.e., they do not provide a solution that improves components' capabilities for composition in general.

Interface bridging and *interface standardization* are two major mechanisms for the solving of component mismatches. They can be further classified according to whether they handle composition at the point of the procedure call (*procedure-oriented composition*) or at the point of objects (*object-oriented composition*) (see Konstantas [Kon95] and Wegner [Weg95]). Remote procedure calls (RPC) are a common way to handle procedure-oriented composition. Composition in object-oriented systems is more difficult because objects cannot simply be decomposed into sets of independent operations and data.

7.3.1 Interface Bridging

Interface bridging overcomes the differences between interfaces. Interface transformation languages are used to express how an offered interface can be transformed to the requested interface [Kon95]. This allows clients in a distributed environment to access services from different servers without using different interfaces for each server.

Problems with procedure calls arise when interfaces requested by clients do not match, at least not exactly, interfaces offered by servers. In this situation languages can be used to declare how actual parameters of a client's procedure call have to be transformed and arranged in order to match the formal parameters of the server's procedure. Based on such a declaration, code can be generated automatically for handling needed transformations at run-time. Typically, parameter transformations are restricted to basic types like integers, characters, strings, arrays, etc.

Object-oriented interface bridging requires two steps: *interface adaptation* to define relations between types on different environments and *object mapping* to support the interoperation at run-time. The static part of object mapping is responsible for the creation of classes which implement the specified interoperation. The dynamic part has to instantiate and manage the objects which are used during the interoperation.

Procedure-oriented interface bridging is provided in the *Polylith* system, while the *Cell* framework is an example of object-oriented composition by interface bridging [Kon95].

7.3.2 Interface Standardization

Interface standardization addresses interfaces under which services are offered. Interface definition languages are used to express specific interfaces in a programming language independent way [Kon95] (see Section 6.3.3 on page 80).

Object models like Corba [MZ95] provide interface standardization. They provide a common layer for the transparent exchange of messages (see Section 7.1.9 on page 92).

7.4 Summary

We distinguish between activities of software engineers and activities of components. Software engineers put components together; i.e., they compose or interconnect components to build new, more complex components. Once components are interconnected, they can communicate, interact or interoperate. We do not further differentiate these and use the terms *composition* and *interoperation* for the two activities. Composition and interoperation are closely interrelated. For example, if two components cannot interoperate, we cannot put them together. In this case they are incompatible and we have a composition mismatch or an interoperability mismatch.

Composable software has a higher degree of flexibility than monolithic software. Different languages and environments facilitate software composition to different degrees by supporting different notions of components and compositions. It is easier to recompose software in order to meet new requirements instead of modifying a monolithic creation. There exist examples of successful application of software composition in certain domains like user interfaces, application frameworks, programming environments and 4th generation languages, but a general model of software composition does not yet exist [NM95].

There are a variety of components and plugs. The crucial point in component-oriented software development is having a selection of reusable components that are plug-compatible. The higher the granularity of the components is, the higher the increase in software productivity can be. Putting objects or applications together is more effective and productive than plugging macros together.

Object models as platforms for component plugs are gaining importance in the field. Currently much work is being done in this area and we can expect improvements in the near future.

Many topics on languages, tools and methods are open for research in software composition. For example, composition languages that support the glue for the composition of components are a current topic for research (see Nierstrasz [Nie95]).

8. Component Attributes

Contents

In the previous chapters we identified various aspects of software components, such as platforms, composition and interoperation. Now we deal with various attributes of components that allow us to better classify components. Some of the attributes are platform specific, others are component-specific. Attributes may also be specific to certain platforms and specific to components on other platforms.

In this chapter we identify and describe the following attributes of software components: functionality in Section 8.1, interactivity in Section 8.2, interaction in Section 8.3, concurrency in Section 8.4, distribution in Section 8.5, adaptation in Section 8.6 and quality control in Section 8.7. A summary follows in Section 8.8.

8.1 Functionality

The functionality of a component is essential for its reusability in a certain context. If we need to sort items, a component for binary searching is useless. A functional component typically offers a certain service such as sorting or searching (it *does* something).Components with higher level of abstraction like classes and applications provide behavioral interfaces that include several operations.

It is easy to determine whether a function's functionality fits the needs for a reuse scenario: it is either needed or not. When components comprise many operations, this question becomes harder to answer. Components' functionality may partially overlap, be too specific or too general, or be incomplete.

Applicability, generality and completeness of a component are important for their reusability [BR92].

Component applicability. The applicability of a component is its likelihood to be a reuse candidate in the range of software systems for which it was designed to be reused. A component's applicability can be high for a certain application domain and low or zero for others. For example, a component for handling an aircraft's landing gear can have high applicability in the aviation domain, but is completely useless in the programming environment domain.

Component generality. The generality of components typically increases their reusability. A component sorting numbers is less likely to be reused than a component sorting arbitrary objects. High generality of a component means also high applicability of this component. However, care has to be taken not to overgeneralize a component. Excessive generality leads to complex components and unnecessary overhead in both execution time and resource consumption.

Component completeness. Completeness of a component is difficult to capture, yet important for reuse. We can say that a component is complete when it offers the functionality expected by reusers in its intended reuse scenarios. A clear example of an incomplete component is a stack missing the *pop* operation. A missing *top* operation is less severe as it can be imitated with a *pop* and a *push* operation. Yet the component is considered to be incomplete if the *top* operation is frequently needed.

8.2 Interactivity

Interactive components have unpredictable inputs from an external environment. Macros and functions are noninteractive components. Objects and applications are typically interactive. We demonstrate some general differences between noninteractive and interactive components by comparing functions to objects (see Wegner [Weg93]).

Table 8.1 summarizes basic differences between functions and objects. Function-oriented systems transform an initial state to a final state (transition systems). All the input has to be specified before computation can begin. The result is delivered when the function stops computation. Endless loops are considered to be erroneous because they prevent the function from yielding the expected results. By contrast, objects are reactive. They react to messages they receive from other objects by doing some computation and/or sending messages to other objects. The connections among objects are looser than among functions, which makes incremental changes easier.

Functions do not have memory. Here we do not consider global or static variables which can be used to add memory to functions. Thus functions' computations always yield the same results with the same inputs. Objects

Table 8.1. Properties of functions and objects [Weg93]

Properties	Functions	Objects
Behavior	like verbs, they *do* something	like nouns, they *are* something
Specification	with input/output functions	with behavioral interfaces
Memory	no memory (same effect on every invocation)	memory of past events (time-varying behavior)
Persistence	self-destruction after completed invocation	persist while reacting to multiple invocations by clients
Complexity measure	by computation cost	by life-cycle cost
Computation models	functional and algorithmic	interactive

have an internal state and a certain behavior, which usually depends on the internal state and thus can vary from time to time. Once the results of a function are delivered, there is no need for the function to exist any longer on the machine. Objects may be destroyed also, but their lifetime usually spreads over a much longer period and is not constrained by single computations. Functions are destroyed and are simply newly created if their computation is needed again. The behavior of objects is too complex to be described with simple input/output functions.

The complexity of functions is often measured by computation costs. Consider the variety of available sort functions like bubble sort, insert sort and shell sort. Their main characteristic is their run-time, which depends on the number of elements to be sorted. For large n it is crucial whether an algorithm sorts in $n \, log_n$ or in n^2. Typically, such considerations are less important for objects because their operations are less complex. Part of the complexity shifts from objects themselves to their interaction. This makes the development of software systems more difficult because the complexity of interaction extends far beyond the internal complexity of functions.

Another distinction can be made between *proactive* and *reactive* components. *Reactive components* become active only when they get a request from another component. *Proactive components* become active on their own. For example, a timer component might become active whenever a certain amount of time has passed and might broadcast a timing signal (broadcast control). This, on the other hand, can cause reactive components to become active.

8.3 Interaction

A component can interact with other components (*component interaction*) but also with the human user (*user interaction*). Both forms influence the reusability of a component.

Component interaction. Reusable components should have *high cohesion* and *low coupling*. This means that the interface of a component should have a high degree of conceptual unity and that the dependence on other components should be small [BR92].

For example, classes can easily be reused in their programming language domain if they have no dependencies on other classes. Often they strongly depend on classes of a certain library, e.g., an application framework. In this case certain dependencies of some classes in this set may restrict the reuse of all classes. If an application framework is implemented on top of a certain window system, then its use may be restricted to this window system unless its designers have considered portability to other window systems.

High coupling can discourage the reuse of a component even if it is technically feasible, because all the components on which it depends might have to be incorporated into the design. Additionally, this can lead to penalties in execution speed and memory usage [BR92].

User interaction. A component can interact not only with other components but also with humans. In this case it needs some sort of a user interface like a window or textual input/output facilities. For reuse it is essential whether a component has a user interface directly attached to it. In most cases having an attached user interface will decrease its reusability.

User interaction does not necessarily exclude a component from being reused in a software system. For example, editors can be integrated in programming environments. However, user interaction of a component might interfere with user interface guidelines of a software system or even be inappropriate because, for example, the system sets parameters rather than letting the user do so.

8.4 Concurrency

Execution of concurrent components overlaps in time. The textual order of the computations does not define the order of execution. Thus concurrent components can behave nondeterministically; i.e., they do not necessarily deliver the same results when run with the same input data [BD93]. Reasons for running components concurrently include [BD93]:

- *Gains in execution speed*
  by assigning different physical processors to different processes

- *Elimination of potential processor idle time*
  by sharing the processors among a number of components running as concurrent processes

- *Inappropriateness of sequential model*
  for inherently concurrent and nondeterministic problem domains

Concurrent components can be defined in a certain programming language and can be compared to functional abstraction. Usually they are executed on a single processor and communicate via shared variables. However, they have their own thread of control and need a means for communication. In contrast to functions, invoking a concurrent component does not require waiting for completion. Synchronization is necessary if two components, for example, share any kind of resource.

Generally, source code components are not concurrent unless programming languages are used that explicitly support concurrency. However, executable components are usually inherently concurrent.

In the context of components we can distinguish between *intraconcurrency* and *interconcurrency*. Concurrency may happen within a component but not among components. For example, tools my be implemented concurrently in a concurrent programming language. Yet these tools may be interconnected via the Unix pipe mechanism, resulting in sequential processing. On the other hand, sequential components may run concurrently and communicate on different processors, e.g., client/server programs.

8.5 Distribution

Distributed components are logically and sometimes geographically separate. The main reasons for the popularity of distribution are not cost considerations but increased capabilities, greater flexibility of incremental expansion, and choice of vendors [QW93]. For increased reusability we want to use, buy and sell components for a variety of platforms. Thus components must be able to communicate and exchange data, i.e., interoperate among distributed platforms.

Distributed computing systems can be realized on a variety of architecture models such as the following:

- *Vector computers*
  same arithmetic operations applied to different data

- *Data flow machines*
  different operations applied to different data

- *Multiprograms*
  multiple processes on one processor

- *Multiprocessors*
  multiple processes on multiple processors sharing memory
- *Multicomputers*
  multiple processes on multiple processors passing messages
- *Networks*
  multiple processes on multiple processors connected by local area and/or wide area networks

This creates a distinction between logically and physically distributed software and hardware. Logically nondistributed software can be executed on physically nondistributed hardware (traditional configuration) and on physically distributed hardware (vector computers, data flow machines). From the viewpoint of reuse, physical distribution does not have any advantage over physical nondistribution. Logically distributed software can also be run on physically nondistributed hardware (multiprograms, multiprocessors, multicomputers) and on physically distributed hardware (multicomputers, networks). Logical distribution opens the door for software reuse. As long as the communication protocol between two processes is met, they can easily be replaced and/or reused in other contexts.

In a distributed system the unit of parallelism is not necessarily a process. The unit of parallelism offered by various programming languages ranges from processes to objects, statements, clauses and even expressions [BST89]. However, in the context of software reuse we are only interested in high abstractions; thus we neglect low-level units like statements and expressions. Distinctions can also be made according to the kinds of interprocess protocols being used. One common form of distributed system architectures is the client/server organization [And91, GS94].

For reuse we consider a distributed system simply as consisting of several interacting components. Strongly coupled components as encountered on vector and data flow machines are excluded. We are primarily interested in weakly interdependent components and their compatibility. This essentially relates to communication issues, which determine whether components can be replaced by other components, whether components can be reused in the context of a new system, and whether an existing system's functionality can be extended by adding a new component.

A distributed system consists of independently executing components. They can be implemented in the same programming language using communication mechanisms provided by that language. However, they can also be implemented in different programming languages and paradigms using language-independent mechanisms for communication. Besides data sharing, message passing is the central means for these components to communicate.

8.6 Forms of Adaptation

What happens to a component between the time a decision is made to reuse it and the time it becomes part of the software systems is referred to as *adaptation* [MMM95]. We can distinguish between adaptations that were foreseen and provided for by the creators of a component and adaptations made possible through a component's technology. We call the former *customization* and the latter *modification*.

As an example of customization, consider Unix tools that can be used as filters. For most of them, options can be specified which enhances the potential of their reuse. Object-oriented technology is a good example of inherent adaptation means for components. The inheritance mechanism allows modifications that have not necessarily been foreseen by the developers of a class to be reused. However, adaptation is still limited. Components have to be designed for reuse and must provide means for customization.

On the source code level, templates/generics provide a limited means of adaptation. Copying a component and modifying the copy is always a possible form of modification but creates multiple versions and inconsistencies of components. A component has to be designed for reuse. Technical support for this purpose is available at different levels of abstraction and varies among the various kinds of components.

P++ is an example of a language that offers subsystem abstractions (see Section 7.1.6 on page 88). Realms as presented in P++ provide advanced customization features at the source code level. Having components as parameters for components can simplify the customization of large software systems like operating systems. This can also lead to increased design reuse by simplifying the reuse of application frameworks. However, widely used programming languages still lack features at this level of abstraction.

8.7 Quality Control

The availability of high-quality, reliable software components is essential in order to build high-quality, reliable software systems. A market of reusable software components will not evolve without some sort of guaranteed quality. Unfortunately, the dream of formal verification is unrealistic and achievable at best with small source code components. We cannot expect to formally guarantee the correctness of software components in order to build large-scale software systems. Thus we have to build our software systems out of components that may be faulty. The goal of fault tolerant software is to make sure that a software system does not fail even when it contains faulty components [Jal94]. Fault tolerance also concerns faulty input, unpredicted events, hardware failure, etc.

The idea of designing by contract has been realized in the programming language Eiffel [Mey92]. Preconditions, postconditions and variants are used to characterize classes and to assure their correct behavior. Preconditions are boolean expressions that are used to check that input arguments are valid and that an object is in a reasonable state to do a requested operation. Similarly, postconditions assure that a method has successfully performed its duties, i.e., fulfilled its contract with the caller. Invariants are checked every time a method passes control to a separate object. Checking boolean expressions can help in improving the quality of source code components and the correct cooperation of components. However, the correctness of the assertions remains to be proven. If a check fails, an exception is raised.

Exceptions are another means of improving quality and fault tolerance of source code components [Str94]. Exceptions are conditions that require immediate action and are especially important for error handling. Compared to function calls, exceptions occur infrequently in a (typical) software system. Usually, subsystems, i.e., a collection of functions/modules/classes, rather than single functions are provided with this kind of fault tolerance. From the perspective of reuse exceptions provide a means of making components more reliable. The interface to the component becomes more sophisticated and requires careful treatment of all possible exceptions raised by the reused component. These exceptions become part of the interface to the component. Exceptions can be either built-in or user-defined. They make components more reliable by handling exceptional situations and by allowing other components to take corresponding actions.

Two methods for organizing diverse designs in order to build fault-tolerant software are the recovery block approach and N-version programming [Jal94]. The main idea of these approaches is to use multiple components for the same functionality.

Distributed components not only solve problems but also introduce new ones, e.g., partial failure and deadlocks. They pose the possibility of independent failures; i.e., individual components can fail while others still run. Usually the system should continue working after one or more components have failed. Components can either provide some handling of certain failures themselves (e.g., by using backup processes) or leave that responsibility to another component (e.g., a supervisor process). Especially in loosely coupled systems, components also have to deal with unreliable communication channels. For example, messages may get lost even if both the sender and the receiver are working. Various levels of fault tolerance exist, e.g., reliable point-to-point messages and atomicity of actions.

8.8 Summary

Table 8.2 summarizes attributes of components and provides examples in each category. The upper part of the table (*functionality*, *component interaction*, and *user interaction*) is more component-specific. The lower part (*form of adaptation*, *concurrency*, and *distribution*) is more platform specific. *Quality*

Table 8.2. Attributes of components

Attribute	Examples
Functionality	sorting, menu handling, database management
Component interaction	function call, database query, server contact
User interaction	dialog-box, window display, terminal input
Quality control	tests, verifications, compiler checks, assertions, process backups
Form of adaptation	parameters, inheritance, modification
Concurrency	semaphores, critical regions, monitors
Distribution	client/server, World-Wide Web, file transfer

control is somewhere in the middle because platforms can provide tremendous help for it (e.g., type checks of compilers), but quality still is a component-specific matter which, for example, requires thorough testing and long-term experience with a component.

Some attributes are more specific for components than for component platforms. For example, components may be concurrent and/or distributed. This is specific to a certain component, but the component's platform determines whether concurrency and/or distribution are possible at all.

9. Component Taxonomy

Contents

A taxonomy for reusable components provides a framework for creating and retrieving components. Component categories make it easier to determine the reuse potential of specific components. A taxonomy also helps in evaluating the state of today's component reuse and in recognizing future potential for reuse.

In this chapter we provide a taxonomy for software components. In Section 9.1 we introduce a taxonomy based on the contents of the previous three chapters. A comparison with existing taxonomies is presented in Section 9.2. A summary follows in Section 9.3.

9.1 Taxonomy

In Chapters 6, 7 and 8 we described various aspects of software components. Now we factor out distinguishing characteristics and provide a taxonomy for components. We base the taxonomy on components' interfaces, composition techniques, platforms and attributes.

9.1.1 User and Data Interfaces

Components (especially applications) that do not provide explicit reuse support can be combined and reused under certain circumstances. Even if they

Table 9.1. User interface levels

| Level 2: Graphical user interface |
| Level 1: Command-line interface |
| Level 0: None |

do not provide a programming interface, user interfaces and data interfaces may be used for that purpose. Below we summarize user and data interfaces and present different levels of reuse support.

Components are not restricted to one interface, but may have several. Any one of the interfaces can be used for reuse purposes. Programming interfaces are considered in the next section.

User interfaces. We distinguish three different levels of user interfaces (see Table 9.1). Various ways exist to reuse components by means of their user interface, e.g., pseudo ttys or *dynamic data exchange* (DDE).

Unless components have been designed for reuse, their reusability is reciprocal to their user interface level. Components without a user interface are easier to reuse than components which interact with the user. This is true both for source code components and for full-fledged applications.

Compound documents provide a means for the composition of components with graphical user interfaces. However, the composition is done by means of programming interfaces.

Data interfaces. Input and output of components can take many forms. From the point of reuse, only simple input/output is worthwhile because complex data formats limit the number of components available for reuse. Additionally, data formats may change over time; e.g., when new requirements arise, old components may have to be modified accordingly.

Table 9.2 lists data interface levels. Textual input/output has proven successful for reuse. However, similar to user interfaces, the reusability of components is reciprocal to the data interface level. We refrain from making an extensive classification for extensive data I/O and differentiate only *specific file I/O* and *database I/O*.

Unix filters and pipes are the prominent example of successful reuse with (textual) data interfaces. Putting two filters together with a pipe does not require any programming. This eases reuse, but also limits possibilities of application. Also, the structure and semantics of text can take different forms.

Table 9.2. Data interface levels

| Level 3: Database I/O |
| Level 2: Specific file I/O |
| Level 1: Textual I/O |
| Level 0: None |

Table 9.3. Composition categories

Level 8: Open platform composition
Level 7: Specific platform composition
Level 6: Object model composition
Level 5: Subsystem composition
Level 4: Object-oriented composition
Level 3: Modular composition
Level 2: Functional composition
Level 1: Textual composition
Level 0: None

Thus two components may have textual input/output and be composed, but their interoperation may not be useful if they are based on different semantic structures of the text.

9.1.2 Composition and Interoperation

Programming interfaces represent the most important aspect for reuse. In Section 7.1 on page 83 we discussed various forms of component composition, ranging from simple textual composition to open platforms. Composition levels for reuse are summarized in Table 9.3. We do not know yet exactly what an *open platform* will be and how it will look. Component composition at this level is an area of quickly changing technology and the next couple of years might drastically change/extend the upper part of the compositional landscape.

In Section 7.1 on page 83 we also mentioned source code parameterization, distributed computing, compound documents and compound applications in addition to the levels listed in Table 9.3. These items are not included because they can be assigned to the given levels. For example, *compound documents* are realized by means of *object models*.

In the taxonomy we do not explicitly consider forms of interoperation as depicted in Section 7.2 on page 98. The interoperation categories describe the way components interact. This is influenced by the kind of composition that is used. However, various forms of interoperation can be used for certain levels of composition. For example, two functions can simply call each other without any data transfer, use global data, use other functions for data access, or use function variables for dynamic calls.

Table 9.4. Platform categories

Level 4: Programming languages
Level 3: Libraries
Level 2: Programming system
Level 1: Operating system
Level 0: Hardware

9.1.3 Platforms and Attributes

Many aspects and attributes of components are determined by their platforms, e.g., programming language, operating system or distribution. Other aspects and attributes are specific to individual components, e.g., user interaction or quality.

In order to support systematic reuse, we have to overcome the boundaries of component platforms. The goal is to have highly reusable components available in many reuse scenarios, not only for projects developed on/with a certain operating system and/or programming language.

Table 9.4 lists five platform categories. This is only a rough representation of platforms. A more detailed classification is possible. We stick to this simple form because components can be assigned to more than one platform and because platforms in the same category can have different reuse characteristics. Therefore a more detailed classification is not necessarily more useful.

The standardization of platforms is important for increased reusability of components. For example, the definition of *virtual machines* is one step in this direction. Java is a programming language whose programs can be executed on many different platforms without recompilation, even when they have a graphical user interface. This portability not only increases widespread use of such programs, but also provides a platform for increased reusability of components.

Component attributes as described in Chapter 8 are not suitable for component classification. As with interoperation some attributes are influenced by the kind of composition that is used; for example, component interactivity is a matter of fact for classes, modules and applications. Means of adaptation are partly determined by the technology used. Inheritance is possible only when using object-oriented composition. Adaptation is also specific to individual components and depends on what component designers have foreseen for adaptation.

In order to come closer to the goal of developing software systems out of reusable components, we need open platforms and flexible techniques for composition.

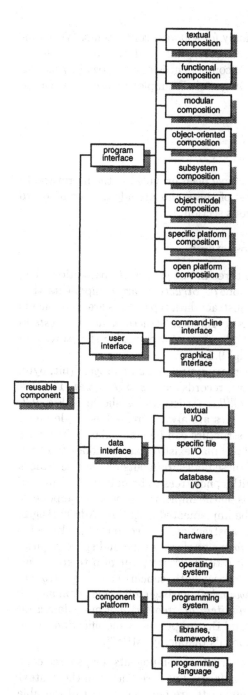

Fig. 9.1. Reusable software components (taxonomy)

9.1.4 Summary

Fig. 9.1 presents the complete taxonomy for software components. We distinguish three different types of interfaces (user, data and programming interface) and platforms of components. A component is characterized by assignments to several of the presented categories. Examples presented in Chapter 10 demonstrate this.

9.2 Related Work

Several classifications of components have been provided in the literature. In this section we briefly discuss several of these and provide a comparison to the approach presented in the previous section.

9.2.1 Structures, Tools and Subsystems

Booch has divided components into three major groups of abstractions, i.e., structures, tools and subsystems [Boo87]. *Structures* are components that denote objects or classes of objects (abstract data type), *tools* are components that denote algorithmic abstractions targeted to structures and *subsystems* are components that denote logical collections of cooperating structures and tools. This distinction is shown in Fig. 9.2.

Structures are derived from elementary types, i.e., *atomic types* (bit, byte, integer, etc.), *composite types* (arrays, records) and *pointer types*. The distinction between *monolithic* and *polylithic* structures, as shown in Fig. 9.2, is made based on whether the structures are always treated as single units, i.e., whether individual parts of the structure can be manipulated. Trees are considered polylithic structures, as links may exist to various nodes of a tree, allowing individual modifications of these nodes from outside the tree. Stacks do not necessarily have to be monolithic, nor trees to be polylithic. Which of these attributes is applicable depends on the implementation of a component. Booch sees structures and tools to be implemented as generic Ada packages, whereas subsystems represent larger abstractions (collections of packages).

Additionally, Booch introduced *forms* to classify time and space requirements. Forms are applicable primarily to structures, but also to tools and subsystems. The categories of forms deal with concurrency (e.g., *sequential, concurrent*), space (*bounded, unbounded*), garbage collection (*unmanaged, managed, controlled*) and iterators (*noniterator, iterator*). For more details on forms, see Booch [Boo87]. Margono and Berard propose a modification to the *temporal* and *spatial* behaviors in Booch's taxonomy [MB87].

Comparison. Booch classifies data structure components, i.e., source code components. This provides a fine granularity, but is restricted in the context of reuse because data structure components are only one aspect of reusable software components.

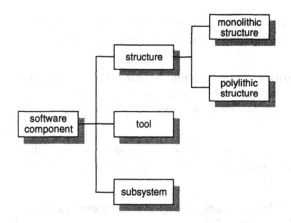

Fig. 9.2. Booch's taxonomy of reusable components

Booch suggests the three abstraction groups *structures*, *tools* and *subsystems* in the context of Ada packages. We regard structures and tools as components with modular composition. Booch's subsystems correspond to subsystem composition. However, Ada does not provide language support for the notion of subsystems. We do not reflect Booch's distinction between structures and tools or his *forms* to classify time and space requirements. We provide a much broader range of components and do not consider detailed distinctions in all (sub)categories.

9.2.2 Scope, Purpose, Granularity and Abstraction

Kain uses the characteristics scope, purpose, granularity and level of abstraction to categorize components [Kai96] (see Table 9.5).

- *Scope*
  Specification components capture the characteristics of problems, e.g., object models, specifications and designs. Source code or executable code constitutes *implementation components*, e.g., functions, classes, programs.

- *Purpose*
  Components with *domain purpose* capture problems in application domains. Components that are not specific to an application domain but

Table 9.5. Kain's component categories and values

Category	Values	
Scope	specification	implementation
Purpose	domain	technology
Granularity	fine	coarse
Abstraction	general	specific

focus on technical aspects of a software system are said to have *technology purpose*, e.g., components for database access or the user interface.

- *Granularity*
  Fine-grained components are small and have limited capability, e.g., a function or class. *Coarse grained* components are more complex and provide extensive capabilities, e.g., subsystems or full-fledged applications.

- *Abstraction*
  Components are considered to be *general* if they apply to at least two different applications. *Specific* components are limited to a particular problem that is specific to an application.

The combination of the two values for each of the four categories yields 16 different component categories (see Fig. 9.3).

Similarly, McGregor et al. use components' level of granularity and scope of responsibility for distinction. They identify architecture-level components, design-level components and code-level components [MDK96]. *Architecture-level components* correspond to independent units like subsystems. *Design-level components* are represented by design patterns. Finally, *code-level components* are either single classes or clusters of tightly coupled classes.

Comparison. Kain uses *scope, purpose, granularity* and *abstraction* as characteristics for component classification. We reflect these general categories only partly.

Granularity is represented by the different composition categories. Fine-grained components are those using textual, functional, modular, and object-oriented composition. Coarse-grained components correspond to components with subsystem composition, object models, and open platform composition.

Scope, purpose and abstraction can be used in addition in order to further characterize the functionality of components.

9.2.3 Active and Passive Components

Dusink and van Katwijk propose two types of components, *active* and *passive* [DvK87]. Functions in libraries are considered passive components to be used as building blocks in a system. Executable programs are active components that require some kind of interprocess communication for composition. The different levels of abstraction reflect the historic evolution of abstraction mechanisms provided by programming languages.

- *Active components*
  Active components run on their own. The environment, e.g., the operating

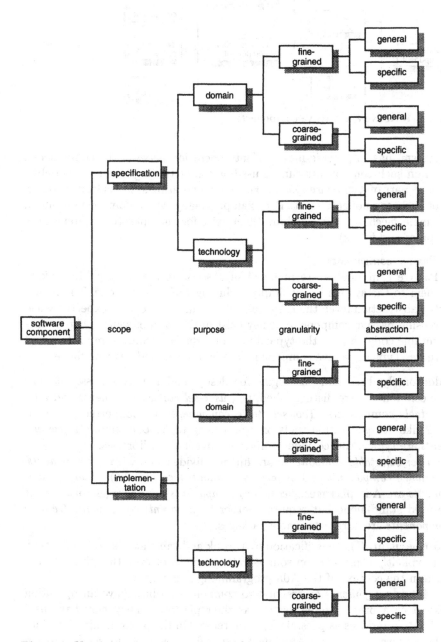

Fig. 9.3. Kain's component category combination

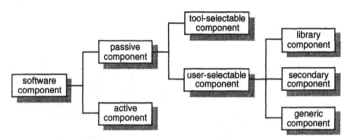

Fig. 9.4. Active and passive components

system, has to provide means of interoperation between the components. Often such components can be used as complete programs by themselves or as part of a software system. For many operating systems large catalogs of such components exist. For example, many active components plus a simple mechanism to combine them exist for the operating system Unix (pipes and filters) .

– *Passive components*
Passive components are included in a software system, e.g., by linking them to the system or by simply including their source code. The higher the abstraction level, the more gains in productivity can be expected when reusing passive components. They exist in the form of source code or executable code and are the typical unit of today's software composition and reuse. Typical passive components are functions, modules and classes.

Additionally, based on paradigms for design and use, two classes of passive components are distinguished, i.e., *user-selectable* components and *tool-selectable* components. *Tool-selectable components* are supported by meta-tools like 4th generation tools or prototyping tools. *User-selectable components* are typical source code components available in libraries.

User-selectable components are further divided into *library components*, *secondary components* and *generic components* (see Fig. 9.4). *Library components* are Ada packages. *Secondary components* are packages that cannot be used stand-alone but require another (i.e., *parent*) component. *Generic components* are parameterizable packages.

Comparison. The classification by Dusink and van Katwijk is rudimentary, but explicitly considers non-source-code components, even though it was defined in the context of the Ada programming language.

Active components correspond to components which have an operating system or a programming system as their platform. They may have user and data interfaces as possible forms of reuse. On the programming interface side, active components are assigned to specific or open platform composition (levels 7 and 8).

Passive components are source code components (programming language or library platform) with their composition ranging from textual to subsys-

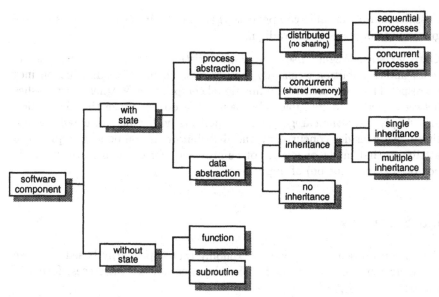

Fig. 9.5. Wegner's taxonomy of software components

tem composition. In fact, as Ada packages are primarily considered, modular composition is the appropriate category.

Library components correspond to components based on a programming language platform. *Secondary components*, i.e., components requiring other packages, fall into the category library platform.

9.2.4 State, Inheritance, Concurrency and Distribution

Even though published already in 1984, Wegner provides a general classification of software components of different languages [Weg89]. He uses state, inheritance, concurrency and distribution as discriminating characteristics. This results in the following components: functions and subprograms, packages and modules, classes with single inheritance, classes with multiple inheritance, concurrent tasks with shared memory, distributed concurrent processes, and distributed sequential processes (see Fig. 9.5).

Wegner states that this taxonomy is tentative, with the technology of software components being in a state of transition. For example, he writes that process abstraction may become the central abstraction mechanism, with data and function abstraction becoming a specialized form thereof.

Wegner's taxonomy was primarily motivated by classifying programming languages, i.e., components provided by these languages. The other taxonomies we have presented were motivated by classifying components provided by a certain programming language like Ada. In contrast to these taxonomies, Wegner provides a general approach which is more useful for a classification of reusable components that may be implemented in any programming language and paradigm.

Comparison. Wegner uses the characteristics state, inheritance, concurrency and distribution to classify components. His functions and subroutines correspond to components with functional composition. Wegner distinguishes between single and multiple inheritance. We do not make this distinction and simply have one category for components with object-oriented composition. We consider concurrency and distribution as component or platform attributes that might or might not be provided. For component reuse this is not (and should not be) of importance.

9.3 Summary

We have proposed a component taxonomy that is primarily based on reuse considerations. Aspects used for the classification are interfaces, forms of composition and platforms.

The reuse taxonomy classifies components based on whether components can, in general, be put together. Only if composition and reuse is possible in general, do more detailed aspects of a component have to be determined, like its functionality, its quality, its reuse status, etc.

We have also presented component taxonomies that were created in different contexts and with different motivations. None of them meets the need to classify arbitrary components that may be candidates for reuse. Many taxonomies concentrate on source code and do not take higher levels of abstractions into consideration.

The component categories defined in this chapter are used in Chapter 10 to classify sample components that exhibit a high degree of reuse.

10. Component Examples

Contents

There have been several successful attempts in increasing the reusability of software components. All of these approaches are applicable only in certain contexts and do not provide general solutions to software engineering problems, but they demonstrate that productivity can be increased considerably when special attention is paid to software composition.

In this chapter we discuss two component examples of programming languages and three examples of application components. VisualBasic and Java are described in Sections 10.1 and 10.2, respectively. Unix filters, Frame-Maker, and Field are discussed in Sections 10.3, 10.4, and 10.5, respectively. We have chosen these examples for discussion for the following reasons:

– VisualBasic is often referred to as *the* success story of software reuse.
– Java enjoys increasing popularity as *the* Web language.
– Unix filters represent a simple but successful reuse story.
– FrameMaker provides an example of a reusable application with a complex graphical user interface.
– Field is an example of reuse in an integrated programming environment.

In Section 10.6 we rate the example components according to the taxonomy we introduced in Chapter 9.

10.1 VisualBasic: Reuse of Visual Controls

In the past years visual programming has attracted widespread attention by promising to make programming much easier. Visual programming comprises areas like visual programming, program visualization, and programming by example [Mye86] (the term 'visual programming' is used here with two different meanings). Although mechanisms for program visualization and programming by example can supply helpful support for software reuse purposes, they do not provide additional abstractions for software components and their compositions. Yet some visual programming environments have emerged that seem to cast a new light on software reuse. In this context it is not important whether a system is "really visual". Instead, we are interested in the concepts that are provided in modeling and combining (reusable) components.

Microsoft VisualBasic is a popular visual programming language [Mic93a, Mic93b]. It provides programmers with a quick and easy method of developing applications. An integrated environment with various tools can be used to quickly create graphical user interfaces and to use event-driven programming techniques. The integrated development environment has sophisticated editing and debugging tools which allow attaching code to the interface and writing code to respond to specific events which occur as a result of user input. The fact that all components react on events makes it easy to arbitrarily combine them and to select among a large number of existing components. There are three main steps to creating a VisualBasic application:

1. Create the user interface.
2. Set properties.
3. Write code.

The user interface is made of controls, forms and other objects. Controls are used to click buttons to perform actions, to display and enter text, to present choices to the user, etc. VisualBasic programs are event-driven. Forms and controls recognize events and respond by executing event procedures. Events are caused by the user (e.g., keystroke or mouse click) or by other forms or controls [Mic93c]. A VisualBasic application consists of:

– form modules (containing visual elements of a form, including controls and basic code associated with forms),
– code modules (containing Basic code), and
– custom controls.

Code and form modules can contain declarations, event procedures and general procedures (i.e., procedures not directly associated with an event).

Custom controls are Windows DLL files and highly dependent on Visual-Basic. Custom controls are designed and implemented with control classes. A control class is composed of a control model (property information table, event information table) and a control procedure (e.g., determines when an event is recognized, handles the painting of the control). Custom controls can also (with little or no modification) be used in the Visual C++ environment. Control classes can be subclassed.

Evaluation. VisualBasic components are clearly based on a programming system; i.e., VisualBasic is the platform. On whatever machine this system is offered, the components can be reused. Composition with different platforms is possible, as long as it is supported by the VisualBasic platform, e.g., with Visual C++ and with OLE.

VisualBasic components can have a graphical user interface and data interfaces, but these interfaces are not used for composition purposes. The platform provides an event handling mechanism, which makes it easy to add components to a system and to remove them. Due to the extension features and the event handling, VisualBasic's composition features can be assigned somewhere in between object-oriented composition and subsystem composition. OLE access provides the possibility for integration with object models.

Despite their usefulness and contribution to increased software productivity and reuse, components of visual programming systems share one common handicap. They need their specific support environment and cannot easily be combined across different systems.

10.2 Java: Reuse on the World-Wide Web

Java is an object-oriented programming language with interesting features for software reuse [GM95]. Java's designers addressed many problems of today's software developers. For example, many hardware architectures with different operating systems and incompatible graphical user interfaces make it difficult to develop software running on all these platforms. Additionally, applications are increasingly required to run in distributed client/server environments. Programming languages like C and C++ can be used to cope with such situations, but they also provide many pitfalls that require experienced and disciplined engineers willing to put much extra work into achieving these goals.

Java was developed at Sun Microsystems as a portable, interpreted, high performance and simple object-oriented programming language. A characterization of the language is given by the goals that were set for Java's development [GM95]:

− *Simplicity and familiarity*
  When switching to a new programming language necessitates extensive programmer training, this can keep the language from being quickly adopted on a broad basis. Java is both syntactically and semantically similar to C and C++, which, considering the hordes of programmers using C and C++, should positively influence its wide acceptance.

− *Object-orientedness*
  There is no doubt any more that object-oriented programming has many benefits and is more than just another way of organizing the source code. Object-orientedness is a must for any modern programming language.

- *Robustness and reliability*
  Considering the fact that our software systems are growing larger and
  larger, building reliable software is a key problem. The majority of today's
  systems are built with inappropriate tools like C and C++ that offer an
  enormous variety of unchecked, potential errors. Eliminating many of these
  features and adding both extensive compile-time and run-time checking
  has made Java suitable for building highly robust and reliable software.
  Automatic garbage collection is one improvement over C++.

- *Security*
  Security is of utmost importance in distributed environments. Java provides checks for recognizing dangerous code, thus avoiding dangers by
  viruses and other intruders.

- *Portability*
  In order to support portability over many platforms, a *virtual machine*
  has been defined. An interpreter is used to execute Java code on this machine. This slows down performance but guarantees the same semantics on
  all platforms. This contrasts to the portability of C and C++, for which
  many features are defined as machine dependent. Additionally, standard
  class libraries, including a window toolkit, are defined and available on all
  supported platforms.

- *High performance*
  In order to compete with the performance of compiled languages without
  giving up portability, code fragments of a Java program can be compiled
  on the fly, i.e., at run-time. It is also possible to rewrite certain parts in
  machine code and interface them to the Java system.

- *Heterogeneity and distributed networks*
  Multiple threads, as lightweight processes are called in Java, together with
  synchronization mechanisms are supported directly in the language.

- *Architecture neutrality*
  Java code can be interpreted on any machine to which the interpreter and
  run-time system have been ported.

- *Dynamic adaptability*
  Despite its strict static checking at compile-time, Java programs can be
  extended and adapted by dynamically loading and linking classes on demand.

A World-Wide-Web browser was among the first applications to be implemented with the Java language. Besides the features listed above, the most
compelling characteristics of this browser are mini-applications, called *applets*, that are shared across the net (local or wide-area) and executed locally.

The HotJava browser provides a good example of how Java applications
can be dynamically configured and adapted even over the Internet and at the

user's discretion. HotJava can be extended dynamically and adapted to support new protocols by adding the appropriate components. This can be done even over the Internet in a transparent way (see Fig. 7.3 on page 96). Thus software components can be reused world-wide and incorporated in one's own system automatically. This mechanism cannot cross language boundaries, but it is independent of any constraints from hardware architectures, operating systems and/or graphical user interfaces.

An enhancement to the Java platform is JavaBeans, a component architecture for Java [Sun96]. This platform allows more dynamic interaction and the definition of more independent components.

Evaluation. At first sight, there seem to be no major differences between Java and other object-oriented languages like C++. We have object-oriented composition and Java as platform. However, the platform might make the difference. The platform includes not only the language but also extensive libraries with support for graphical user interfaces. This guarantees portability of components among many computer systems. In addition, the platform offers not only source code, but also object code compatibility and some sort of security.

The ability to download applets from the net and to extend the functionality of a running browser adds a new dimension to software reuse. Currently the main application of this feature is to control the display of (animated) data in Web pages. Additional functionality and a new kind of Internet software may come into existence. Whether this is an important contribution to traditional software engineering is not clear yet. However, continued extension and modification of software is important to comply to ever changing requirements.

The (commercial) success of Java remains to be seen. In case it continues its increasing popularity it will provide a better platform for software reuse than languages like C++.

10.3 Unix Filters: Reuse based on ASCII Pipes

In the well-known pipe and filter approach each component reads input data and produces output data, usually by applying local transformations to the input stream. These local transformations are done incrementally; i.e., output is generated before the whole input is consumed, thus the term filter. To make filters highly interchangeable, they do not share states with each other and do not know the identity of other filters (their input generators and their output consumers). Common specializations of pipes are [GS94]:

– *Pipelines*
  are linear sequences of filters.

– *Bounded pipes*
  have the amount of data restricted.

Fig. 10.1. Unix pipes and filters

– *Typed pipes*
have a type defined for their data.

In Unix shells these components can be arbitrary programs as long as they read streams of input data and produce streams of output data. Filters are integrated by piping the output from one component into the input of another component (see Fig. 10.1). Filters can easily be combined, added and replaced when they agree on the same form of data transmission, e.g., text files. However, pipe and filter systems lead to batch processing and cannot (easily) be integrated with interactive applications. A lowest common denominator on data transmission (e.g., ASCII files) requires each filter to parse and unparse data leading to added complexity in the filters and a loss of performance [GS94].

Unix provides many components that can serve as filters. Consider the following example, where three components are used in order to determine how often the word 'filter' is used in a set of files:

```
more *.tex | grep filter | wc -l
```

First, the component *more* inputs and outputs the contents of all files that end with the extension .tex. This output is used by the second component, *grep*, which outputs all lines containing the word 'filter'. This output is used by the component *wc*, which counts lines. The '|' is used to pipe the output of one component to the input of another component. The output of the last component could be directed to a file. In the example there is no output file specified for the last filter; thus the result is simply output on the console.

Simply typing the above example at the prompt of a Unix shell would mean to 'use' these components, rather than to 'reuse' them. However, it is possible to create new components by reusing existing ones (e.g., using *shell scripts*).

Evaluation. Components are complete programs (filters) that are purely computational and do local processing and data stream to data stream mapping [Sha95]. Filters do not communicate with each other. They simply read input and write output. Reuse is accomplished by means of a textual data interface, rather than a program (or user) interface.

Filters are executable programs. They can be implemented in any programming language and paradigm. A set of filters to be used together has to share the same execution platform (e.g., Unix). This platform has to provide a mechanism (pipes) for the interconnection of the output of one filter to the input of the next filter.

Filters do not have a user interface, but parameters can be specified on invocation. In the example above, the components *more*, *grep* and *wc* are invoked with parameters. For example, the option -1 for *wc* specifies that only lines should be counted rather than characters and words also.

Unix filters are often implemented as shell scripts and not self-contained when they invoke other components by name. Thus they may behave differently under different environments, as their 'subcomponents' may be different.

10.4 FrameMaker: Reuse of a Desktop Publishing Application

FrameMaker is a complex commercial application for publishing. It contains a word processor with spell checking, hypertext links, cross-references, a page designer, a graphics editor, a book builder, and much more [Fra95b]. FrameMaker is available on many platforms (operating systems), e.g., Unix, Apple Macintosh and Microsoft Windows. The document format is the same on all of these platforms.

FrameMaker appears as a monolithic application with a complex graphical user interface and complex functionality. However, reuse is possible by means of an application programming interface (Frame API) and a development environment (FDE).

With the API it is possible to write C programs to control FrameMaker, communicate with the user, add functionality, modify the user interface (e.g., menus), and do anything a user can do. Programs using the API (called *clients* in FrameMaker terminology) can add various types of functionality to FrameMaker, e.g., grammar checkers, reporting utilities, version control systems, filters for file exchange with other applications [Fra95a].

The development environment supports the development of platform-independent clients. It provides platform-independent support for input/output, string handling, memory allocation, etc. It provides the (software) platform to guarantee portability of FrameMaker clients to all platforms supported by Adobe.

Fig. 10.2 depicts the general structure of FrameMaker and its clients. More than one client can be used simultaneously. FrameMaker starts the clients as separate processes and communicates via the C library. Clients perform simple function calls and do not have to worry about interprocess communication.

Evaluation. FrameMaker is a complex component. Its reuse is possible by means of a functional application programming interface. Naturally, reuse is limited to the platforms supported by FrameMaker. Even though interprocess communication is used between FrameMaker and its clients, composition is solely functional. For the reuser, i.e., the programmer writing a

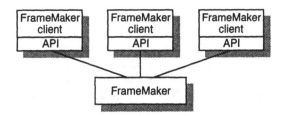

Fig. 10.2. FrameMaker with clients

FrameMaker client, it does not matter whether the client is called beyond process boundaries or, for example, linked dynamically. Interoperation between FrameMaker and its clients is static; i.e., specific functions are called and specific data is used.

The FrameMaker Development Environment (FDE) provides C interfaces as *application programming interface* (API) to access FrameMaker. FrameMaker *clients* can be programmed in any language as long as the language provides access to C functions. Clients can be implemented, for example, in C++.

10.5 Field: Reuse in a Programming Environment

Field is an integrated programming environment on Unix platforms by Reiss [Rei95a]. Its development started in the mid 1980s at Brown University. A major criterion in developing the environment was simplicity and the provision of a base for existing tools. The integration of existing tools is important for programming environments because programmers want to stick to their favorite editor. But it is also important to integrate existing compilers, debuggers, configuration management tools, etc. Otherwise it is almost impossible to support various programming languages. Moreover, especially from our viewpoint of reuse, it does not make sense to reimplement all these existing tools only for the sake of having them integrated in the environment.

Integrating and reusing existing tools was not the only goal in the development of Field, however. The production of a friendly, easy-to-use (for students) environment that also provides a showcase for programming environment research was another goal.

A *message server* forms the nucleus of the Field environment. This server supports a broadcasting mechanism for messages containing commands or pieces of information. Tools register with the server and send messages which are then broadcast to other tools. In order to reduce the amount of message traffic, the broadcasting mechanism is selective. Thus tools not only register with the server but also notify the server of messages they are interested in and of command requests other tools can make from them. If the server receives a message, it will broadcast it only to those tools that have explicitly expressed interest in getting such a message.

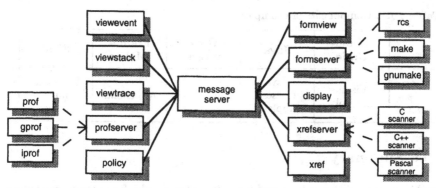

Fig. 10.3. Architecture of the Field environment

Existing tools are not aware of the message server and will not communicate with it. In order to reuse such tools the environment has to provide tools that send and receive messages and also communicate with the tools to be reused. These mediator tools are called wrappers and have to map messages from and to commands of the tool they wrap. An alternative way of integrating existing tools into a message-based environment is to augment them with the code that is necessary to communicate with the message server. This is *white-box reuse*, as the tools to be reused have to be modified, i.e., extended. The source code has to be available in order to apply this integration mechanism. Using wrappers corresponds to *black-box reuse* and is less susceptible to changes in new versions of tools. In Field tools from the underlying Unix environment are wrapped by creating subprocesses that run using pipes or pseudo ttys.

Fig. 10.3 shows the general architecture of Field, presenting only a few of the components available. The message server plays the central role in this architecture and communicates with tools that have been specifically developed for this purpose. These tools deal with outside communication to tools that do not have an integrated message mechanism. Programming environments with similar tool integration include Fuse from DEC, SoftBench from Hewlett-Packard, SparcWorks from Sun Microsystems, and Sniff from TakeFive (see also [Rei95a]).

Evaluation. The reuse approach demonstrated in integrated programming environments can be regarded as quite successful. The user is provided with a uniform user interface and can handle different task with different tools. However, integrated environments do not solve reuse problems on a broader basis. Only certain kinds of components can be included, i.e., reused. It is not possible to take arbitrary components, e.g., a class browser from a different vendor, and include it in one's favorite environment. Integration work remains to be done. Components to be reused have to be either modified or endowed with a wrapper.

Table 10.1. Components of examples

	Visual-Basic	Java	Unix filters	Frame-Maker	Field
Components	Visual controls	Java classes, applets	Unix filters	API clients	Programming tools

10.6 Summary

In this chapter we have discussed five different examples for component reuse, i.e., VisualBasic, Java, Unix filters, the application FrameMaker and the Field programming environment. Below we briefly summarize the reuse aspects of these examples.

Components. The components of the examples are summarized in Table 10.1. VisualBasic offers visual elements that are used to form part of the user interface and to generate and react to various kinds of events. For Java we distinguish between classes used to write the source code of programs and applets, which are used as dynamic extensions to Internet browsers. Unix filters provide high flexibility in terms of components. Any executable program can serve as filter as long as it reads from standard input, writes to standard output, and does not require any other interaction with the user. FrameMaker interacts with API clients that have to be created by means of the provided functional interface. Components of the Field programming environment are tools that communicate with the *message server.* Various composition techniques can be exploited to enable the reuse of existing tools that are not endowed with the necessary communication skills. Wrapping tools with command-line user interfaces or filters are examples of that activity.

Composition. Table 10.2 summarizes the classification for component composition. Unix filters are most peculiar among the example components, as they use solely a data interface for composition and interoperation. The other components use functional and object-oriented programming interfaces.

Components of VisualBasic, Java, FrameMaker, and Field may also use a data interface for interoperation, but typically this is not the case. Unix filters must not have a user interface, but they may provide the option to specify arguments when invoking a filter. VisualBasic components often contain/specify part of the user interface, e.g., a button or dialog. FrameMaker clients typically enhance the user interface of FrameMaker, but may also use some separate means of user interaction. The composition between FrameMaker and its clients is done solely by means of the programming interface.

Attributes. Table 10.3 summarizes attributes of the example components. The functionality of Unix filters is limited to textual transformations, and

Table 10.2. Interfaces and platforms of example components

	Visual-Basic	Java	Unix filters	Frame-Maker	Field
Program-ming interface	object-oriented	object-oriented	–	functional (1)	functional
User interface	–	–	– (2)	– (3)	any (4)
Data interface	–	–	textual	–	– (5)
Platform	Visual-Basic	Java	Unix	Frame-Maker (6)	Unix

(1) FrameMaker provides a functional C interface.
(2) Parameters can be specified on invocation of a filter.
(3) FrameMaker does have a graphical user interface, but it is not used for reuse purposes.
(4) Most Field tools have graphical user interfaces which are not used for reuse purposes. However, some (legacy) 'background' tools are wrapped by means of pseudo ttys.
(5) Tools may use data interfaces for individual interoperation.
(6) This includes any platform where FrameMaker is available and whatever provides possible composition with C functions, e.g., C++.

there is no component interaction. VisualBasic components interact by means of events. Java classes have method invocation with dynamic binding. Frame-Maker clients are limited to a functional programming interface. Tools in the Field programming environment use a selective message broadcast.

User interaction is possible for any components except for Unix filters. Features for quality control are not available, except simple compiler checks like type compatibility. An example of additional quality control are Eiffel's preconditions and postconditions.

Java and VisualBasic components can be adapted by means of inheritance. Unix filters can be wrapped; i.e., before and after a filter's transformation some additional transformations can be performed. FrameMaker clients and Field tools may have various differing forms of adaptation.

Distribution is a matter of fact for FrameMaker clients and Field tools. Unix filters can be executed on separate processes, but the pipe mechanism requires serial execution on a single process. VisualBasic and Java components are typically not distributed, but provide the possibility. Java applets

Table 10.3. Attributes of example components

	Visual-Basic	Java	Unix Filters	Frame-Maker	Field
Functionality	any	any	any text transformation	any [1]	any [2]
Component interaction	event-based	dynamic binding	–	via API	via message server
User interaction	usually yes	possible	no	possible [3]	possible [4]
Quality control	–	security [5]	–	–	–
Form of adaptation	inheritance	inheritance	wrapping	arbitrary [6]	arbitrary [7]
Concurrency	no	no	no	no	no
Distribution	yes/no	yes/no	no	yes	yes

[1]   typically in the context of desktop publishing
[2]   typically in the context of programming environments
[3]   User interaction is typically done through FrameMaker itself.
[4]   Tools may have separate user interaction.
[5]   Security features are provided for applets.
[6]   FrameMaker clients can be implemented in any programming language that is compatible to C.
[7]   Tools can be implemented in any programming language and/or paradigm.

are distributed over the Internet. Upon their invocation, however, they are copied over the net and executed on the local machine.

Part III

Software Engineering

11. Software Engineering

Contents

Cost-effective production of high-quality software systems is the primary goal of software engineering. Quality in this respect comprises attributes like reliability, robustness, user-friendliness, efficiency and maintainability. Software reuse and software components provide crucial contributions in this direction; this is the topic of Part III.

In this chapter we give an overview of *classic* software engineering. Large software projects are broken up into various project phases. In the following sections we describe these. Various divisions of the phases are possible depending on project size, project kind, etc. We describe software management in general in Section 11.1 and the phases specification in Section 11.2, design in Section 11.3, implementation in Section 11.4, testing in Section 11.5 and maintenance in Section 11.6. A summary follows in Section 11.7.

11.1 Software Management

Software projects tend to run over budget and behind schedule. Reasons for this are that projects are often distinct from previous projects, that software process models are only simplifications of the real software process, and that software is intangible. Software management has to plan a project, establish objectives, consider alternative solutions, identify constraints, and select and evaluate personnel. It comprises the following major activities (see Pressman [Pre92] and Sommerville [Som92]):

- *Project planning*
  The progress of a project must be thoroughly planned. Planning is an interactive process. The initial plan will not be static but will have to be

modified with advancing time. It is important to anticipate problems, to prepare different solutions (risk analysis), to establish milestones, etc. Various plans may be necessary for effective management, e.g., development plan, validation plan, testing plan, staff training plan, configuration management plan, etc.

- *Project measuring*
Despite the intangible nature of software, many measurements can be done in software projects. Software measures can focus on technical, productivity and quality aspects. They are used to indicate software quality, to assess staff productivity, to assess tool, training and methodology benefits, and to provide data for cost estimation.

- *Project estimating*
Cost and effort estimations are necessary to predict profit or loss of a project. Systematic steps can be taken to provide estimates with acceptable deviations. Different techniques for cost estimation have been proposed, e.g., algorithmic cost modeling, expert judgement, estimation by analogy, top-down/bottom-up estimation. Different techniques should be used and their results compared. A well-known and well-documented cost estimation model is Boehm's CoCoMo (Constructive Cost Model) [Boe81, Boe96]. A project must be estimated continually in order to stay within budget/time and to detect cost overruns or delays as soon as possible.

- *Project scheduling*
Software project scheduling involves identifying project tasks, establishing interdependencies among these tasks, assigning resources to tasks, and developing a time-line schedule. Some of the tasks are usually carried out in parallel. Coordination of these tasks and optimization of work force is essential for project scheduling. Task dependencies and staff allocations are typical outputs of project scheduling.

- *Project controlling*
Project plans and schedules are used to administer resources and to direct staff members. Keeping track of and controlling project progress requires various activities, e.g., comparing actual and planned dates for tasks, conducting periodic meetings for status or problem reports, determining the accomplishment of milestones, etc.

All these activities depend on each other; e.g., cost estimation requires measurements and controlling is impossible without planning and scheduling. Software reuse influences software management, for example, measurement issues (see Section 4.4 on page 48) and organizational models (see Section 4.3 on page 40).

11.2 Software Specification

Software specifications serve as contracts between customers and manufacturers of software systems. (Likewise, specifications of components serve as contracts between component manufacturers and component reusers.)

For complex systems or components, requirements analysis may be necessary. This involves steps like *problem analysis, document analysis, data analysis, weak-point analysis, feasibility study,* etc. [Pom84]. Software components are typically less complex and do not always require all these activities.

A software specification should specify the external behavior of a component, specify constraints on the implementation, be easy to change, serve as a reference tool for maintenance, and characterize acceptable responses to undesired events [Som92]. Functional and nonfunctional requirements are among the most important parts of a specification. Other parts include user interfaces, error behavior, acceptance criteria, system environments, etc.

– *Functional requirements*
   services that are expected by reusers of a component

– *Nonfunctional requirements*
   constraints under which a component has to operate

Specifications should completely and consistently define the requirements on components. A component's specification not only serves as a contract between component developer and reuser but also as a valuable source of information for evaluating a component's reuse value in a certain context (also see Section 17.2.4 on page 208).

11.3 Software Design

After software requirements have been analyzed and specified, a design has to be made. Software design is an iterative process and involves describing a component at different levels of abstraction. Design is a creative process and requires experience, which can be gained by the studying good designs. This makes well documented, good designs valuable. Design includes various activities:

– *Architectural design* defines subcomponents and their interrelations.

– *Component or interface design* defines components' interfaces in detail.

– *Data structure design* defines data structures that are used for the implementation.

– *Algorithmic design* defines the algorithmic decomposition of components.

Top-down design is typical for components being built from scratch. Tasks are decomposed into subtasks until these can easily be formulated as algorithms. *Bottom-up design* proceeds in the opposite direction. Fundamental components are defined first and used to realize the next level of abstraction. Each level comprises what is called an *abstract machine*. Bottom-up design is essential for the reuse of existing components.

Good design is crucial for the quality of a software component. There is no exact definition of what a *good* design is, but good designs are considered to have the following characteristics [Pre92, Som92]:

− *Modularity*
A component should be logically partitioned into subcomponents that perform specific functions.

− *Coupling*
Loosely coupled components are as independent of other components as possible. For example, they do not have a shared state and do not interchange control information with other components.

− *Cohesion*
Cohesive components represent single entities including all operations on these entities.

− *Understandability, adaptability*
To make components understandable and adaptable, they should be loosely coupled and well documented.

All these characteristics are related to each other. For example, loose coupling supports both understandability and adaptability.

Various categories of design methods exist, for example, function-oriented (like stepwise refinement), data-oriented (like Jackson Structured Programming) and object-oriented design methods (as proposed by Booch and Rumbaugh).

Design methods and software reuse interact in two ways [BR92]. First, a design method may or may not encourage designers to consider the reuse of existing components (*design with reuse* or *application engineering*). Second, the products of a design method (anything from design documents to source code) will turn out to be more or less reusable (*design for reuse* or *component engineering*). We cover this in more detail in Chapters 14 and 15.

11.4 Software Implementation

Implementation is the process of transforming a design into an executable form. For software systems this typically means coding in a certain programming language. According to our definition, software components can have a variety of forms. They can be implemented in a programming language or be composed of components of any kind.

Ideally, the design of a component is independent of its implementation. In practice, however, this is often impossible. As shown in subsequent chapters, we have to consider reusable components already during the design. Depending on what kind of components we consider, we make assumptions about the implementation of the component under development.

We refrain from dealing with implementation in greater detail. This typically comprises subjects like choice of programming language, choice of names, programming style, comments, portability considerations, etc. These issues lose importance for systems being composed of components. They have to be considered, however, in order to implement a component in a certain programming language.

11.5 Software Testing

The purpose of testing is to ascertain whether a component satisfies its requirements by discovering as many errors as possible. Tests can be applied to different aspects of components. Various kinds of tests include the following:

− *Specification test*
  Specification tests check for the completeness, clarity, consistency and feasibility of a component specification. This should be done together with potential component reusers.

− *Component test*
  Component tests reveal discrepancies between a component's specification and its implementation.

− *Integration test*
  Composing tested components can reveal new kinds of errors that stem from the interaction of components. Integration tests are applied to subsystems or components being composed of lower-level components.

− *Acceptance test*
  The development of software products ends with an acceptance test where real operating conditions are used. This may not be possible for software components where potential reuse candidates might not even be known at the time.

Various testing methods and strategies include:

− *Static/dynamic testing*
  Static testing involves activities to find errors via static and semantic analyses. For dynamic tests components have to be executed or simulated.

- *Black-box/white-box testing*
  Black-box tests involve input/output relationships of components. White-box tests consider the inner structures of components as well.

- *Top-down/bottom-up testing*
  In top-down testing the main components are tested first by using stubs for components that are not yet available. In bottom-up testing basic components are tested first, followed by higher-level components that rely on lower-level components.

Debugging is closely related to testing. Testing means detecting errors; debugging involves the activities of finding and removing errors.

With software reuse, software quality can be increased and testing efforts can be decreased. A component developer will do any kinds of tests that seem appropriate to guarantee a component's quality. The component reuser should be able to trust a component's quality. Dynamic black-box tests are sufficient on the reuser's side. For composition of systems from components, bottom-up tests are suitable in most situations.

11.6 Software Maintenance

Software maintenance is the modification of a software component after its first delivery. Such modifications include error corrections, performance or other improvements, functionality extensions, or adaptations to changed environments.

Software maintenance is by far more than just fixing bugs. Maintenance activities fall into the following categories:

- *Adaptive maintenance*
  to make a software component usable in a changed environment, e.g., adapting a component to a new (version of an) operating system or application framework

- *Corrective maintenance*
  to overcome existing errors, i.e., diagnosing and correcting bugs

- *Perfective maintenance*
  to improve performance, maintainability, or other software attributes, e.g., enhancements demanded by users

- *Preventive maintenance*
  to prevent future maintenance activities, e.g., redesigning, recoding, and/ or retesting, sometimes complete re-engineering

The cost of maintenance has been steadily increasing over the past decades. Most companies spend by far more than 50 percent of their software life cycle budget on maintenance. This causes a dramatic decrease in software productivity. Maintenance costs are related to both technical and nontechnical factors. Technical factors include component dependencies, programming languages/paradigms, quality of documentation, etc. Dependencies on the external environment (e.g., taxation changes), system lifetime, and staff stability are examples of nontechnical factors influencing maintenance costs.

Reuse can have a positive influence on maintenance costs when high-quality components are available and reused for the development of software systems.

11.7 Summary

At the beginning of this chapter we mentioned that the cost-effective production of high-quality software systems is the primary goal of software engineering. For more details the reader is referred to various software engineering books, e.g., by Blum [Blu92], Pressman [Pre92], Sommerville [Som92] and Goldberg/Rubin [GR95].

With the reuse of software components, the definition of software engineering has to be slightly modified to be the cost-effective production of high-quality software components and the composition of high-quality software systems. The terms software specification, software design, software implementation, software testing and software maintenance can simply be replaced by component specification, component design, component implementation, component testing and component maintenance. However, effective reuse requires additional activities to compose systems and to extract commonalties of groups of common systems. This is discussed in Chapters 13, 14 and 15.

Documentation is not covered in the chapters at this point. Like maintenance, documentation is often seen as an appendage to the process of software development. However, the importance of documentation increases with the reuse of software and particularly with the reuse of software components. We take this into account by dedicating a whole part of this book to *Software Documentation* (Part IV).

12. Software Process Models

Contents

In the previous chapter we described the most important steps for the creation of software. In order to define the order of these steps and to establish transition criteria to progress from one step to another, models for the software development process were derived from other engineering activities [Boe88]. The major advantage of software process models is their guidance regarding the order in which to fulfill certain tasks.

In this chapter we discuss various software process models. The original model, known as the *waterfall model* and depicting the classic software life cycle, is described in Section 12.1. Modifications and enhancements made to this model follow in Sections 12.2 to 12.4. The twin life cycle, depicting the general idea of reuse, is described in Section 12.5. A summary follows in Section 12.6.

12.1 Waterfall Model

According to the waterfall model, the software development process is divided into well-defined phases (see Fig. 12.1). Each phase must be finished before the next one can start. After completion of static specifications, software developers must prepare a tailor-made design and a corresponding implementation. The better the implemented program fulfills the given requirements, the better was the work of the software developers. The waterfall model has been widely adopted because it can be clearly divided into various steps and documents can be defined as the result for each step. This enables management to inspect the development process and assess its progress. Every step is considered to be complete when the documents defined for this step are produced, reviewed and accepted. The waterfall life cycle comprises the following steps:

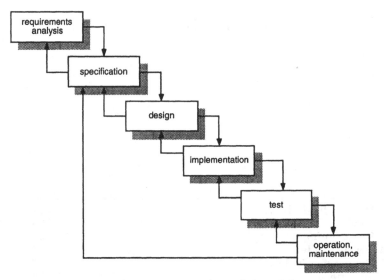

Fig. 12.1. Classic software life cycle (waterfall model)

— *Requirements analysis*
  The purpose of this step is to identify and document the requirements
  to the software system. Interaction between customers and developers is
  necessary if the requirements are not clear. This step focuses on the end
  user and may already include the creation of user manuals.

— *Specification*
  Once the requirements are clear, software developers write the exact specification of the software system. The specification focuses on the system
  itself, and all the user requirements have to be considered. The resulting
  document serves as the base for the subsequent development process. The
  final system will be said to be correct if it meets the specification.

— *Design*
  The design of a software system usually comprises two stages, architectural
  or high-level design and detailed design. Architectural design establishes
  the overall structure of the design, e.g., module structure and class organization. The results of the architectural design are refined by outlining the
  structure of the modules and/or classes.

— *Implementation*
  In this step the actual code of the software system is produced.

— *Test*
  All parts of the software system have to be tested individually. After that,
  the parts are integrated and the system is tested as a whole.

– *Operation and maintenance*
  After successful testing the system is delivered to the customers. Any modifications after delivery are part of the maintenance phase.

Any step might uncover problems in a previous step and necessitate returning and partly or even completely redoing earlier work. In practice a step might start before the previous has been totally completed. Some activities of the software process are not depicted as separate steps because they span the entire life cycle. These activities encompass documentation, verification and management.

The waterfall model enforces a linear process, which implies that executable programs are available late in the process. Any misunderstandings between customers and developers remain hidden for a long time. Misconceptions are likely to occur because specifications, which are the contract between customer and developer, are written in a style customers are seldom familiar with. Another drawback is that any technical problems cannot be perceived before the test phase. Modifications become costly because they are so late. The classic software life cycle presupposes static requirements and does not deal with incomplete and inconsistent specifications. This approach contradicts reality, because experience has shown that programs need continuous modification and extension.

Despite its drawbacks, the classic software life cycle continues to provide structure for many software projects. However, despite the weaknesses, it is better to develop software according to this life cycle than to use a haphazard approach.

12.2 Exploratory Model

The classic software life cycle is not practical for many of today's software systems. When requirements and environments are changing quickly, it becomes impossible to foresee all aspects of a system from the start. Exploratory software development helps in this respect [SS92, Som92].

In the exploratory model a working system is developed as quickly as possible. Thereafter modifications are made to the system until it meets all its requirements. This model is especially useful when the requirements are not known or not well understood from the beginning. Thus exploratory software development also means the production of software to meet partially known requirements. Testing the product leads to more requirements and results in modifications to fulfill them. This process is repeated until the developed software system performs satisfactorily. As there is no complete specification, the system cannot be evaluated by comparing it to its specification. Instead, adequacy of the system has to be demonstrated and evaluated, which can only be done by subjective judgments.

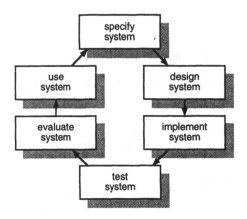

Fig. 12.2. Exploratory software development

Large, longevous software systems are usually not developed by using exploratory programming. This is because managing an exploratory software process is difficult due to the lack of well-defined stages and regular documents. Thus evaluating the progress of a project becomes difficult.

Exploratory software development is best suited when an inherent goal of the project is to identify elusive requirements (specification), to establish a suitable system architecture (design), or to explore possible implementation techniques. Exploratory software development involves repeatedly applying small steps. Each step ideally results in an improvement of the current version of the software system until both customers and developers are satisfied with the result (see Fig. 12.2). One step may last several weeks, several hours, or even less. The usefulness of exploratory software development emerges from the lack of alternatives in many situations.

Both customers and developers not yet knowing exactly what they really want is a typical development situation that lends itself to exploratory development. Programmers also might not know how to solve certain implementation problems. In such cases it is appropriate to work with experimental versions of a software system. Experimenting gives both customers and developers new insights into their problem domains and thus brings them closer to better solutions.

The waterfall model aims to provide customers with the complete product by a certain date. The exploratory model delivers various operational but incomplete products which satisfy only a subset of the customers' requirements. Each delivery is supposed to fulfill more requirements until finally the complete product can be provided. This gives customers the possibility to work with the system without having to wait for the final product. It also enables them to assign priorities to outstanding functionality and to refine requirements. However, a contractual framework has to be provided to avoid endless requirement changes.

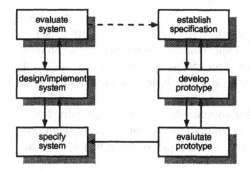

Fig. 12.3. Prototyping

Exploratory development challenges software engineers in that they have to create an open architecture. Any additions have to be incorporated into the structure of the existing system without destroying that structure and without yielding to an unmanageable, unextensible and unmaintainable system. The difficulties encountered in the exploratory model should not lead to its general rejection but to its restriction to areas where it is applicable.

12.3 Prototyping Model

Rapid prototyping has become popular for the development of software systems with complex user interfaces. It shares similarities with exploratory programming, but its main objective is to determine requirements for the system to be developed. This is done by building a prototype that can be employed for user experiments. A prototype is a working model with a subset of the end product's functionality, which is often constrained to the user interface. The prototype is changed and adapted until the user is satisfied (see Fig. 12.3).

The purpose of the prototype is to enable customer and developer to agree on what the software system is supposed to do. This is a much better means of communication than a written specification. Once the prototype has been created, revised and accepted by the customer, software development can start. The development process can be carried out by adopting the waterfall model, the exploratory model, or whatever seems appropriate. Since the prototype has been validated through interaction with the customer, the resulting specification can be expected to be less prone to changes than it would be by agreeing on a written document. This should result in less feedback loops in the subsequent development process.

Prototyping has many variations. For example, prototypes can be either thrown away or enhanced to the final system. Often prototypes are built with special prototyping tools or 4GL systems which may require disposal of the prototype. Many user interface tools provide a means of building a prototype and then extending it to the full system.

Prototyping is most effective for systems with complex user interfaces. Customers and developers must agree that the prototype is built to serve as a means for the definition of the requirements. There may be problems when customers get confused and see a prototype as a working version and are unaware of the efforts needed to transform it into a high-quality end product.

Prototypes are useful for software components as well, especially those with complex user interfaces. However, many components provide functionality via a programming interface only, making prototyping less applicable and useful.

12.4 Spiral Model

Despite its difficulties, the waterfall model has been widely adopted by large software companies. Despite their usefulness, exploratory programming and rapid prototyping are not really an option for the large software systems these companies have to build. The main reason for this is that management of projects based on theses processes is difficult because of the lack of documents. Documents are needed by management to assess project progress. The waterfall model defines documents for being the result of each stage. In exploratory software development, iterations may be so rapid that updating documents after each iteration is too expensive and time-consuming. The main goal of rapid prototyping is deliver a running system rather than a written document. After the completion of the prototyping phase, a written specification may be created and followed up with the waterfall model. However, during the initial phase creating and updating documents remains too expensive and time-consuming. Furthermore, the document-oriented approach of the waterfall model has its drawbacks [Som92]:

- *Regular intervals*
  In order to assess project progress, management needs documents at regular intervals. Regular intervals usually do not correspond with the time required to complete certain activities and to produce the needed documents.

- *Document approval*
  Problems discovered during a process may be covered to avoid iterations and the need to change approved documents.

- *Transition*
  Smooth transition from one phase to the next is rare. Very often phases are started before the documents of the previous phase have been completed and approved.

- *Inadequacy*
  There are problems that are not well suited for a linear process as suggested

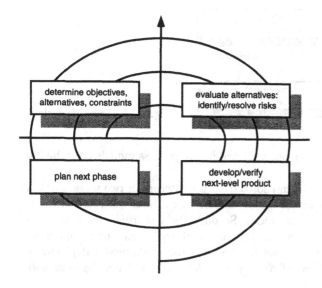

Fig. 12.4. Boehm's spiral model

in the document-driven waterfall model. Blind application of the model can lead to unnecessarily high project costs.

A possible alternative is the spiral model, which is risk-based rather than document-driven or code-driven [Boe88] (see Fig. 12.4). The key characteristics of this model are regular assessments of management risks and actions to counteract these risks [Som92]. Risk includes anything that can go wrong. Usually risk is a consequence of incomplete or inadequate information. Uncertainties can be reduced by gathering and discovering further information.

Each cycle of the spiral begins by specifying objectives like performance, functionality or resource consumption. The next step is to list alternatives, and their constraints, towards achieving these objectives. This is followed by assessing each of the alternatives against each objective. The result is the identification of risk sources that have to be evaluated in the next step. Risk evaluation may require a more detailed analysis, prototyping or simulation.

The spiral model incorporates other process models. Prototyping may be used to resolve risks based on requirements. In addition, formal transformations or the waterfall model may be used for the whole or for parts of the system.

12.5 Twin Life Cycle

Incorporating reuse changes software process models. We have seen in Section 4.3 that different organizational groups are involved in systematic reuse. We introduced *domain groups*, *component groups* and *application groups*. The

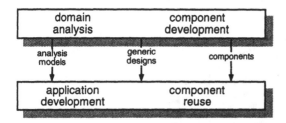

Fig. 12.5. Twin life cycle

activities of these groups are not reflected in the process models described in the previous sections.

Software process models and software reuse interact in two ways. First, a model may or may not encourage developers to consider the reuse of existing components (*design with reuse*). Second, the resulting products (anything from design documents to source code) will turn out to be more or less reusable (*design for reuse*). The *twin life cycle* model depicted in Fig. 12.5 gives an overview of *development for reuse* and *development with reuse* [Kar95].

The twin life cycle model provides only a rough overview, but it clearly demonstrates activities of domain, component and application groups. These activities, i.e., *domain engineering*, *component engineering* and *application engineering* are the topics of Chapters 13, 14 and 15.

12.6 Summary

We have considered various software process models, i.e., the traditional waterfall model, the exploratory model, the prototyping model and the spiral model. In traditional software life cycles, software reuse is not considered to be an explicit part of the process. Instead, systems are designed to be developed from scratch. In the implementation process some implicit reuse might happen. Programmers may adapt previously written code or even get some source code from a library or other projects and adapt it to the requirements encountered in the new system. The primary goal is to get the system finished. Typically, no attention is paid to whether there might be some components of the system to be considered for reuse in other projects.

The twin life cycle distinguishes between *development for reuse* and *development with reuse*. Subsequent chapters describe this in more detail.

13. Domain Engineering

Contents

Software reuse can be improved by identifying objects and operations for a class of similar systems, i.e., for a certain domain. In the context of software engineering, domains are application areas. Examples of domains are airline reservation systems, software development tools, user interfaces and financial applications. The scope of a domain can be chosen arbitrarily, either broad, e.g., banking, or as narrow as simple text editing. Usually broad domains are built on top of several narrow domains. For example, the user interface domain may be regarded as subdomain of the airline reservation systems domain (and several others) [Pri87, Pri90].

In this chapter we provide an introduction to domain analysis (Section 13.1) and depict activities (Section 13.2) and methods (Section 13.3) of domain analysis. In Section 13.4 we describe Foda as an example of a domain analysis method. The context of domain implementation is described in Section 13.5. A summary follows in Section 13.6.

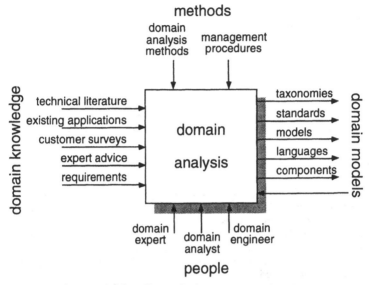

Fig. 13.1. Context of domain analysis

13.1 Domain Analysis

Common objects and operations are likely to occur in multiple applications within a domain and thus are candidates for reusable components. A domain is analyzed by studying several of its representative systems and by developing an initial view of the structure and functionality of these systems. During software development, information of several kinds is generated. One of the objectives of domain analysis is to make all this information readily available. When familiarity with the domain has been achieved and the representative systems are understood, information used in developing these systems as well as their common and variable parts are identified, captured and organized for later reuse in developing new systems in that domain.

Domain analysis stresses the reusability of analysis and design, not code. This is done by deriving common architectures, generic models or specialized languages that substantially increase the power of the software development process in the specific problem area of the domain. Domain analysis can be seen as a continuing process of creating and maintaining the reuse infrastructure in a certain domain. Fig. 13.1 shows the inputs, outputs, controls and mechanisms of domain analysis [Pri90].

A vertical domain is a specific class of systems. A horizontal domain contains general software parts being used across multiple vertical domains. Examples of horizontal reuse are mathematical function libraries, container classes and Unix tools.

Domain-specific reuse is usually accomplished by separating domain engineering and application engineering. The goal of domain engineering is to identify objects and operations of a class of similar systems in a particular problem domain. Typical activities in domain engineering are domain analysis, architecture development, reusable component creation, component recovery and component management. Application engineering means software engineering taking the results of the domain engineering process into consideration, i.e., identifying reuse opportunities and providing feedback to the domain engineering process (see Chapter 15).

13.1.1 Information Sources

There are several sources of information that can be used for domain analysis (see Hess et al. [HCK+90]). The most important sources are existing applications and domain experts. Requirements of applications can be used for the domain model. Their designs show the architecture of typical applications of the domain. Domain experts often have knowledge that is unavailable elsewhere. Additionally, they can serve as consultants during domain analysis, identify future trends, and help to validate the outputs of domain analysis. Theories, techniques and methods may be taken from technical literature. Existing standards and customer surveys provide other inputs for the analysis of a domain.

13.1.2 Products

Domain analysts extract relevant information and knowledge from existing applications. They are supported by experts in the domain of consideration. Any source of information like source code, requirements, design documents, user manuals, etc. can be used for this purpose. The domain engineer helps in organizing and encapsulating the extracted knowledge in the form of the shown outputs, i.e., taxonomies, standards, models, languages and reusable components. The whole process is guided by management procedures and domain analysis methods [Pri90].

Domain analysis is not a single process but a continuing effort of considering new systems and refining the results. Specific outputs of domain analysis activities have been described by Braun [Bra94d], Hooper/Chester [HC91] and Prieto-Díaz [Pri90]:

- *Domain definition*
  description of a domain's context

- *Domain model*
  identification of objects, operations, and relationships that are likely to occur in more than one application and characterize applications in the domain (also identification of areas of variation in systems of the domain)

- *Domain requirements model*
  identification of requirements that are likely to occur in more than one application and characterize applications in the domain

- *Architecture model*
  design and implementation structure of software in the domain

- *Domain taxonomy*
  single hierarchies, semantic nets, faceted classification schemes, etc.; the taxonomy can have different levels of complexity and can be developed incrementally with increasing knowledge about the domain.

- *Domain language*
  a common vocabulary for describing these objects, operations and relationships, and for creating a standard for classifying and describing components in the domain

- *Domain standards*
  design methods, coding standards, management policies, development procedures like walk-throughs, etc.

- *Reusable components*
  common objects within the domain are candidates for reusable components, possibly resulting in a reference architecture and/or a common design framework

The goal of domain analysis can also be to support the generative approach of software reuse by building an application generator. In an attempt to formalize the process of building application generators, Cleaveland has identified activities that are closely related to domain analysis [Cle88].

We are primarily interested in components. In the context of domain analysis we can distinguish the following categories:

- *General-purpose components*
  can be used in various applications of different domains (horizontal reuse).

- *Domain-specific components*
  are more specific and can be used in various applications of one domain (vertical reuse).

- *Product-specific components*
  are very specific and custom-built for a certain application; they are not reusable or only to a very small extent.

13.1.3 Benefits

Domain analysis can be viewed as a gathering of domain experience and domain knowledge of experts. Domain knowledge contains information about how problems in a certain domain are addressed in software systems [HC91]. Experience and knowledge are accumulated until they reach a threshold at which abstractions can be formed and prepared for reuse. The benefits of domain analysis can be summarized as follows [Kan89]:

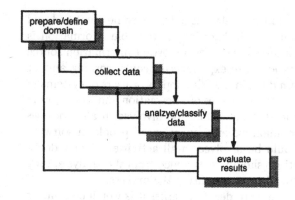

Fig. 13.2. Steps of domain analysis

- reuse of domain knowledge
- reuse of components in a certain context, i.e., domain-specific components
- domain-specific model for classification, storage and retrieval of components
- framework for tooling and systems synthesis from reusable components
- large-grain reuse across products (in the same domain)
- identification of reusable software components

The reuse of domain knowledge is of increasing importance as the areas to which software is applied become larger. This makes it difficult for companies to find software engineering personnel with the required application domain knowledge. Results from domain analysis can be used not only for reuse but also for the education of new staff providing them with general structures and operations of systems in a particular domain.

13.2 Domain Analysis Activities

Activities involved in domain analysis have been described by various authors, e.g., Arango [Ara94a, Ara94b], Karlsson [Kar95] and Prieto-Díaz [Pri87, Pri90, Pri91a, Pri93a]. Arango has compared several domain analysis methods and extracted a common process [Ara94b]. We have distilled the following activities from this comparison and descriptions by the other authors (see Fig. 13.2).

13.2.1 Domain Definition and Preparation

It is important that a domain be clearly defined and its boundaries be established. A domain's width determines where the domain ends and another one begins. Its depth fixes the subdomains to be included or excluded in the analysis. A narrow definition of a domain should be the goal.

After the definition of the domain, relevant data has to be identified and collected for the acquisition of domain knowledge. Reusable information is likely to be found in existing systems. Another important information source is domain experts. Domain experts are experienced people working and/or developing software in a certain domain, i.e., developers or users of systems in the domain. They are crucial both as sources of information and as reviewers for results of the analysis process. They should be involved in all processes of domain analysis. Besides domain experts, experienced people in software design and software reuse should be involved in all activities. Poorly documented and designed applications should be excluded from the analysis; they would otherwise increase costs without benefiting the process.

An important part of this step is to decide whether it is worth continuing domain analysis. For example, considering the business objectives the chosen domain might not be the 'right' one because the expected *return on investment* might not be attractive enough. Once the domain has been defined and the decision to continue the analysis process has been made, the next steps should be planned.

13.2.2 Data Collection

Different approaches for data collection can be used, e.g., reviews of literature, interviews of experts, analysis of applications.

Analyzing applications will reveal candidates for reusable components as well as models of the domain. Domain-specific components (objects, operations, relationships, constraints) have to be selected and/or defined. Product-specific and general purpose components should be removed.

In determining reusable components various levels can be chosen for analysis: a whole system, subsystems, individual source code components like modules, classes, functions, etc., or individual items of the requirements. Simple questions can help in identifying reusable components [HC91], e.g.:

- How common is a component's functionality within the domain?
- Is there duplication of a component's functionality within the domain?
- Do components exist in various specializations, generalizations, or variations?
- Is the design optimized enough for reuse in another implementation?
- Can nonreusable components be made reusable by parameterization?
- Are components reusable in many applications with only minor changes?
- Can a nonreusable component be decomposed to yield reusable components?
- How valid is a component decomposition for reuse?
- Can a component be modified and adapted for reuse?
- Is a component hardware dependent?

In analyzing applications, care must be taken to not deduce wrong abstractions or bad ones that may have been used. It is important to rely on several sources to complete and/or validate information gathered from a single source. Data must be verified for correctness, consistency and completeness. Irrelevant data must be recognized and discarded [Ara94b].

Different sources of information provide different types of information. Experts are better in providing general information, principles and explanations. Applications reveal detailed information on architectures and design.

13.2.3 Data Analysis and Classification

The results of domain analysis can be manifold and differ among domains. It is important to classify and catalog them for future reuse. Guidelines will help to decide whether certain components may be used in certain contexts. Reuser manuals have to be written that help in reusing, adapting and modifying components.

It is crucial to analyze similarities, variations and combinations of data. Data at this level can be entities, operations, events and relationships in the domain. Entities are reusable components of any abstraction level, depending on the kinds of components to be reused later, e.g., Ada packages, C functions.

The activities in this step are not entirely different from activities in developing a single software system, i.e., in requirements analysis, data modeling, object modeling, etc. The main difference is that these activities are done for a set of applications, i.e., the applications of the particular domain for which the analysis is being done.

Domain information is prepared by abstracting and generalizing functions, objects and their relationships. Different views and levels of abstractions of static and dynamic structures can be captured. Various models can be developed, e.g., functional models, process models, conceptual models. Taxonomies and standards might also be useful for the domain and should be defined.

Existing components can be re-engineered and redocumented in order to comply with quality standards set for the domain.

13.2.4 Evaluation

Domain analysis is an iterative process. New requirements might have to be added. Domain boundaries might change, or subdomains may might to be defined.

Besides using and refining the models, it is helpful to evaluate the domain, i.e., its models and components. This can be accomplished, for example, by a test, i.e., by describing a specific system in the domain. Real application developments are the best evaluation and test of a domain, and constant refinement and tuning will be likely.

13.3 Domain Analysis Methods

Analyzing domains is not an easy task. In the previous section we discussed many difficult activities that are involved, e.g.:

- recognizing domains
- identifying the boundaries of domains
- recognizing 'fundamental' concepts of domains
- deciding when analyses are complete
- validating domain models

Domain modeling is a continuous and incremental learning process. Similar to software engineering, it is hard if not impossible to do domain analysis without some sort of systematic proceeding. Domain analysis methods have been introduced for that purpose.

Arango has presented, compared and evaluated eight domain analysis methods [Ara94b]. These methods were found to be essentially similar, with the main differences in:

- emphasis on certain data acquisition means over others
- approach to modeling, e.g., functional vs. object-oriented techniques
- overlapping subsets of notations
- different groupings of activities with different names
- same names with slightly different meanings

We have chosen one of these methods, Foda, and describe it as representative. Foda comes close to being the union of techniques in other methods [Ara94b]. It has had a major impact on the state of domain analysis [Pet96] and has also been used in the industry [CSPK92, PC91, Zal96]. Additionally, there are detailed publications on this method with examples showing results using the method, e.g., Hess et al. [HCK+90].

13.4 Foda: Feature-Oriented Domain Analysis

The Feature-Oriented Domain Analysis (Foda) method was developed at the Software Engineering Institute [HCK+90]. It defines a process and establishes specific products. The following subsections briefly describe the three basic phases of Foda, i.e., context analysis, domain modeling and architecture modeling.

13.4.1 Context Analysis

Defining the scope of the domain and its relationships to other domains is the purpose of *context analysis*. A *context model* documents the results; it defines the boundaries of the domain. Context models consist of structure diagrams and data flow diagrams.

Structure diagrams show target domains in relation to other domains and define subdomains, superdomains, and peer domains. *Data flow diagrams* show the flow of data among all the domains. All subsequent analysis activities, i.e., feature analysis, entity relationship modeling, functional analysis, and architecture modeling (see below) are performed within the scope defined in the context model. Thus the scope of a domain has to be chosen carefully. Commonality of domains, availability of domain expertise, and expected applications have to be taken into consideration when performing context analysis.

13.4.2 Domain Modeling

Analyzing commonalties and differences of problems being addressed by applications in the domain is the purpose of *domain modeling*. A variety of models that represent different aspects of these problems are the results of this phase. Domain modeling consists of the activities feature analysis, entity relationship modeling and functional analysis:

– *Feature analysis*
  Feature analysis captures the understanding of end users about general capabilities of applications in a domain. This primarily includes services provided by applications, but also covers additional aspects like performance considerations or hardware platforms of applications.

– *Entity relationship modeling*
  Entity relationship modeling captures and defines domain knowledge for the implementation of applications in a domain. Entity classes represent object abstractions. Generalization (*is-a*) and aggregation (*consists-of*) relationships specify commonalties, differences and composition structures.

– *Functional analysis*
  Functional analysis identifies functional commonalties and differences of applications in a domain. Structural and behavioral aspects of applications are depicted, and major decision points with alternative decisions are captured (called *issues* and *decisions*).

The development of components is considered during functional analysis. Features and issues/decisions are incorporated into the model by developing separate (refined) components for alternatives, by developing parameterizable components (to be adapted to alternatives), or by developing general components with separate instantiations for alternatives [HCK+90].

13.4.3 Architecture Modeling

Providing a software solution to problems defined during domain modeling is the purpose of *architecture modeling*. The architecture model serves as a base for detailed design and component development.

The Foda architecture model is a high-level design of applications in the domain. Common components are identified and related with features, functions, and data. The architecture may be defined at various levels of abstraction having components in each of the layers.

13.4.4 Summary

Table 13.1 summarizes the inputs, processes and outputs of the three Foda phases *context analysis, domain modeling* and *architecture modeling*.

Context models describe the environments in which applications will be used. *Feature models* describe end users' perspectives of applications in domains. Developers' understanding of domain objects and their interrelations is covered in *entity relationship models*. The functionality of applications from requirements analysts' perspective is reflected in *data flow models* and *finite state machine models*. Finally, architectural aspects of applications from designers' points of view are depicted in *process interaction models* and *module structure charts* [HCK+90] (see Table 13.1). For more details on Foda the reader is referred to Hess et al. [HCK+90] and to Peterson/Cohen [PC91].

13.5 Domain Implementation

Domain engineering involves domain analysis and domain implementation [FI94]. In the domain analysis phase commonalties and differences of systems in a domain are discovered and recorded. Domain implementation means the use the information collected in domain analysis to create reusable components and new systems.

The creation of new components is part of *component engineering* (see Chapter 14). The process of creating new systems is called *application engineering* (see Chapter 15).

13.6 Summary

We have described aspects of domain analysis, including products, benefits, activities and methods. Foda has been presented as a representative of domain analysis methods. Domain engineering comprises not only domain analysis but also domain implementation. This is regarded to be part of component engineering and application engineering, described in subsequent chapters.

Table 13.1. Summary of the Foda method

Phase	Input	Process	Output
Context analysis	operating environments, standards	context analysis	context model
Domain modeling	features, context model	feature analysis	feature model
	application domain knowledge	entity relationship modeling	entity relationship model
	domain technology, context model, feature model,	functional analysis	data flow model
	entity relationship model, requirements		finite state machine model
Architecture modeling	impl. technology, context model, feature model,	architectural modeling	process interaction model
	entity relationship model, design information		module structure charts

Ways to effectively analyze domains and to represent and use results of the analysis are still major fields of research. Example issues in domain analysis research are knowledge acquisition and knowledge representation. Knowledge has to be represented in a way that it can be understood by humans and processed by computers. Arango has identified weaknesses of domain analysis methods, which pose additional areas of needed research [Ara94b].

14. Component Engineering

Contents

Component engineering is software development for reuse. Systematic reuse requires a foundation of high-quality components with proper documentation. Such components cannot be simply extracted from existing applications. Getting reusable components requires more effort. Components in applications are usually designed for special requirements. They have to be generalized to satisfy a wider range of requirements and documented to meet the information needs of potential and actual reusers. Reusable components should also be self-contained and coherent.

In this chapter we describe steps involved in the process of component engineering. Development of components is described in Section 14.1. Generalization and certification of components follow in Sections 14.2 and 14.3, respectively. Software repositories are depicted in Section 14.4, followed by classification of components in Section 14.5. A summary follows in Section 14.6.

14.1 Component Development

Even though software development based on reusable components will eventually surpass development from scratch, new development will still be necessary. Ideally, new developments result in generalized, reusable components rather than in specialized ones that are used only once. By developing *with* reusable components we search for, evaluate, adapt and integrate existing components in new contexts. By developing *for* reuse we develop components for reuse in other contexts than the one it was initially developed for.

Unfortunately, most existing software has little or no reusability. In order to develop reusable components, we have to focus on attributes that influence reusability, i.e., generality, completeness, cohesion/coupling, portability and quality. For example, the following requirements on reusable components have been identified by Di Felice [DF93] (for reusable mathematical source code components) and Braun [Bra94d]:

- generality, self-containment
- high cohesion/minimal coupling
- use of standardized architecture models and standardized interfaces (created during domain analysis)
- use of coding standards and naming conventions
- modular/object-oriented design (high degree of information hiding)
- possibility of parameterization
- independence from hardware/compiler/operating system
- proper documentation

More general guidelines for the design of reusable components have been proposed by De Mey [dM95]:

- Concepts used in a number of different places should probably be components, e.g., user interface components.
- If components require an undetermined or variable number of resources, these resources should probably be components, e.g., role components.
- Composite components should contain only a small number of components and take advantage of hierarchical decomposition.
- Components should strike a balance between abstraction and concreteness.

Some of the above guidelines were given in the context of source code components. However, most of them can be applied to any kind of components. For more details on the guidelines, although some of them are a little vague, the reader is referred to the given references [Bra94d, DF93, dM95].

Existing design methodologies, e.g., the Constantine Method or the Jackson Method, explicitly consider neither the creation of reusable components nor the reuse of existing components. However, different design techniques certainly have peculiar suitability for software reuse. Process-driven design and function-oriented design are typically done in a top-down manner. Starting at a high-level, functional views are repeatedly refined into more detailed designs. The data is defined only in relation to the functions. Data-driven designs concentrate on the data rather than the functions. Here a software system's data is identified in order to derive a design, and the functions are only a by-product. In both cases an attempt is made to achieve a good design with respect to the given specification, i.e., to have functions and/or data that are needed for the software system to be built. This tends to result in custom-made components. However, the experience and talent of a software designer impact on the reusability of the resulting components. As Mittermeir and Rossak state [MR90]: "An excellent programmer can write highly reusable software with most methodologies."

Object-oriented decomposition of software is a design approach that to some extent supports the reuse of components. However, this approach does not implicitly lead to reusable components either. Attention must be paid to the requirements mentioned above as well. Principles for designing reusable components have been identified, e.g., to increase correctness, composability, reusability and understandability of Ada components [Hol92]. Still, there is not a complete method for designing reusable components [FI94].

Besides developing and maintaining components, it is also necessary to observe the market and possibly buy certain components instead of developing them.

14.2 Component Generalization

Components should be independent of applications for which they were initially developed. They should also be sufficiently general to allow their reuse in future projects. However, specific characteristics of future potential clients should not be considered.

Karlsson has identified techniques for generalization by analyzing reusable components [Kar95]. These techniques can be applied to components in order to make them more reusable.

– *Widening*
  Components can be generalized by widening their scope, i.e., by extending the requirements. It is more likely that a widened component can be reused in future applications. The drawback of this approach is that initial development costs are higher and that the complexity of the component may become unnecessarily high. High complexity may hinder the comprehension process when the component is reused. Another drawback is that a component may have more functionality than is needed in many reuse contexts. This may lead to inefficiencies in execution speed and memory usage.

– *Narrowing*
  In contrast to component widening, we can also narrow the scope of components and limit their functionality to a set which is needed by several customers. Narrow components build the base for various extensions that are implemented in separate components. Narrowing is very common in

object-oriented programming, where the inheritance mechanism supports this concept. Narrowing addresses the problems and drawbacks of widening. Its own main drawback is the fact that an immense number of similar components may make it difficult to decide which one to choose in a certain context.

- *Isolation*
  Isolating specific requirements to certain components or parts of components helps in constructing the rest independently of whatever specialization had been chosen. Isolation is used to separate components from system-specific parts like operating systems or hardware. Parameters can also serve as a means of isolation; they can express various requirements.

- *Configurability*
  Instead of building a component satisfying all requirements, it may be useful to develop a set of smaller components which can be composed in various ways in order to meet different needs. This approach is especially useful for optional requirements and for the separation of variant and invariant functionality. Application frameworks are examples of component sets that can be combined in various ways.

These techniques are independent of a component's size and/or its development process.

Reusable software components should have broad and general functionality in order to increase their reusability. Generalized components may be reused even if the needs in a certain software system are more specialized and limited. This can cause an overhead which must be seen as the price for increased productivity. Consider the reuse of a component that provides several services, but only one or some of them are needed. A typical example is the reuse of an entire application framework of which only a few components are needed. Because of the interdependencies, extracting the needed components from the framework may not be practical. Redundancy may also occur when different components provide the same functionality but are needed because of some other functionality.

Generalizing components is important, but there is also the danger of over-generalization. Additionally, a proper balance must be found between reuse potential and ease of implementation [DvK87].

14.3 Component Certification

We can build reliable and high-quality software systems only by using components of high quality and reliability. Reused components must be free of design and implementation flaws. Users of software repositories often mistakenly assume that only components of high quality are included. Software developers should only reuse components they can trust and should refuse to reuse components of either low or unknown quality. Usually components benefit from multiple reuse in that they are more thoroughly tested. However, some effort has to be made in order to quantify their characteristics. By focusing on testing only, important aspects of quality are not being considered. The idea behind the certification of components is to guarantee that a specific set of quality guidelines has been met [DK93].

14.3.1 Component Properties

To establish a certified component repository, we begin by defining properties for components. Developers must demonstrate that a component to be included into the repository has the required properties. Reusers are urged to inquire about a component's properties and make sure they meet their needs. Properties may cover various aspects of components, e.g., an assumption about its environment. It is possible to define several sets of properties, and components can be certified according to all or parts of these sets. The defined properties may vary among organizations and/or projects. There is no limit in size or precision. Anything that is considered relevant can be included. Example properties for source-code components are the following [DK93, PSC+92]:

– *Guidelines*
  A component should comply with certain sets of programming guidelines, e.g., an assignment operator and a copy constructor should be defined for C++ classes that declare a pointer member. Also see the guidelines in Section 14.1.

– *Testing standards*
  A component in a repository should have been tested already according to certain testing standards.

– *Performance standards*
  A component should comply with certain performance standards, e.g., memory utilization, numeric accuracy. A variety of efficient implementations may also be desirable.

– *Conceptual clarity*
  A component should be clear and understandable. The interface should contain only what is necessary to reuse the component.

– *Coupling and cohesion*
  A component should have high cohesiveness and low coupling. Any dependencies on operating systems, compilers, hardware, etc. should be isolated and clearly documented.

Some of these properties are still vague and have to be refined in order to be used for certification. It is clear that these properties are not restricted to a component's reusability. They are desirable for any piece of software.

However, multiple reuse of a component justifies putting more effort into enhancing the quality of components.

14.3.2 Certification Levels

Depending on the nature, reuse frequency and importance of components, the effort invested in their certification may vary. Four levels of certification are proposed by Merrit [Mer94]:

1. A component is described with keywords and an abstract and is stored for automatic retrieval. No tests are performed; the degree of completeness is unknown.
2. A source code component must compile to be worthy. Metrics are determined if defined for the particular language.
3. Testing, test data and test results are added.
4. A reuse manual is added.

Step 2 is clearly intended for source code components but can easily be made more general for other components as well. More on testing is provided in the next section. Documentation in general and reuse manuals in particular are described in Chapters 16 and 17, respectively.

14.3.3 Quality Assurance

We can demonstrate that components have certain quality properties by means of static analysis, formal inspections, testing, usage modeling, formal verification and benchmarking [DK93, WR94].

– *Static analysis*
  Static analyzers can check various properties, especially of source code components, without the need for execution. Properties that can be checked include unreachable code, set/use anomalies of variables, component cohesion, etc.

– *Formal inspections*
  Certain properties of components may escape automatic examination and require human inspection. Such properties include specification consistency, documentation quality, design correctness, test coverage, etc.

– *Testing*
  Testing can be applied to any executable components, i.e., primarily source code components, but also their specifications and designs (in case they are expressed in executable notations). Testing cannot demonstrate the absence of errors, but rather it is helpful in finding them. Nevertheless, testing can be beneficial in establishing a certain degree of trust in the reliability of a component.

Table 14.1. Quality assurance techniques

Emphasis	Advantages	Disadvantages	Typical uses
Static analysis	automated	limited application, lack of available tools	checking simple design rules
Formal inspection	widely applicable, exploits human skills	labor intensive, checking possibly incomplete	checking functional correctness
Testing	flexible, gives some confidence in components	resource intensive, not rigorous	checking the implementation
Usage modeling	simply to understand and apply, gives confidence in components	labor and resource intensive	checking the implementation (mean time between failures)
Formal verification	high degree of assurance	time consuming, lack of available tools	checking safety-critical components
Benchmarks	provides quantification	limited application	measurement of time and space performance

- *Usage modeling*
  Usage models are adopted to model the external view of a component's usage. They provide a basis for statistical quality control. A component can be certified by modeling its usage, deriving usage profiles, generating and executing test cases, collecting failure data, and predicting future reliability [WR94].

- *Formal verification*
  The best guarantee of any property is by means of formally proving it. Formal verifications are common for individual algorithms, for example, where it is necessary to show that loops terminate. Unfortunately, showing that a component's whole implementation is correct with respect to its specification is often too costly if not impossible. Besides, errors can also be made in the proof itself; this becomes more likely for complex components.

- *Benchmarks*
  Performance measures like execution speed, response time and memory usage of components can be determined by benchmarks.

Table 14.1 summarizes advantages, disadvantages and typical uses of these quality assurance techniques (see Dunn/Knight [DK93] and Wohlin/Runeson [WR94]).

14.4 Component Repositories

A component repository is a database for the storage and retrieval of reusable components. It contains software components with all relevant information about them, including their design, history, interactions with other components, classification (for retrieval) and documentation. A repository is the link between development for reuse and development with reuse. Ideally, a large set of components should be available for reuse. Component repositories are needed because it is impossible for humans to be familiar with all the information about these components or even to know about the existence of all components. The chance that a programmer will reuse a certain component instead of developing a new one depends on the availability of potentially reusable components in the repository, but it also depends on the mechanisms provided by the repository to find components and on the programmer's ability to search in the repository.

We distinguish local, domain-specific and reference repositories [Moo94]:

– *Local repository*
   Local repositories stock a broad range of general-purpose components. They have little depth in their supply.

– *Domain-specific repository*
   Domain-specific repositories provide special-purpose components within a well-defined scope and offer more depth; i.e., they provide alternative components for specific tasks.

– *Reference repository*
   Reference repositories assist in finding components in other repositories. They archive (references to) published components and serve as *yellow pages*.

Potential reuse can be significantly enhanced by providing access to component repositories spread over networks. In addition to accessing a central repository within (part of) an organization, developers can utilize components over cooperating departments, cooperating companies, and even over the whole world by using the Internet. Naturally, copyrights become essential in this respect, depending on whether repositories are private, commercial, nonprofit, government or public-domain.

Banker et al. have found some interesting facts in an evaluation of repositories [BKZ93]:

– The level of reuse does not grow as the number of available components grows.
– Most of the components are reused within the same projects.
– Programmers tend to reuse components that they developed themselves.

This suggests that search mechanisms provided by repositories are either inadequate and/or not fully exploited.

Griss et al. suggest the use of different search mechanisms depending on the size of a repository [GFW94]. For small repositories (up to 50 components) an on-line file or a printed list may be sufficient. Repositories with up to 200 components have been used effectively with well organized indices sorted under various headings. For larger repositories more sophisticated tool support is required (see the next section, *Component Classification*).

14.5 Component Classification

Finding and retrieving software components can be prohibitively difficult. The problem is often analogous to finding a book in a cluttered junkyard rather than in an organized library [Bra94d]. Browsing a library or searching it by specific attributes such as author and date of creation can help in finding certain components, but for effective retrieval a meaningful organization of a collection of components is essential. The better the organization is, the easier it is for reusers to spot suitable components.

Classification is used to group similar components, i.e., all members of a group sharing one characteristic that components of other groups do not. Classification amounts to attaching search information to components which can then be used for retrieval. Several classification methods are applicable to software components, such as free text, keywords, facets and attribute-value pairs [FP94, Kar95]. In the next sections we describe these methods.

In the literature the term *component classification* is used with two slightly different meanings. First, it can mean a component taxonomy as we have described in Chapter 9, i.e., the classification of components in general. Second, it is used for the classification of particular components, i.e., how to classify concrete components in order to retrieve them for reuse in certain contexts. The latter is the topic of this section.

14.5.1 Free Text and Keyword Classification

Free text is the simplest form of identifying suitable components for reuse. Apart from the rigorous documentation that should accompany any component intended for reuse, this approach requires no particular preparation for storage in the repository; searching is full-text in nature [FP94, Kar95].

Attaching keywords to components is another means of identification. Keywords are entered by the developer of a component and describe its properties. Keywords can be chosen either freely or from a controlled vocabulary. For retrieval, users enter keywords which are compared to those of the components in the library. Keyword methods can be refined by enforcing a standard vocabulary, by applying weights to keywords, by adjusting for missing and superfluous keywords, and by adding composite terms [Kar95].

Both the free text and the keywords are matched exactly in a query. This does not account for potential near-matches, which can be achieved

```
000 Generalities
   004 Computer Science
   005 Computer Programming
      005.3 Programs
100 Philosophy
200 Religion
300 Social Sciences
400 Language
500 Pure Science
600 Applied Science
700 Arts & Leisure
800 Literature
   822 English Drama
   822.33 William Shakespeare
900 Geography and History
```

Fig. 14.1. Excerpt from Dewey decimal order classification

by relating similar words (synonyms) and providing a structure for the set of used words. A set of words with structure is called thesaurus. Different relations can be used to form such structures [Kar95].

The major advantage of free text searching is that it can easily be fully automated. This results in lower costs than would be necessary for human indexing. However, it is also quite inaccurate and can allow retrieval of unsuitable components.

14.5.2 Enumerated Classification

Enumerated classification schemes are hierarchical categories divided into subcategories, sub-subcategories, and so on. The Dewey decimal system is an example of an enumerated classification scheme used for the organization of book libraries [Dew79]. Fig. 14.1 shows part of this classification. The advantage of enumerated classifications is that they are easy to understand and use.

A major shortcoming of the enumeration approach is its inflexibility. All categories must be defined initially. New topics can only be inserted at lower levels. This, for example, results in the classification of new technologies low in the Dewey decimal system. Additionally, this results in unbalanced, awkward structures. Another shortcoming of the hierarchical approach is ambiguity because components can fit perfectly into various categories. For example, *structured systems programming* could match any of the classes *systems analysis* (001.61), *software* (001.642.5), *systems* (003), or *systems construction* (620.73) [Pri91b].

14.5.3 Faceted Classification

Disadvantages of enumerated classification have motivated the development of faceted classification [Pri89, Pri91b, PF87]. Facets are based on attribute-value pairs and can be considered as perspectives, viewpoints or dimensions

Table 14.2. Faceted classification example

Facet	Terms	Description
Function	add, delete, move, compare, ...	performed function
Object	characters, arrays, files, ...	manipulated objects
Medium	buffer, table, file, tree, ...	where action is executed
Type	file handler, lexical analyzer, scheduler, ...	functional or application-independent area
Functional area	bookkeeping, database management, ...	application-dependent activity
Setting	car dealer, insurance, computer store, ...	where action takes place

of particular domains [PF87]. Important vocabulary of a domain is identified and analyzed into basic terms that are organized as facets. Components are then classified by synthesizing facet term pairs.

Table 14.2 shows an example faceted classification scheme introduced by Prieto-Díaz and Freeman [PF87] (also see Poulin and Yglesias [PY93]). This scheme aims at the classification of software components with a size of up to about 200 lines of code. The facets *function, object* and *medium* are used to characterize the functionality of a component. The other three facets describe the environment of a component, i.e., the type of the component, the functional area and the setting/location of the component (domain).

Facets can be contemplated as a component's attributes with multiple values. A set of keywords with any kind of structure can be used for their representation. Advantages of the faceted classification scheme are that complex relationships can be created by combining facets and terms, and that modifying the scheme is much easier than modifying a hierarchical scheme like the enumerated one. Facets can be changed individually without affecting other ones.

14.5.4 Attribute-Value Classification

A set of attributes and values is used for the attribute-value classification. Attributes can take arbitrary values. Retrieving components requires the exact specification of values for (all or a subset of) attributes [PY93].

Attribute-value classification is very similar to faceted classification (a simplification thereof). The difference is that faceted classification typically uses a small number of facets (seven or fewer). This limit is not common for attribute definitions. Additionally, facets and terms usually have an ordering, which is not typical for attributes and values. Finally, with simple attribute-value pairs, synonyms cannot be handled properly (see Frakes and Pole [FP94]).

Similar to enumerated classification, a shortcoming of attribute-value classification is ambiguity. In different components different terms can be used to describe the same (or similar) values. This can be counteracted by a controlled terminology setting (see Section 14.5.6).

14.5.5 Automatic Indexing

Indexing software components manually is difficult and expensive. Automatic indexing is a low-cost way to construct retrieval systems. Many information systems (such as WAIS, Archie and Veronica on the Internet) already provide automatic, yet primitive searching capabilities. Identifying software components requires more precision. A distinction can be made in automatic software indexing based on whether only the lexical level is used or whether syntactic and semantic analysis are included also.

With only the lexical level, attributes for software components are automatically extracted from their natural language documentation. This requires neither any understanding of the documentation nor any kind of syntactic or semantic knowledge.

Classification based on knowledge bases with semantic information about application domains requires human resources to build these bases.

An approach for automatic indexing of software components from natural language descriptions has been pioneered in the Rosa project [RGI94, RGI95]. In Rosa the system extracts lexical, syntactic and semantic information from software descriptions. This knowledge is used to build a 'frame-based internal representation' for the software components.

14.5.6 Indexing Vocabularies

Fig. 14.2 shows a taxonomy of indexing vocabularies [FP94]. The main distinction is made depending on whether a controlled or uncontrolled vocabulary is being used.

– *Controlled vocabularies*
  Controlled vocabularies limit the terms used for classification. For example, the *Library of Congress Subject Headings* lists acceptable and unacceptable terms to be used in descriptions. They are used in many public library catalogs. A syntax can also be given to limit the combination of terms.

– *Uncontrolled vocabularies*
  Uncontrolled vocabularies do not have restrictions on the terms to be used. The terms either are extracted from the text under consideration or originate from some other source. Automatic indexing is typically used for the extraction of terms.

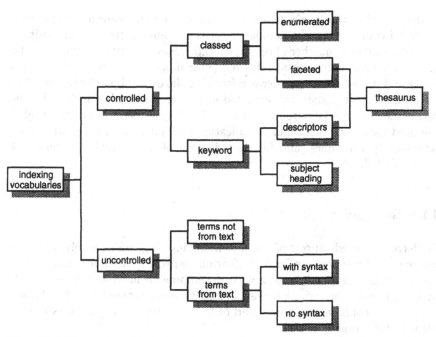

Fig. 14.2. Taxonomy of indexing vocabularies

Free text classification has no vocabulary at all. Keyword classification has a controlled vocabulary. Enumerated, faceted and attribute-value classification use a controlled vocabulary. A thesaurus is often used for controlled vocabularies.

14.5.7 Comparison

Systematic classification of components is crucial for effective retrieval in large repositories. This is less important when only small numbers of components are stored, when primarily generative reuse is used, or in organizations with low staff turnover (as people may accumulate information about available components over time) [FP94].

Frakes and Pole have presented an empirical study for the comparison of keyword, attribute-value, enumerated and faceted classification, which concludes the following [FP94]:

- The four methods did not show any significant differences in search effectiveness (but produced partly different results).
- All four methods did only 'moderately well' in terms of search effectiveness (see below).
- Users did not clearly prefer any of the four methods.
- Differences in user search times were significant, with the best results for enumerated searching, the worst for keyword searching.

Search effectiveness was measured by the number of relevant components retrieved compared to the number of relevant components in the repository (*recall*) and by the number of relevant components retrieved compared to the total number of components retrieved (*precision*). For more details on this study and its results, the reader is referred to the original publication [FP94].

Poulin and Yglesias have reported experiences with the faceted classification method in a large repository at IBM. Their experiences have revealed the need for a combination of classification methods, for an integration with text search techniques, and for the adoption of a hierarchical ordering of facets [PY93].

14.6 Summary

We have discussed aspects of component engineering, which involves the development of components for reuse. Various aspects have to be considered in order to make components reusable; e.g., components must be general enough to be applicable in various contexts. Quality plays a major role for the acceptance of components. Some kind of formal process for quality assurance helps in this respect as well.

The classification of components is important for effective retrieval. Various classification techniques exist. Depending on the size of repositories, different techniques and/or combinations thereof may be useful.

15. Application Engineering

Contents

Application engineering is software engineering with the systematic reuse of existing components and domain knowledge. Applications should be built by assembling components. In case needed components are not available they have to be specified and provided by the component group. The component group is responsible for finding and possibly adapting suitable components. The application group is encouraged to consider the use of components from the beginning of the project. This should maximize the reuse of existing software components and reduce overall development costs.

In this chapter we discuss aspects of application engineering. Reuse-driven development is described in Section 15.1. Reuse considerations for the software life cycle are discussed in Section 15.2. The incorporation of domain analysis is the subject of Section 15.3. A summary follows in Section 15.4.

15.1 Reuse-Driven Development

In the traditional reuse approach, developers are encouraged to look for needed components after most of the design work has been done. Rather than waiting until the design is done (and then looking in vain for matching components), software products need to be designed around available software components [Gri93].

Too often reuse is incorporated too late in the development process. This is demonstrated in Fig. 15.1 and Fig. 15.2, which show the stages of development with reuse and of reuse-driven development.

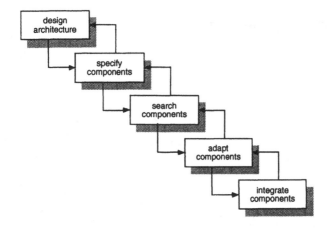

Fig. 15.1. Development with reuse

— *Development with reuse*

First a high-level design and specifications of needed software components are created. This is followed by a search for suitable components which, possibly after making adaptations, will be incorporated into the system.

— *Reuse-driven development*

In reuse-driven development the system specification and the architectural design are already influenced by available software components. The design is based on available components and, compared to development with reuse, results in a higher degree of reuse.

Reuse-driven development may induce compromises in the specification, causing the design to be less efficient, but this is compensated by lower development costs and higher system quality.

Development based on existing components is done in a bottom-up fashion rather than top-down. For example, object-oriented programming requires bottom-up design in order to utilize existing classes. This approach is different from designing a system top-down and creating custom-made and specific (sometimes highly coupled) components.

Many aspects of component reuse have been described in Chapter 14 about component engineering, e.g., repositories and classification. In the following, we consider activities not covered so far, i.e., component reuse in general and component adaptation/modification in particular.

15.1.1 Component Reuse

For effective reuse, it must be easier to find components than to develop them from scratch. (Component repositories and classification techniques are described in Chapter 14.) Finding suitable components does not mean finding exactly what is needed. Locating similar components can be sufficient.

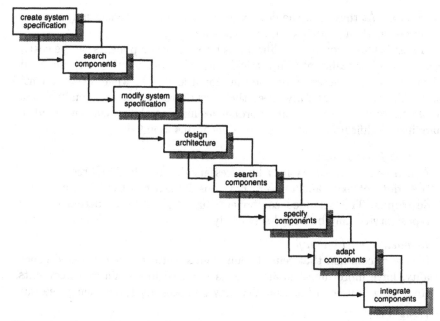

Fig. 15.2. Reuse-driven development

After components have been found, they must be understood in order to reuse them. Finding and understanding are related because selecting a component for reuse requires knowing what the component does. Understanding becomes even more important when the component has to be modified. Adequate documentation is significant for this step.

Building a software system out of a set of unmodified components is the ideal scenario. Typically, at least some of the components have to be adapted to specific needs of the particular software system to be built. Components can be modified in various ways, e.g., by changing internals or by adding new features.

Once a component provides the required functionality, it has to be incorporated into the software system. The goal is to maximize reuse and to minimize basic development efforts. However, typically, existing components will not suffice to build new systems. At least a few components will have to be built from scratch. Ideally, these components are developed for reuse and added to the repository as well.

15.1.2 Component Modification and Adaptation

In many cases a component does not perfectly fit the required needs, and modifications are required. A good understanding of a component is essential to perform this task. The means of possible modification plays a role in the evaluation process and influences the selection of a component from possible candidates. At this point the development of a new component may turn out to be better than modification of an existing one.

Investigating required modifications for several components can be costly, especially when sufficient information is not provided for this purpose. Modifications can be necessary on the functional level, i.e., when a component's functionality does not fully meet the reuser's requirements. Nonfunctional modifications include qualitative properties like portability, efficiency and reliability. Modifications may take different forms [Som92]:

– *Adding functionality*
Additional functionality may be necessary due to additional requirements that did not exist and/or were not considered when the component was developed. The extended component may replace its predecessor in the repository or may be added separately.

– *Removing functionality*
It is very common that reused components, through their required generality, have more functionality than is required in certain reuse contexts. Removing unneeded functionality may be necessary for efficiency reasons.

– *Generalizing*
Modifications to a component's implementation suggest that the component may not be general enough. In this case reviewing the component for possible generalizations is recommended. For more information on component generalization, see Section 14.2.

In the literature the terms *modification* and *adaptation* are not clearly differentiated. We suggest using the term adaptation for minor modifications, i.e., modifications that were in some way planned by component developers (e.g., parameterization) and/or are supported by component technology (e.g., inheritance). For example, re-engineering components clearly goes beyond adaptations and can be seen as white-box reuse.

15.2 Component-Based Life Cycle

Reuse must be seen as an integral part of the software life cycle. This is the only way to systematically get away from simple code reuse or no reuse at all. Boehm's spiral model is a good starting point for this challenge as it offers a combination of other life cycles and explicitly addresses the important factor of risk. Even though every software project is exposed to many risks, projects employing software reuse seem to be open to greater risks due to uncertainties of components to be reused. This discourages project managers from applying reuse in their projects. Developing from scratch is seen as harboring far less uncertainty. Applying Boehm's spiral model can help in identifying and resolving risks in general and reuse risks in particular. Many risks involved with software reuse stem from a lack of information about reusable components. Information provided with a component should include the following [BM92]:

- detailed information about a component's functionality
- guarantees that the component successfully performs the functions it claims to do, e.g., test results
- information about possible modifications/adaptations and their consequences for the overall function of a component

Appropriate documentation is a necessity in assessing risks involved with a component's reuse. Additionally, component validation, verification and certification are means of reducing uncertainty for component reuse.

15.2.1 Reuse Activities

The software engineering process comprises activities that are needed to transform users' requirements into a software system. Hooper and Chester [HC91] and Kang [Kan87] have proposed refinements to the life cycle by adding reuse activities to the various phases of the life cycle as follows:

1. *Understanding*
   understanding the problem and identifying a solution structure based on the predefined components

2. *Reconfiguration*
   reconfiguring the solution structure to improve the possibility of using predefined components available at the next phase

3. *Retrieval*
   acquiring, assessing and instantiating predefined components

4. *Adaptation*
   modifying and adapting the components

5. *Integration*
   integrating the components into the products for this phase

6. *Evaluation*
   evaluating reusability prospects of components that must be developed and components obtained by modifying predefined components for contribution to the set of predefined components

The suggested activities include both development with reuse (steps 1 to 5) and development for reuse (step 6).

For systematic reuse these activities have to be incorporated into the software life cycle. The spiral model offers the enough flexibility to accomplish this. Incorporating the reuse activities results in the *reuse spiral*.

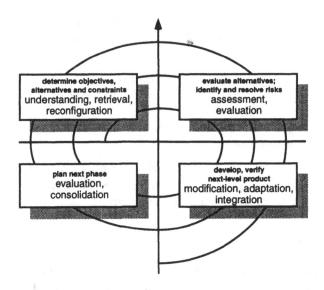

Fig. 15.3. Reuse spiral

15.2.2 Reuse Spiral

Boehm's spiral model allows explicit and early consideration of reuse by identifying alternate means for the implementation of components of the system to be built. This is done at the beginning of each spiral and concedes the evaluation of suitable reusable components. Fig. 15.3 shows the spiral model with activities involved for software reuse in each of the four quadrants.

The reuse spiral is not meant to replace Boehm's spiral, but rather constitutes one of the many options that are intrinsic to the spiral model anyway [BM92]. We discuss these activities in the four quadrants in more detail below.

– *Quadrant 1: understanding, retrieval, reconfiguration*
  The first quadrant of the spiral model we identify objectives of the system to be developed, alternatives for the realization of components of the system, and constraints imposed on these alternatives. In the context of reuse this means that we have to understand the problem and retrieve components that can potentially be used in the given scenario. The components have to be evaluated and the solution structure may have to be changed based on the availability and functionality of components.

  Result of quadrant 1 is a number of components that are candidates for reuse for the realization of components of the system, and various solution structures based on the functionality of these components.

– *Quadrant 2: assessment, evaluation*
  In the second quadrant of the spiral we evaluate alternatives and identify and resolve risks. Thus we have to determine needed modifications of components, the effort needed to accomplish these modifications, and the risks

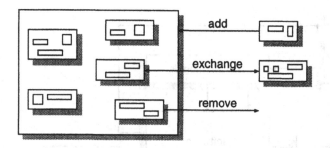

Fig. 15.4. Software evolution

involved in doing so. Different alternatives are evaluated by risk and effort assessment. Existing risks have to be resolved, e.g., by retrieving more information about components or by experimenting with them.

The result of this quadrant is the decision on how to implement the system part under consideration, i.e., which components to reuse and which modifications/adaptations to make.

– *Quadrant 3: modification, adaptation, integration*
The third quadrant of the spiral comprises the development of the next-level product. The selected components have to be modified/adapted and integrated into the subject system.

Result of quadrant 3 is the implementation of the system part to be developed.

– *Quadrant 4: evaluation, consolidation*
The fourth quadrant of the spiral involves planning for the next phases. In the context of reuse we first have to look back and evaluate reusability prospects of modified or new components for contribution to the component repository. If a separate team is available as component group, then all the information should be handed to this group; feedback about reused components and experiences made in quadrant 3 should be given to this group for reuse evaluation.

The reuse spiral as presented above is not isolated from the original spiral model. Rather, it is one possible way of running through a cycle. New development will always be an alternative to reusing existing components. Thus, even though a spiral starts with reuse in mind, it might end with a traditional waterfall model for new development of parts of the system.

15.2.3 Software Evolution

Requirements on software systems are not static but change over time. Maintenance efforts become increasingly difficult when a system has not been designed for later extensions and modifications. Software systems are constantly changing products.

Fig. 15.4 portrays the evolution of software systems. Components are continuously added, changed and removed from a system. This is a constant

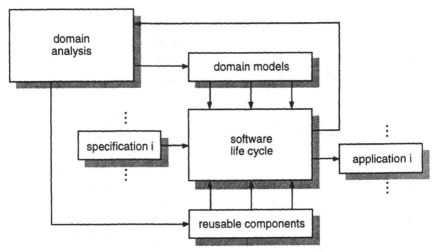

Fig. 15.5. Domain analysis and the software life cycle

process over the lifetime of the system and replaces the traditional development/maintenance steps. Typically, any changes in the set of components involve one or more cycles in the reuse spiral presented above.

15.3 Domain Analysis and the Software Life Cycle

Domain analysis is an ongoing process with constant refinement of domain models based on experiences in the development of new applications. New applications should lead not only to refinements of domain models, but to new reusable components and to modified/improved existing components.

Fig. 15.5 is adapted from Prieto-Díaz [Pri90] and depicts the integration of domain analysis and the software life cycle. Domain analysis starts with existing domain knowledge, e.g., existing applications of the domain. Subsequently, its output is used as input for the software life cycle. Any life cycle model can be used that is appropriate either for the whole domain or for a certain application thereof.

The domain models support or even control various phases of the development of new applications. Data gained during development is used as feedback for refinement of the domain models and for updating the repository with reusable components. Thus every new development contributes to an increase of the maturity of both the domain knowledge and the component repository.

15.4 Summary

In this chapter we have described aspects of application engineering. For the design of applications, it is important that reusable components be considered early in the design process and that the design process be adapted to increase the potential reuse of components. The reuse spiral provides a framework for these considerations. Domain analysis should be done in parallel to component and application development and provides various inputs like components and/or domain models.

Application engineering is component-oriented software development. We design and develop software systems in a compositional way; i.e., we create a set of components to work together. The components are not designed in isolation but rather to collaborate and to be reused in various contexts.

Part IV

Software Documentation

16. Software Documentation

Contents

Software systems contain all relevant 'information' in order to be executable on a machine. Human readers need additional information which has to be provided in the documentation of a software system. Documentation has to be produced during the software process for various categories of readers.

All statements made subsequently about documentation apply to software components and/or software systems. The documentation of software systems composed of software components should be a collection of the components' documentation plus additional information. This means that the documentation of a component has to fulfill requirements similar to those on the component itself. For example, the documentation should be self-contained, adaptable and extensible (in case the component is being adapted and/or extended).

In this chapter we give a general introduction to software documentation. Reuse related topics of documentation are covered in Chapters 17 to 20. In this introduction we describe various categories of documentation in Section 16.1 and describe each of these categories, i.e., user, system and process documentation in Sections 16.2 to 16.4, respectively. A summary follows in Section 16.5.

16.1 Documentation Categories

Documentation of a software product has to contain information for various readers. Information has to be provided for end users, management, developers and maintenance personnel (see Pomberger [Pom84] and Sommerville [Som92]).

Different reader groups have different information needs which are addressed in different kinds of information. End users need information that enables them to efficiently and effectively use and administer the system (*user documentation*). Management needs help for planning, budgeting and scheduling current and future (similar) software processes (*process documentation*). Developers need information about the overall system structure, about components and their interaction (*system documentation*).

In contrast to a software product, a software component needs additional information for developers who reuse the component. In the following sections we depict the classic documentation categories as described by Pomberger [Pom84] and Sommerville [Som92]. Reuse documentation is described in Chapter 17.

16.2 User Documentation

Good user documentation is important for the commercial success of a software product. Users need different kinds of information and there are different kinds of users, e.g., novice and experienced users. Users must be able to use a software system with the information provided in the user documentation. Additional assistance and/or further information should not be necessary.

A component may or may not be (directly) used by end users; thus user documentation of components is optional. However, components that are not full fledged applications but do interact with users may have user documentation. The user documentation of an application being composed of such components may be composed of the documentation of these components.

Sommerville proposes five parts for user documentation [Som92]. Depending on the size and kind of a software system, some of these may be optional or be combined with other parts. The five parts are:

– *Functional description*
  outline of system requirements and provided services
  (for system evaluation)

– *Installation manual*
  detailed information on how to install the system in a particular environment (for system administrators)

– *Introductory manual*
  informal introduction to the system and description of standard features
  (for novice users)

– *Reference manual*
  complete description of all features and error messages
  (for experienced users)

– *System administrator manual*
  more general information for system administration
  (for system administrators)

Other authors propose similar structures. For example, Pomberger suggests three parts, i.e., a general system description (*functional description*), an installation and user manual (*installation document, introductory manual, reference manual*), and an operator manual (*system administrator's guide*) [Pom84].

16.3 System Documentation

System documentation has to capture all information about the development of a software component/system. It should contain sufficient information such that a new member of the development or maintenance team can make modifications and extensions without further information and/or assistance. System documentation includes the following information [Pom84, Som92]:

- *Requirements*
  contract between component user (end user and/or reuser) and component developer
- *Overall design and structure*
  subcomponents and their interrelations
- *Implementation details*
  e.g., algorithmic details
- *Test plans and reports*
  for integration tests and acceptance tests
- *Used files*
  in case component/system uses external files
- *Source code listings*
  too often the only accurate and complete description of a component or system

System documentation of components composed of smaller-grained components typically contains the documentation of the components it is composed of. As mentioned at the beginning of this chapter, it is important for documentation composition that a component's documentation be self-contained, modifiable and extensible.

Due to time pressure, system documentation is often neglected. Thus information is often incomplete and inconsistent. Literate programming as described in Chapter 18 provides a means for improving documentation completeness and consistency.

16.4 Process Documentation

In contrast to user and system documentation, which describe a component at a certain point of time, process documentation describes the dynamic process of its creation. The reason for documenting the process is to support effective management and project control. Whereas user and system documentation have to be kept up-to-date, much of the process documentation becomes outdated.

Process documentation is a collection of information that depicts the whole development process. Its documents include the following [Pom84, Som92]:

- *Project plan*
  individual phases with estimates and schedules (for prediction and control)

- *Organization plan*
  allocation and supervision of personnel

- *Resource plan*
  allocation and supervision of resources other than personnel (e.g., machine time, travelling expenditures)

- *Project standards*
  e.g., design methodology, test strategy, documentation conventions

- *Working papers*
  technical communication documents that record ideas, strategies, and identified problems (contain information about the rationale of design decisions)

- *Log book*
  discussions and communication between project members (design decisions)

- *Reading aids*
  e.g., index of documents, word index, table of contents

Process documentation helps in controlling the current project, i.e., controlling project progress (project plans and estimates), controlling quality (standards, check points), and determining production costs (personnel cost, machine time). Another reason for the creation of this kind of documentation is that its information can be used when creating similar components or systems.

16.5 Summary

In this chapter we have introduced various kinds of documentation for software systems. For the reuse of components, we additionally need reuse information as described in Chapter 17. Fig. 16.1 summarizes the structure and contents of software documentation.

Software documentation can be divided into user, system and process documentation. Software systems and software components have to be documented equally carefully. Depending on the kind and size of a component, its documentation may have different focal points; for example, user documentation may be missing or process documentation may be only rudimentary for small source code components.

Many books on software engineering provide further information on software documentation (e.g., document quality, standards and preparation). Some software engineering books, however, reprehensibly ignore documentation aspects; by doing so, they at least reflect the priority of documentation in many real software projects. By contrast, Bell et al. provide a focus on technical communication, history, strategies and processes of documentation [BBC+94].

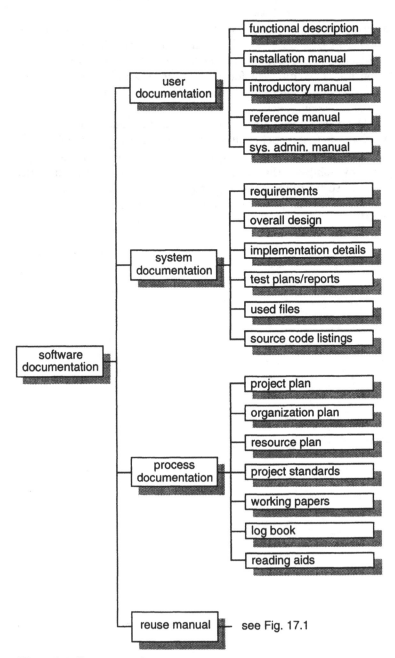

Fig. 16.1. Documentation structure

17. Reuse Documentation

Contents

In addition to the documentation we use for software systems (user, system and process documentation) we have to provide reuse documentation for software components. Reuse documentation has to contain all the information needed for component selection, effective reuse, component modification, etc. The target audience is software engineers who have to decide whether a certain component fits their needs and who need extensive information about components' interfaces. For black-box reuse, implementation details of components are not necessary for effective reuse.

In this chapter we propose a structure for reuse documentation. Section 17.1 provides a motivation for supplying reuse information. In Section 17.2 we propose the structure for a component's reuse manual. A summary follows in Section 17.3.

17.1 Motivation

In order to effectively and correctly reuse a software component, information about various aspects of it has to be provided. This includes information that enables:

– the evaluation of components in a set of possible candidates,
– the understanding of a component's functionality,
– the use of a component in a certain environment, and
– the adaptation of a component for specific needs.

Good documentation of components is essential to software reusability. Regular documentation does not meet these needs.

The amount and kind of information needed strongly depends on the form of a reusable component. Reusing assembler routines requires different information than reusing an object-oriented class or a self-contained application.

Documentation must be valued as an essential part of a software component. Without proper documentation, a component is useless. Neither can it be retrieved when needed, nor can it be reused and adapted with reasonable effort. Documentation standards have to be established in order to guarantee the availability of important information and the completeness and consistency of this information. A consistent structure makes the documentation more readable and better understandable. It helps the reuser in finding relevant components and decreases the time needed for evaluation, actual reuse and adaptation of components.

Another important aspect is that each component has its self-contained documentation. Letting the reuser filter out a component's documentation from a big document describing a set of components is bad practice. A component's requirements, design, test and reuse information must stand alone. and its dependencies and references to other documents should be minimal. Additional requirements on the documentation are its availability in machine-readable form. This allows us to reuse the documentation for derivative components and modify it according to the modifications made to the component. Clarity and understandability should be a matter of course for any documentation. This is of special importance in fostering reuse.

Imagine a repository with all possible kinds of components. In order to find and select components for reuse in a certain context, various questions have to be answered about these components:

– *What kind of component is it?*
An indication about the nature of a component is its platform. This specifies, for example, the programming language for source code components or the operating system of processes.

– *What is the component's functionality?*
Despite the technical subtleties of composition, a component's functionality remains a crucial factor for its reusability. We have seen that completeness, generality and applicability are factors influencing the reusability of components.

– *Can the component be reused in our context? How?*
Whether a component can be reused in a certain context depends on many factors. Let's suppose a component has the right functionality and is of the right kind (platform). Interaction plays an important role for reuse as it can either support or hinder it. High coupling with other components may require the reuse of (many) other components that would badly influence

performance and/or lead to overlapping functionality. User interaction may also prohibit a component's reuse.

- *What else is needed to reuse the component?*
Component interaction may require the reuse of other components as well. For example, certain libraries or an application framework may be necessary in order to use a function or class. The reuse of an application may require a certain operating system.

- *Can the component be customized/adapted/modified? How? To what extent?*
Whether a component can be adapted to certain needs depends on several factors. If a component's functionality is close to our needs, it is more likely to be a reuse candidate. Whether the needed adaptations have been foreseen by the components' developers is another crucial aspect. Finally, the kind of component plays a role in how easily modifications can be made to the component. For example, object-oriented components are more likely to enable adaptations than procedure-oriented ones.

- *Can the component be interconnected with our components?*
This question can be answered by considering the platforms of a component. Sometimes reuse over platform boundaries may be possible. Components running on their own offer a greater variety of interconnection and need more attention in this respect.

- *Is the component's quality sufficient for our purposes?*
In critical parts of a software system, quality control at the reuse end may inhibit the inclusion of arbitrary components without proven quality. Some sort of component certification and defined levels of certification are required. More details on the certification of components are provided in Section 14.3 on page 174.

Information with answers to these questions has to be provided in the reuse documentation. The answers to some of the questions may be obvious depending on the kind of a component. For example, a C++ class can obviously be reused in a software system written in C++; it can be customized by writing subclasses. The class' functionality may be obvious from its interface description, but typically some documentation will be mandatory. To what extent the class can be customized depends on its design and should be described in the documentation. The implementation of the class may use other classes and/or library routines that are not listed in its interface. The availability of these other components must be guaranteed in order to reuse the class. Even if reuse is possible, additional parameters may determine whether a component is actually reused, e.g., performance and cost considerations.

17.2 Reuse Manual

A reuse manual should be defined and created for each component. The size, layout and contents of such a manual will vary according to the type of a component. However, it must contain all relevant reuse information. The kind of information needed for reuse has been proposed by many authors, e.g., Braun [Bra94d, Bra94a], Karlsson [Kar95], Krueger [Kru92] and Meyer [Mey94]. We suggest an outline consisting of the following five parts [Sam96]:

- *General information*
  general information for evaluation purposes (overview)

- *Reuse information*
  detailed information for actual reuse

- *Administrative information*
  information about legal constraints and available support

- *Evaluation information*
  detailed information for evaluation purposes

- *Other information*
  additional information, e.g., references

These parts are described in the subsequent sections. We assume that we have components of different types in a repository. In case a repository contains only components of one kind, e.g., C++ classes, then some of the entries may be superfluous, e.g., type of component.

17.2.1 General Information

This part contains general information about a component and serves evaluation purposes. It should provide enough information to decide whether a component is a candidate in a certain reuse scenario, but should refrain from being too detailed. If the information in this part contains too many details, the evaluation process will be encumbered. However, a final decision on which component to choose out of a set of candidates may require the inspection of information of the other parts as well.

1. *Introduction*
   Is the component a candidate for potential reuse in a certain scenario? The introduction should contain a clear, concise initial statement about the component's function for initial selection, including name, identification and overview of the component.

2. *Classification*
   What information is used for the classification of the component? Classification information may be taken from other areas of the reuse manual, e.g., a component's functionality and platforms.

3. *Functionality*
   What is the general functionality of the component? This item gives an overview of all externally visible operations and provides interface descriptions.

4. *Platforms*
   On what platforms can the component be used? Examples are C++, C and OpenDoc.

5. *Reuse status*
   What is the status of the quality of the component with regard to test, maintenance, finances, etc.?

17.2.2 Reuse Information

This part contains the essential information for actual reuse. It should include all the details necessary for installing, reusing and adapting the component.

1. *Installation*
   Which steps (if any) have to be done to incorporate the component into a system, e.g., installation of an application?

2. *Interface descriptions*
   What are the exact interface definitions for the entire functionality?

3. *Integration and usage*
   How can the component be reused (correctly)? This has to contain detailed information for effective reuse of the component, including interfaces, sample scenarios and diagnostic procedures (what to do if a problem occurs).

4. *Adaptation*
   How and to what specific needs can the component be adapted? This information includes means of adaptation to specific needs with detailed information about how to accomplish this, e.g., available options, subclassing.

17.2.3 Administrative Information

This part contains administrative information such as legal constraints and available support.

1. *Procurement and support*
   What is the point of contact to get help (e.g., in adapting the component)? What are the source (if component is not directly available in repository) and ownership (any legal or contractual restrictions)?

2. *Commercial and legal restrictions*
   What are the commercial or legal restrictions on the use of the component, e.g., purchase, special license or permission required?

3. *History and versions*
   What is the history and current version of the component (including all prior versions, their developers and dates of release)? What are the main differences compared to older versions?

17.2.4 Evaluation Information

This part contains more detailed information for the evaluation of a component, including known bugs, limitations and quality statements.

1. *Specification*
   What is the component's functionality in full detail, including functional and nonfunctional requirements? See Section 11.2 on page 145.

2. *Quality*
   What is the quality of the component? This has to contain information about verification, applied tests, test results, available test data, retesting procedures, etc.

3. *Performance and resource requirements*
   What (amount of) system resources are required for using the component (e.g., memory, processor, communication channels)? What are the performance characteristics?

4. *Alternative components*
   Are there similar components that could be used instead of this one?

5. *Known bugs/problems*
   Are there any reports of unresolved problems, e.g., known bugs, desired enhancements?

6. *Limitations and restrictions*
   What are the (technical) limitations and restrictions on the use of the component (e.g., capacities, programming language, operating system dependencies)?

7. *Possible enhancements*
   What are possible enhancements, e.g., to make the component more robust, to improve performance/maintainability, or to extend the component's scope of reuse?

8. *Test support*
   Are test cases and/or a test environment available for the component?

9. *Interdependencies*
   Can the component be used stand-alone or must other components be used with it?

17.2.5 Other Information

Any other information not covered by the first four parts is subsumed in the last part.

1. *System documentation*
   How is the component implemented? The system documentation includes requirements, design, implementation, etc. (see Section 16.3 on page 199). When a component is reused as a black box, its system documentation is not necessary for reuse purposes.

2. *References*
   Are there references to any literature or other documentation which are useful for the reuse of the component?

3. *Reading aids*
   Additional reading aids like index, table of contents, list of figures, and list of tables help in navigating through extensive documents.

17.3 Summary

Separate documentation is essential for effective reuse. Specific needs of reusers have to be addressed explicitly. In this chapter we have proposed a structure for a reuse manual. The outline of a reuse manual should be defined and consistently created for all components in a repository. Naturally, adaptations may be appropriate depending on the nature of the components being stored. Fig. 17.1 summarizes the proposed structure and contents of a reuse manual.

Any existing guidlines for documentation have to be applied for the reuse manual as well, e.g., compliance with accepted documentation standards; use of consistent structures, styles, and formats; consistency with the code; writing in clear and understandable form; etc.

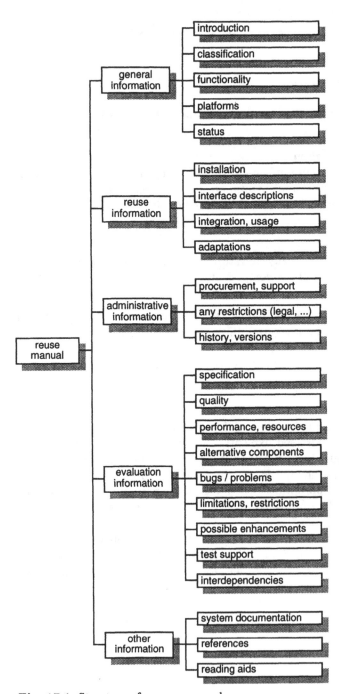

Fig. 17.1. Structure of a reuse manual

18. Literate Programming

Contents

The central idea of literate programming is to improve documentation quality by describing problems and solutions rather than executable programs. An important aspect is the integration of source code and documentation. Literate programming is primarily for system documentation. Thus reusers benefit from it only when doing white-box, glass-box, or grey-box reuse and when reading about the implementation in the system documentation. However, interface descriptions of source code components (i.e., parts of the reuse manual) may be created in a literate manner for the reuse documentation as well.

In this chapter we present aspects of literate programming. We discuss concepts in Section 18.1 and tool support in Section 18.2. Reasons for the lack of widespread acceptance of literate programming are given in Section 18.3. Reuse aspects of literate programming are considered in Section 18.4. A summary follows in Section 18.5.

18.1 Concepts

Programs are written to be executed by computers rather than to be read by humans. However, when writing programs, the goal of telling humans what we want the computer to do should be more important than instructing the computer what to do.

Literate programming was proposed by Knuth [Knu84, Knu92]. Its idea is to make programs as readable as ordinary literature. The primary goal is to obtain not just an executable program but also a description of a problem and its solution, including assumptions, alternative solutions, design decisions, etc. Literate programming is a process leading to more carefully constructed software systems with better documentation.

There are often misconceptions about what a literate program is. Childs has provided a list of requirements from a practitioner's point of view [Chi91]:

- *Integration of source code and documentation*
  The source code and the system documentation have to come from the same source files.

- *Problem descriptions*
  Literate programs should contain problem descriptions and an examination of alternative solutions rather than just a description of the final solution. Graphical representations should be used to communicate problems and solutions.

- *Logical subdivisions*
  Literate programs should have logical subdivisions like chapters and sections.

- *Logical order*
  The order of presentation of literate programs has to be based upon logical considerations rather than syntactic constraints of a programming language.

- *Reading aids*
  Additional readings aids like cross references and indexes should be provided automatically.

Literate programs as produced with Knuth's Web system (see next section) consist of a series of sections. Fig. 18.1 shows part of a simple literate program [Knu92]. It consists of two paragraphs of documentation followed by the outline of a Pascal program. The complete program is given in [Knu92]. Each section of a literate program contains documentation text and source code. Documentation text explains the subsequent source which contains containers that can be filled in later sections, e.g., ⟨Other constants of the program 5⟩. The sections are numbered (we have section 2 in Fig. 18.1) and the containers are suffixed by a number that indicates in which section the containers are defined.

Besides documentation text and source code Knuth used macro definitions. They served as a remedy for language deficiencies of Pascal and, thus, are not explained here.

18.2 Tool Support

The original Web system was developed by Knuth as a superset of the programming language Pascal and the text formatting language TEX. The two languages were chosen for practical reasons. A Web source contains documentation text in TEX and program text in Pascal. Additionally, some extra

2. This program has no input, because we want to keep it simple. The result of the program will be to produce a list of the first thousand prime numbers, and this list will appear on the *output* file.

Since there is no input, we declare the value $m = 1000$ as a compile-time constant. The program itself is capable of generating the first m prime numbers for any positive m, as long as the computer's finite limitations are not exceeded.

⟨Program to print the first thousand prime numbers 2⟩ ≡
program *print_primes*(*output*);
const m = 1000; ⟨Other constants of the program 5⟩
var ⟨Variables of the program 4⟩
begin ⟨Print the first m prime numbers 3⟩
end.

This code is used in section 1.

Fig. 18.1. Literate program excerpt

features like code containers (mentioned in the previous section) can be used. Both the executable program and a high-quality documentation are generated from the same source. An architectural overview of the Web system is given in Fig. 18.2.

Fig. 18.3 shows the source of the literate program excerpt of Fig. 18.1. Horizontal bars (| |) are used in the documentation text to enclose source text. At-signs and angles (@< @>) are used in the code to identify containers.

A number of Web and Web-like systems have been developed. They have been adapted to different programming and formatting languages, e.g., CWeb [KL93, Lev93], FWeb [AO90, Kro90] and NoWeb [Ram94]. Levy created CWeb based on Knuth's Web, but using the C and C++ programming languages. Krommes' FWeb is based on CWeb and supports several programming languages. NoWeb was created by Ramsey and is an example of a literate programming tool that works with any programming language and supports TeX, LaTeX and HTML back ends. Thus you can produce printed

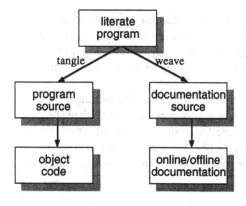

Fig. 18.2. Architecture of the Web system

```
@ This program has no input, because we want to keep it simple.
The result of the program will be to produce a list of the
first thousand prime numbers, and this list will appear on
the |output| file.

Since there is no input, we declare the value |m = 1000| as
a compile-time constant. The program itself is capable of
generating the first |m| prime numbers for any positive |m|,
as long as the computer's finite limitations are not exceeded.

@<program to print the first thousand prime numbers@>=
program print_primes(output);
  const m = 1000;
   @<other constants of the program@>
  var @<variables of the program@>
   begin @<print the first |m| prime numbers@>
   end.
```

Fig. 18.3. Source of literate program excerpt

documentation with page numbers as cross-references and/or on-line documentation with hypertext links. NoWeb was designed to be as simple as possible but still meet the needs of literate programmers. NoWeb's primary advantages are simplicity, extensibility and language independence. The primary sacrifice relative to Web is that code is not prettyprinted and that indexing is not done automatically.

Most literate programming tools automatically provide extensive reading aids like tables of contents and indexes. These tools can and should be used for the entire documentation of software components, of which only a small part will have source code included. The advantage of using a literate programming tool for the entire documentation is that components are documented in a consistent way.

18.3 Acceptance

There are positive reports about the successful use of literate programming in industry, e.g.,Elliot [Ell96] and at universities, e.g.,Childs [Chi91]. Still, despite its apparent advantages literate programming has not gained widespread acceptance, primarily due to the lack of tool support and tool integration.

The more complex software systems get, the more important good, systematic documentation becomes. However, tool support to visualize the manifold relations and to effectively browse through a system becomes equally important. For example, the complexity of class and object interrelations in object-oriented systems is difficult or impossible to manage without adequate tool support.

Unfortunately, we lack reasonable compositions of programming environment components like browsers and literate programming tools. This has hindered general acceptance of literate programming considerably, but will perhaps vanish when better tool (component) integration becomes available.

Another drawback of most existing literate programming tools is their batch processing. Most computer users are used to modern word processing tools with graphical WYSIWYG (what you see is what you get) user interfaces. Even though the TEX text formatting system provides better quality output than most word processing systems, users are not willing to sacrifice ease of use and graphical user interfaces.

Acceptance of literate programming has also been hampered by misconceptions like 'literate programs have to be monolithic' or 'literate programming is the opposite of hypertext.'

18.4 Reuse Considerations

Literate programming is an important concept for increased quality of both software and documentation. It provides help in keeping documentation complete and consistent. In this respect it is important for the reuse of software as well.

Literate programming is clearly aimed at *system documentation*. When we reuse components as black boxes, we are not interested in their internals. Thus system documentation and literate programming are not necessary.

For white-box (also glass-box and grey-box) reuse, system documentation becomes important for the reuse process. Thus literate programming is important for reuse when it becomes necessary to modify or enhance a component's behavior, or to eliminate flaws or existing restrictions.

It is important that high-quality documentation describing the implementation of the component be available, and that documentation be kept consistent with any modifications and complete with respect to any extensions. In this context literate programming is important for reuse because it supports both creating high-quality documentation and keeping it consistent and complete.

A scenario of composing components suggests the composition of documentation as well. As with components, the need for modifications and extensions arises for documentation. Available examples of literate programs, e.g., those from Knuth [Knu86b, Knu86d], do not support the notion of reusable components.

18.5 Summary

In this chapter we have presented the concepts of literate programming and discussed tool support, lack of widespread use, and reuse considerations.

Literate programming was designed to allow sequential reading of programs like books. Hypertext features were not explicitly mentioned originally, but can easily be incorporated. For example, the NoWeb system allows the creation of hypertext links in literate programs.

Literate programming is applicable primarily for system documentation. However, as Childs has elaborated, it is more than just the integration of source code and documentation text. High-quality, complete and consistent documentation is important for reuse, making literate programming an option to be considered.

In Chapter 19 we present a case study on the reuse of documentation. In this case study we demonstrate reuse measurement based on line and word runs (see Section 4.4 on page 48) and white-box reuse in literate programs.

19. Reuse Measurement in Literate Programs

Contents

Documentation requires mechanisms for systematic reuse similar to these for software. As a motivation for this statement, we present a case study on reuse measurement in some literate programs. The case study concerns how much reuse was done and how. By using literate programs, we simultaneously measure reuse in source code and documentation.

In Section 4.4.2 on page 49 we introduced a reuse measure based on line and word runs. This measure is applicable to arbitrary texts, i.e., not only to source code but especially to documentation. In this chapter we demonstrate this reuse measure in more detail and—with the results—motivate systematic reuse of documentation. In Section 19.1 a motivation for the case study is provided. In Section 19.2 we describe line and word runs for reuse measurement. The case study itself with a description of the subject systems, the results and consequences is presented in Section 19.3. A summary follows in Section 19.4.

19.1 Motivation

In the case study presented in this chapter we use line and word runs to determine the amount of ad-hoc reuse in literate programs. Literate programs allow us to investigate documentation and source code.

The case study serves several purposes. It provides an example of reuse measurement with line and word runs, it shows examples of documentation reuse, and it demonstrates the need for systematic reuse of documentation.

$$Reuse_{l,len} = \frac{Identical_{l,len}}{Total_l} \times 100$$

$Reuse_{l,len}$:   line reuse percentage considering runs with
                minimum length *len*.

$Identical_{l,len}$:   number of identical lines in both texts
                (identical lines in runs with length < *len*
                are considered as being different)

$Total_l$:   total number of lines

Fig. 19.1. Reuse measurement based on line and word runs

The case study was originally published in [CS96b, CS97]. Knuth's TeX systems were chosen for examples because they contain source code and documentation, are in the public domain and have consistent and complete documentation.

In the rest of this chapter we demonstrate line and word runs in more detail and provide a small example. Then we present the results of the case study and discuss consequences.

19.2 Line and Word Runs

In order to determine the extent of reuse in a specific case, similarities and differences of texts have to be determined. Comparing lines and words gives a good indication of reuse. If line reuse is high, then obviously much reuse has taken place. If line reuse is low, but word reuse is high, then much reuse has taken place, but the reused text had been modified on a more local basis. Finally, if both line and word reuse are low, then apparently there is not much reuse at all.

Fig. 19.1 shows how to determine reuse based on line runs. In order to evaluate reuse, we determine line and word reuse for various lengths. We denote line reuse with R_l and word reuse with R_w. The lengths used for reuse evaluation may vary depending on the input data.

To give the reader a better idea we demonstrate line and word runs on a small example, the first paragraph of the chapter "Introduction to the syntactic routines" of TeX and MetaFont. The lines of the paragraphs in TeX and MetaFont are listed in Fig. 19.2. Identical lines are marked with '=' at the beginning. Despite the high similarity, there are only three identical lines in these paragraphs. Words that appear in both systems have a box drawn around them. Words are regarded as any sequence of characters separated by blanks or newlines. The text of TeX in Fig. 19.2 contains 12 lines and 128 words. The text of MetaFont contains 13 lines and 135 words. 9 lines or 30 words have to be changed to transform the text of TeX to the text of MetaFont. This results in a line and word reuse of $R_l = 25.0\%$ and $R_w = 76.6\%$.

TEX:

> @* \[21] Introduction to the syntactic routines.
> = Let's pause a moment now and try to look at the Big Picture.
> The \TeX\ program consists of three main parts: syntactic routines,
> = semantic routines, and output routines. The chief purpose of the
> = syntactic routines is to deliver the user's input to the semantic routines,
> one token at a time. The semantic routines act as an interpreter
> responding to these tokens, which may be regarded as commands. And the
> output routines are periodically called on to convert box-and-glue
> lists into a compact set of instructions that will be sent
> to a typesetter. We have discussed the basic data structures and utility
> routines of \TeX\, so we are good and ready to plunge into the real activity by
> considering the syntactic routines.

MetaFont:

> @* \[30] Introduction to the syntactic routines.
> = Let's pause a moment now and try to look at the Big Picture.
> The \MF\ program consists of three main parts: syntactic routines,
> = semantic routines, and output routines. The chief purpose of the
> = syntactic routines is to deliver the user's input to the semantic routines,
> while parsing expressions and locating operators and operands. The
> semantic routines act as an interpreter responding to these operators,
> which may be regarded as commands. And the output routines are
> periodically called on to produce compact font descriptions that can be
> used for typesetting or for making interim proof drawings. We have
> discussed the basic data structures and many of the details of semantic
> operations, so we are good and ready to plunge into the part of \MF\ that
> actually controls the activities.

Fig. 19.2. Sample paragraph comparison

The high difference between R_l and R_w indicates that the text was modified and polished. Some single words, i.e., *that*, *be*, *of* and *the* are identical. Such single words can result in a slightly higher R_w than may be justified by actual reuse.

Table 19.1 contains the run lengths for lines and words of the example in Fig. 19.2. There are no long line runs (none longer than 2). Thus the line reuse percentage drops to zero with a run length of 3. However, there are many word runs with a length of at least 3 (in fact, even much higher). So the word reuse percentage drops slightly when the run length is increased to 2, but then stays at this level. The average length of word runs is 15.3, indicating that even for higher run lengths the reuse percentage will not drop much. This high word reuse percentage and low line reuse percentage indicates high reuse with extensive modifications.

Table 19.1. Line and word runs in sample paragraph comparison

len	n_l	avg_l	M_l	Σ_l	R_l	n_w	avg_w	M_w	Σ_w	R_w
1	2	1.5	2	3	25.0	12	8.2	30	98	76.6
2	1	2.0	2	2	16.7	6	15.3	30	92	71.9
3	0	0.0	0	0	0.0	6	15.3	30	92	71.9

len:	minimum length for runs to be considered
n_l, n_w:	number of line/word runs
avg_l, avg_w:	average length of line/word runs
M_l, M_w:	maximum length of line/word runs
Σ_l, Σ_w:	sum of lengths of line/word runs
R_l, R_w:	line/word reuse percentage

19.3 Case Study

We present sample reuse measurements based on line and word runs for three Webs (literate programming sources) from the TEX system: TEX, a book-quality formatting system [Knu86a, Knu86b]; MetaFont, a system that enables a programmer/artist to create a family of fonts for TEX [Knu86c, Knu86d]; and MetaPost, a close relative of MetaFont that enables the creation of high-quality graphics as encapsulated PostScript files.

An outstanding feature of the TEX system is its implementation in the form of literate programs. The complete documentation allows reuse measurement to reveal similarities that go beyond plain source code.

We first briefly describe the investigated systems and then present the results.

19.3.1 Subject Systems

The TEX system and the Web processors were written in the original Web. The functions of these programs are described at a shallow level. For more details see Childs and Sametinger [CS97] and the references mentioned above.

– *TEX*
  The TEX processor converts a plain text file containing document markup into a device independent graphics metafile. It reads a number of other files in this process to get font characteristics, document styles, etc.

– *MetaFont*
  MetaFont reads a source file that is a metadescription of a font (family). It does significant graphics interpretations, solving of equations, and other items associated with the creation of a consistent family of fonts.

– *MetaPost*
  MetaPost is a close relative to MetaFont. Its inputs have file layouts much like MetaFont sources. Outputs of MetaPost are book quality figures.

Table 19.2. Line and word lengths

System	Lines	Words
TEX	21,541	122,137
MetaFont	20,481	109,307
MetaPost	20,460	104,375

TEX, MetaFont and MetaPost operate on various common files, e.g., device independent files, font metric files, log files. Hence some kind of similarity can be expected. Browsing the sources of TEX and MetaFont in book form [Knu86b, Knu86d] reveals many chapters with the same title. Similarities in these chapters are obvious even from just turning the pages. MetaPost is a direct derivative of MetaFont; this should show the highest degree of reuse.

19.3.2 Results

TEX's source contains about 21,500 lines and 122,000 words. MetaFont consists of about 20,500 lines and 110,000 words. TEX and MetaFont are divided into 55 and 52 chapters, respectively. 26 of these chapters have the same title in both systems. These chapters contain 33.4 percent of the lines of the TEX system.

TEX and MetaFont contain sections of which the only difference is a replacement of the word TEX with the word MetaFont. Also, there are sentences that have been improved by a change of word ordering or by inserting or deleting single words. Additionally, MetaFont has more index entries than TEX, which also has an effect on the resulting reuse percentage.

A high reuse percentage was determined by comparing MetaFont and MetaPost. MetaFont has 52 chapters; MetaPost has 49. 44 chapters appear in both systems with the same title. In Table 19.2 the number of lines and words are summarized for the subject systems.

Table 19.3 shows some detailed results for line and word runs. The abbreviations used have the same meaning as in Table 19.1 on page 220. The left side shows some chapters that demonstrate the highest reuse. It is interesting to note that, despite increasing run lengths for lines and words, the resulting reuse percentages drop only slightly. This is an indication of actual reuse rather than accidental similarities.

The right side of Table 19.3 shows chapters that do not exhibit high reuse. The chapter *"Saving and restoring equivalents"* exposes some reuse with run length 1, but the numbers drops to zero quickly. This is similar to the comparison of two completely different chapters, i.e., *"Reporting Errors"* and *"Character Set"*, and does not result from actual reuse. The chapter *"The command codes"* is interesting in that there are no identical lines at all. Yet the reuse percentage for words does not completely drop to zero even

Table 19.3. Run-based reuse percentages in TEX vs. MetaFont

	Reporting errors	Character set	Input and output	System-dependent changes	Saving and restoring equivalents	The command codes	Reporting errors/ character set
n_l	359	206	301	10	291	163	359
n_w	2,022	1,097	2,333	83	1,803	1,367	2,022
$R_{l,1}$	82.7	81.6	81.1	80.0	3.1	0.0	1.1
$R_{l,3}$	78.0	77.7	76.4	60.0	0.0	0.0	0.0
$R_{l,5}$	69.6	75.7	65.8	60.0	0.0	0.0	0.0
$R_{l,10}$	41.2	69.9	50.2	0.0	0.0	0.0	0.0
$R_{w,1}$	93.3	76.9	93.4	97.6	8.5	19.9	7.3
$R_{w,5}$	91.9	75.8	92.6	96.4	0.5	5.7	0.0
$R_{w,10}$	89.3	72.2	91.3	96.4	0.0	5.2	0.0
$R_{w,20}$	78.2	69.4	82.2	96.4	0.0	2.3	0.0

with a run length of 20. The reason for this is that the first two introductory paragraphs of the chapter share high similarity, as shown in Fig. 19.2 on page 219. The command codes themselves are different in the two systems.

Table 19.4 summarizes the results. It contains the reuse percentages yielded by comparing the entire systems. In the second line only similar chapters are considered. Column *Portion* specifies the amount of these chapters; e.g., considering only 33.4% of TEX for the comparison yields a line reuse of 42.8% and a word reuse of 60.7% (as opposed to 14.3% and 21.5%).

More than 60 percent of MetaFont is reused in MetaPost, even though its size of about 20,000 lines and more than 100,000 words. A total of 24 chapters has a reuse percentage higher than 90%. Except for three chapters all the other chapters have a reuse percentage higher than 70%.

Table 19.4. Summary of reuse percentages

Systems	Portion	R_l	R_w
TEX → MetaFont	100 %	14.3 %	21.5 %
	33.4 %	42.8 %	60.7 %
MetaFont → MetaPost	100 %	63.4 %	67.0 %
	80.8 %	78.5 %	85.1 %

More details on the results of these measurements can be found in Childs and Sametinger [CS96b, CS97].

19.3.3 Consequences

Reuse measurement based on line and word runs can be used for many different purposes. Evaluation of white-box reuse is one example. Other applications are finding the (legal or illegal) reuse in technical/scientific papers, determining the amount of modifications from one version of software to another, finding potential locations for redesign, or finding the amount of "reuse" in programs handed in by students for programming courses [CS96b].

Using the proposed measures, we investigated some sample literate programs. By taking a closer look at these programs, we found, that software reuse had been successfully done, i.e., source code and documentation had been reused.

Each system was created as a self-contained and homogeneous piece of work. In order to achieve this goal, reused parts from other systems had to be reworked and adapted carefully, if not the source code, then at least the documentation. Such adaptations included changing the system name (e.g., TeX to MetaFont), changing the word order or modifying single words for better layout results. This is white-box reuse at its best.

Writing and documenting software systems from scratch leads to different system and documentation structures than building them by reusing existing components. Even when writing and documenting a system from scratch, planning to deliver reusable components as a by-product leads to a different structure or at least to more self-containedness of the various components of the system.

If the TeX systems had been built with object-oriented techniques—which were not readily available at the time they were built—many classes could have been reused not by direct modifications but by inheritance. Documentation needs a similar approach to adaptation and reuse without direct modification. This is the topic of Chapter 20.

The books about the TeX system are perfectly harmonized. For example, the TeX book [Knu86b] has a lion as decoration at the beginning of each chapter. The MetaFont book [Knu86d] has a lioness. In an error message, when all anticipated help has already been given, the TeX user is invited to emulate Hercule Poirot. At the same point the MetaFont user is asked to emulate Miss Marple.

When software systems are written with so much care, it is a pleasure to read them. And it is possible, though not necessary, to read them sequentially from the beginning to the end. We argue that building software systems out of reusable components leads to thinner books with more cross-references. This makes sequential reading less pleasant, but it helps to make reading more efficient. Documentation must be designed for reuse the same way as source code has to be designed for reuse.

19.4 Summary

We have given a description and examples of reuse measurement with line and word runs. The application of this measurement to literate programs has been discussed. The results show the application of this measurement. The systems under investigation cannot be considered representative of a wide spectrum of software systems. However, the results indicate that documentation must be written with care equal to that for source code in order to make it reusable.

The documentation should have the same degree of explicit reuse as source code. Current techniques and tools do not sufficiently support this. In Chapter 20 we demonstrate a systematic way to reuse documentation.

20. Documentation Reuse

Contents

Documentation is an integral part of software components. When a component is reused, its documentation has to become part of the documentation of the system or component to be built. As components are adapted, modified and extended, their documentation must follow suit. We need a systematic way of reusing documentation in a similar fashion as we reuse components.

In this chapter we present inheritance as a means of systematically reusing documentation. After a short motivation in Section 20.1, we give an introduction to source code inheritance in Section 20.2. Subsequently, inheritance and related object-oriented concepts are applied to documentation text in Section 20.3. A summary follows in Section 20.4.

20.1 Motivation

Many components have similar functionality or exist in several variations; they may even have the same functionality but different implementations. Documentation of such components is likely to share many similarities and differ only in some aspects. Similar to components, it is important that documentation be reused in a systematic way.

Reusing software components is a typical task in object-oriented programming. Class libraries and application frameworks provide good examples of such reuse. Modification and extension of software components without the need to make changes to the original component is a big advantage of object-oriented technology. This is accomplished by defining classes by describing

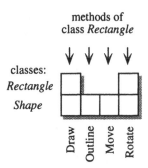

methods of
class *Rectangle*

classes:
Rectangle
Shape

Fig. 20.1. Source code inheritance

their differences, i.e., modifications and extensions to their base classes. Standard behavior is inherited from the base classes. Reusable software components that are realized in an object-oriented manner can have many things in common (through inheritance).

Adequate documentation is mandatory for software maintenance as well as for economic reuse of software components. Overlapping information is typical both for source code and for documentation. Therefore the inheritance mechanism should be applied to the documentation as well.

20.2 Source Code Inheritance

The source code of an object-oriented software system consists of classes containing variables (structure) and methods (behavior). Objects with the same structure and behavior are described in one class. From a documentor's point of view, classes and methods are equivalent to modules and procedures used in conventional programming. However, one of the differences between modules and classes is the inheritance relationship between classes. A class may inherit structure and behavior of another class and additionally extend and modify it.

For example, classes *Rectangle* and *Circle* inherit from a class *Shape*, which defines the structure and the behavior that is applicable to all graphical objects. *Rectangle* and *Circle* are called subclasses (or derived classes), and *Shape* is called the base class. The source code of the classes *Rectangle* and *Circle* contains only the modifications and extensions to the base class *Shape* (see Fig. 20.1).

The boxes in Fig. 20.1 indicate the existence of source code for a method. *Rectangle* objects can be drawn, outlined, moved and rotated, though the class *Rectangle* does not implement the methods *Outline* and *Move*; they are inherited from the base class *Shape*. The methods *Draw* and *Rotate* are overridden; i.e., *Rectangle* objects have their own *Draw* and *Rotate* methods; they do not use the methods of the *Shape* class. The arrows in Fig. 20.1

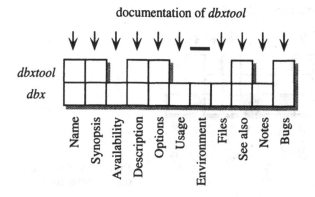

documentation of *dbxtool*

Fig. 20.2. Documentation inheritance

indicate the direction of view in order to determine the methods that are provided and used by class *Rectangle*.

20.3 Documentation Inheritance

As with object-oriented source code, documentation inherits the contents of its base documentation. We use documentation chapters and sections as units for inheritance. Chapters and sections are portions of documentation text with a title. Chapters are subdivided into sections, which may be further divided into subsections, etc. Chapters and sections are defined by the programmer/technical writer and used for inheritance in the same way as classes and methods, i.e., chapters and sections are either left unchanged, removed, replaced or extended.

Fig. 20.2 depicts the structure of the documentation of the Unix tools *dbx* and *dbxtool*. The documentation of *dbx* consists of eleven sections; *dbxtool* has six documentation sections. *dbxtool* inherits the sections 'Availability', 'Usage', 'Files' and 'Notes'. It has its own sections on 'Name', 'Synopsis', 'Description', 'Options' and 'See also'. The section 'Environment' is not applicable to *dbxtool* and thus is hidden. The bugs of *dbx* are also available in *dbxtool*, therefore the 'Bugs' section had been extended. For more details on this kind of documentation inheritance see Sametinger [Sam94].

20.3.1 Documentation Abstraction

In object-oriented programming, abstract classes are designed as parents from which subclasses may be derived. Abstract classes are not themselves suitable for instantiation. They are used to predefine certain structure and behavior which is then shared by a group of sibling subclasses. The subclasses add different variations of the missing pieces. Documentation has similar structure in many domains, e.g., manual pages and software life cycle documents. The

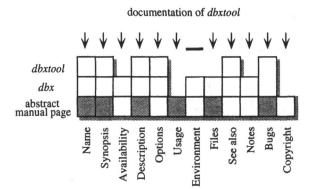

documentation of *dbxtool*

Fig. 20.3. Documentation abstraction

predefined structure for a certain group of documents guarantees uniform and consistent appearance. It is also possible to factor out common information for all the documents, making it easier to make modifications and keep information consistent. The definition of sections of the abstract documentation serves as a guide to consistent documentation and helps identify incomplete parts.

Fig. 20.3 provides another view of the documentation of *dbxtool* in terms of documentation abstraction. The documentation for "abstract manual page" defines twelve sections, of which six are designated for overriding (the sections 'Name', 'Synopsis', 'Description', 'Usage', 'Files' and 'Bugs'). If such a section is not overridden, as indicated in Fig. 20.3 for section 'Usage', then the inherited contents of the section should indicate that this information is missing and has to be provided.

Tool support is useful in checking the completeness of documentation and—if incomplete—in spotting missing sections. The abstract documentation in Fig. 20.3 contains an additional section 'Copyright', which is automatically included for all descriptions inherited therefrom.

Fig. 20.4 shows what the abstract documentation for manual pages could look like. Whenever manual pages for a new tool are written, the presence of "—*information not available*—" (which is inherited from the abstract manual page) indicates that there are still missing parts, i.e., sections of the documentation to be written.

20.3.2 Documentation Inclusions and References

For documentation to be readable, information should not be spread over several files and/or directories. We need either the full documentation of a component with all inherited documentation included, or cross-references to the inherited information (with page numbers for printed documentation or links for on-line documentation).

```
┌──────────────────────────────────────────────────────────┐
│ abstract manual page                                       │
│                                                            │
│ Name                                                       │
│ —information not available—                                │
│                                                            │
│ Synopsis                                                   │
│ —information not available—                                │
│                                                            │
│ Availability                                               │
│ Refer to "Installing OS 4.1" on how to install optional software. │
│                                                            │
│ Description                                                │
│ —information not available—                                │
│                                                            │
│ Options                                                    │
│ no options available                                       │
│                                                            │
│ See also                                                   │
│ OS 4.1 Programmer's Guide                                  │
│                                                            │
│ Notes                                                      │
│ no notes                                                   │
│                                                            │
│ Bugs                                                       │
│ —information not available—                                │
│                                                            │
│ Copyright                                                  │
│ by Horizon Aviation, 1997                                  │
└──────────────────────────────────────────────────────────┘
```

Fig. 20.4. Abstract manual page

Fig. 20.5 shows part of the documentation of a class *Collection*. The section 'Dynamic Creation and Object Copying' is inherited from class *Object* and can be read on page 34 of the documentation. In printed documentation references to page numbers avoid a waste of paper. For on-line documentation the inclusion of inherited sections may enhance readability and avoid the excessive use of links. Then too, it may make the document overly redundant.

It is also useful to have a table of contents for a unit, where for each section (including the inherited ones) the corresponding unit and the page number (printed documentation) or a link (on-line documentation) are specified.

20.3.3 Documentation Views

The amount of available information is constantly growing. Information filtering is important for efficient access. Defining categories for documentation sections is a simple, yet powerful mechanism to provide various views of a document and to meet different documentation needs of various readers. Fig. 20.6 shows what information might be provided to a casual user of *dbxtool*. A professional user would get the other sections as well.

When documenting source code, a useful control mechanism is the distinction among private, protected and public sections, as is done in the program-

---

Class Collection
base class for collections of objects
. . .

Collection Types
The subclasses of Collection implement different ways of storing
and accessing the objects. . . .

Dynamic Creation and Object Copying (class *Object***)**
see page 34.
. . .

Fig. 20.5. Sample (print) output with references

ming language C++. This distinction determines access rights for clients,
heirs and friends of classes. Public sections can be read by everyone and are
devoted to describing how to use a class. Protected sections contain more detailed information that is needed to build subclasses. Finally, private sections
contain additional implementation details that are exclusively intended for
development and maintenance personnel (see Fig. 20.7).

The whole documentation of a class (or a method) is visible only for
friends. Reusers who build subclasses (heirs) see only a subset of this documentation; they do not have access to private sections, which typically
describe implementation details ('Implementation' sections in Fig. 20.7).
Clients' access is further restricted to public sections, which contain general
interface descriptions ('Description', 'Layout', 'Method Descriptions' and 'Interfaces' in Fig. 20.7). Similarly to the source code, private sections of the
documentation are not inherited; i.e., private documentation of the class *Rectangle* does not become part of the documentation of any subclass thereof.

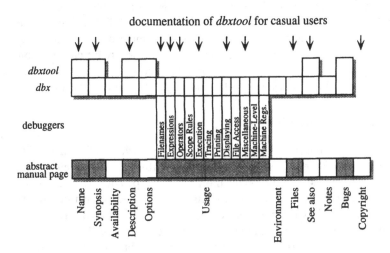

Fig. 20.6. A view of user documentation

documentation of class *Rectangle* for ...

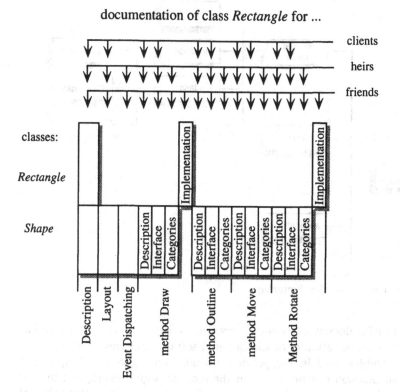

Fig. 20.7. Views for system documentation

20.3.4 Documentation Hierarchies

Documentation inheritance allows the definition of a hierarchy of documentation outlines for different kinds of components, as is depicted in Fig. 20.8. This guarantees a consistent documentation structure for all components, with adaptations according to the type of a component.

If a component is reused for the development of a software system, the component's documentation becomes part of the documentation of the entire system. Any adaptations made to the component have to be clearly documented as well. Ideally, this is done by documentation inheritance [Sam94] without any direct modifications to the original documentation.

20.4 Summary

In this chapter we have demonstrated how documentation inheritance can be used for systematic reuse of documentation. The concepts discussed can be applied to pure documentation (i.e., documentation without any source

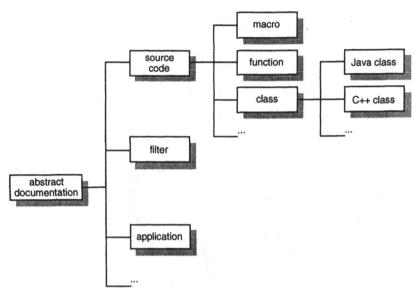

Fig. 20.8. Documentation hierarchy

code) to system documentation of conventional software systems, as well as to system documentation of object-oriented software systems.

The examples used in the previous sections have given a glimpse into how documentation can be reused in the manual page domain, i.e., in user documentation of tools and applications. Documenting an object-oriented software system provides the most obvious applicability of documentation reuse. If system documentation and source code are similarly structured, documentation reuse is a matter of fact.

The goal is to have software systems built from reusable components and to have their documentation built upon these components' documentation. Even though we are still a long way from that scenario, literate programming and explicit documentation reuse can help in improving the quality of software systems and in increasing the productivity of software engineers.

Tool support will be essential for the application of documentation reuse. So far only prototype implementations have been developed (see Childs and Sametinger [CS96a]).

Part V

Closing

21. Conclusion

Contents

There is still a long way to go until systematic reuse of software components, especially beyond company boundaries, will be a matter of fact. It requires more research in various areas as well as commitment from companies to systematic reuse.

In previous chapters we have covered aspects of software reuse, software components, software engineering and software documentation. In this final chapter we provide some concluding remarks. Thoughts on a paradigm shift that is caused by software components and software reuse are presented in Section 21.1. In Sections 21.2 and 21.3 we discuss limits and prospects of component reuse, respectively.

21.1 A Paradigm Shift

Scientists working in a certain field usually accept a set of rules, concepts and procedures. They conduct science in accordance with this set, which is called a paradigm. People working in a certain area try to obtain solutions, but they do not change these rules, concepts and procedures. However, unexpected discoveries may prove inconsistent with the prevailing paradigm. This may trigger a scientific revolution. A new paradigm emerges (*paradigm shift*) and normal scientific activity can be resumed under the new paradigm [Kuh70, Moo89]. Paradigm shifts, although rare, do occur, especially in natural sciences.

Paradigm shifts in software engineering involve the development of new ideas, new concepts, new methods, and also new problems [Fra94b]. A new paradigm gives deeper understanding of phenomena and provides a way of doing software engineering better and more efficiently. We argue that both software reuse and software components contribute to a paradigm shift in software engineering.

21.1.1 Software Components

Building software systems from components produces a major change in the way these systems work and in the way these systems are built. Procedure-oriented programming allows the definition of abstract actions that match the granularity of the tasks to be modeled; a software system is a sequence of actions. Wegner shows that software systems that are composed of collections of interacting entities can be interactive, open, distributed and better suited for change [Weg93].

The evolution of software engineering has not made a quantum leap from procedures to objects, but rather rather progressed in incremental steps. At the beginning algorithms were implemented with machine or assembler languages. High-level programming languages eased this task by providing procedures and functions. Abstract data structures, abstract data types, and finally objects have been important further improvements towards components.

We have defined components as arbitrary reusable entities including macros and functions. This broad definition avoids limitations of unavailability of component technology. Further research is necessary to make the next step beyond object-oriented technology. Then, components will most likely have all the properties that are shown for objects in Table 8.1 on page 109. However, components should have less coupling than objects and should be less dependent on software systems, i.e., not be inherent parts of systems like objects.

Wegner defines a component-based system as a system that has components as primitive description units and communication between components as computation units. "Components have an interface that specifies the interactions (messages) meaningful for that component. Programs are collections of interacting components and computations are patterns of message communication" [Weg93].

Component-based systems can better reflect properties that are needed in order to model large software systems. The software crisis is in part due to the fact that it is not possible to model large software systems as algorithms. Algorithmic programming is programming-in-the-small, whereas building software from interacting components is programming-in-the-large [Weg96]. Not the largeness is the main problem, but the required interactiveness, openness and distribution of today's software systems.

The behavior of software systems composed of objects or components cannot be modeled by algorithms which transform inputs to outputs independent of time [Weg96]. A combination of algorithms yields another, more complex algorithm that can be specified by means of an input/output function. Composing interactive components yields software systems whose behavior cannot be fully specified by the behavior of their components. Wegner shows that interactive systems cannot be modeled by reducible, compositional or complete formal systems [Weg96]. This is similar to Gödel's discovery that it is not possible to completely describe the behavior of integers by logic. Interaction machines are inherently incomplete and cannot be described with Turing machines.

Turing machines are the reference model for algorithmic computation. They are simple thought models that execute state transition instructions and transform finite sequences of input symbols to sequences of output symbols. Turing machines define the transformation power of computable functions. They do not accept any input from the external world during their computations. Thus passage of external time or interaction cannot be modeled. However, Turing machines can be extended to model interaction; the extensions are called interaction machines. Turing machines themselves lose their status as the most powerful computing mechanism [Weg96].

21.1.2 Software Reuse

Frakes argues that systematic software reuse amounts to a paradigm shift in software engineering [Fra94b]. Many new key activities for software engineering are introduced through software reuse as described in this book. Examples are domain analysis, development for/with reuse, reuse measurement, reuse certification, reuse classification and repository compilation. All these activities have spawned new questions and new research directions.

With systematic reuse, software engineering shifts from a discipline concerned with the construction of single systems to a discipline concerned with constructing related systems that share many commonalties and vary in regular and identifiable ways [Fra94b].

Some may think that it is extravagant to speak of a paradigm shift in software engineering. We argue that software reuse and software components provoke so many changes and innovations that this term is justified. For example, there has long been a discussion on whether the (*simple*) step from procedure-oriented to object-oriented programming is a revolution or an evolution. Many argue that object-oriented programming provides just another means of abstraction that can be used in certain situations, but often the *old* concepts are sufficient. We favor the other argument that object-oriented programming has brought a radical change in the way we design software systems, the shift already from algorithmic thinking to the creation of interactive components.

21.2 Limits of Component Reuse

Prevailing problems of component reuse emerge on examination of the steps involved in reusing a component, like classification, retrieval, comprehension, adaptation, integration, certification and generalization. Currently most research is being done in these areas. The most challenging aspect is component integration. Component coordination, communication and interoperation are important terms in this context (see Chapters 6 to 9).

We are still far from the scenario of composing most software systems from existing components. Many questions are still unanswered, and much research has to be done especially in the composability and interoperability of components. However, even if we somehow attain this goal, we will not get rid of all problems. It remains to be seen whether we can raise the abstraction levels of components and at the same time achieve high-performance systems by using these components. Performance is one of the key hindrances to clean software composition. Whenever abstraction levels have risen, lack of performance has resulted as well and efforts were made to circumvent these abstractions. This started decades earlier when compiler-generated code was not fast enough to compete with hand-written assembler code. At that time it was not unusual to write parts of systems that were crucial for the performance in assembler code. Fortunately, hardware has become fast enough that this is seldom necessary any longer. However, at almost any given time we have had abstraction mechanisms that drove our machines to their limits. Object-oriented programming, especially with Smalltalk, has long been unacceptable for production systems due to low performance. Today even interpreted Smalltalk systems are fast enough to be used in a wide range of applications. Communicating over a network or even among processes on a single machine slows down processing, but designing systems as cooperating processes has many advantages in flexibility, reliability and extensibility, and for many application domains the communication overhead is not a crucial point.

The question is whether we will be able to compose software systems out of prefabricated software components or whether we will fail because for many applications the overhead will subvert reasonably fast software systems? "Small is beautiful." Rethinking a problem may yield better solutions than just putting together complex components and summing up the unnecessary burden of multiple computations and needless calculations.

We have to accept a certain amount of overhead in order to increase productivity, but there are limits beyond which we obtain clumsy, oversized and probably useless systems. The goal of software composition is not just to effectively plug together as many components as possible; it is also a challenge to find the right size and functionality of components to justify a compromise between productivity and system performance.

Black-box reuse is another crucial point. For the interchangeability of components, it is necessary to refrain from relying on any internals of components. While we may want to avoid white-box reuse, glass-box reuse may be an alternative in some situations. Influencing the performance characteristics of components by parameterization may help in many situations to reduce performance overhead and to increase the components' reusability.

Kiczales introduces the term "mapping dilemma" [Kic94]. This means that even though certain implementation issues of a component should be hidden in a black box, they affect the performance based on the client's use patterns. There are many examples of such dilemmas. A spreadsheet program could be composed of many (e.g., 100 times 100) components (in fact 10,000 instantiations of one component) that are fully capable of text editing and window display, etc., but it will not work efficiently that way. Even if it works at all, it will take another hundred years until hardware is fast enough to cope with such a design. Virtual memory is another example mentioned by Kiczales [Kic94]. Different page replacement policies are possible. Depending on the application, one policy or another may be an advantage or a big disadvantage. If a graphics editor displays all the graphical objects on the screen there should definitely not be a page fault in the process.

Biggerstaff argues that "formal representation options available today for expressing reusable components—notably, programming languages—are excessively concrete," which "imposes a built-in barrier to widespread and high payoff reuse of those components" [Big93]. A key factor for reuse failure is the lack of abstraction of reusable components. This argument goes against purely compositional reuse and suggests a combination with generative reuse as described by Neighbors [Nei89]. Possible components in today's programming languages are macros, classes, generics and templates. These components are concrete; i.e., implementation details are introduced too early. Reuse has to escape the bounds of concrete representations, which, according to Biggerstaff, requires a mixture of generation and composition [Big93]. We argue that generative reuse will be useful in certain domains, but the limits of component reuse can be surpassed only by higher abstractions that go beyond programming languages. New programming languages are still needed to build these high-level components. Significant reuse benefits will be reaped at the level of interactive, executable components.

21.3 Prospects

Increased reuse of software components represents a different way to build software systems. Not only does reuse provide a more productive way to create new software, systems composed of components also facilitate modifications to these systems. The goal must bei to evolve software. It has long become clear that today's and definitely tomorrow's software systems are too complex and too expensive to be built according to predefined requirements and specifications. Ever-changing requirements have to be taken into consideration from the very start of a software project. Composing systems from components should allow us to add, remove and exchange parts of systems without the need to completely replace systems after a few years. This will help to keep old software up-to-date by integrating new components.

We have to avoid legacy software, i.e., software systems being antique and unmaintainable, but indispensable for companies like the air traffic control system mentioned in Chapter 1. Air traffic is still booming and we can bet that requirements for air traffic control will considerably change (evolve) over the next decades. We cannot build systems that have today's requirements hard-wired in them and expect not to have troubles in the future. Building clean architectures and composing software from components will help in adapting to ever changing requirements even if the components of the system are never reused in another system.

The landscape of software systems will constantly change from closed monolithic systems to open systems composed of reusable components.

References

[And91]   G.R. Andrews. Paradigms for process interaction in distributed programs. *ACM Computing Surveys*, 23:49–90, June 1991.

[AO90]   Adrian Avenarius and Siegfried Oppermann. FWeb: A literate programming system for Fortran 8X. *ACM SIGPLAN Notices*, 25(1):52–58, January 1990.

[Api95]   Steve Apiki. OLE controls from the ground up. *Byte*, pages 169–170, June 1995.

[App95]   Apple Computer Inc. OpenDoc: Frequently asked questions, 1995. http://opendoc.apple.com/info/faq.html.

[Ara94a] Guillermo Arango. Domain analysis. In Marciniak [Mar94], pages 424–434. 1994.

[Ara94b] Guillermo Arango. Domain analysis methods. In Schäfer et al. [SPM94], chapter 2, pages 17–49. 1994.

[Bau93]   Dorothea A. Bauer. A reusable parts center. *IBM Systems Journal*, 32(4):620–624, 1993.

[BB91]   Bruce H. Barnes and Terry B. Bollinger. Making reuse cost-effective. *IEEE Software*, 8:13–24, January 1991.

[BBC+94] Paula Bell, Christine Browning, Saul Carliner, Mary Lou Nohr, and Judy Williams. Documentation. In Marciniak [Mar94], pages 407–419. 1994.

[BD93]   Alan Burns and Geoff Davies. *Concurrent Programming*. Addison-Wesley, 1993.

[BEK+96] Tim Bardo, Dave Elliot, Tony Krysak, Mike Morgan, Rebecca Shuey, and Will Tracz. Core: A product line success story. *Crosstalk: The Journal of Defense Software Engineering*, 9(3):24–28, March 1996.

[Big93]   Ted J. Biggerstaff. The limits of concrete component reuse. In *WISR 6* [WIS93]. 1993.

[BKZ93]   Rajiv D. Banker, Robert J. Kauffman, and D. Zweig. Repository evaluation of software reuse. *IEEE Transactions on Software Engineering*, 19(4):379–389, April 1993.

[Blu92]   Bruce I. Blum. *Software Engineering: A Holistic View*. Oxford University Press, 1992.

[BM92]   Elizabeth L. Burd and John A. McDermid. Guiding reuse with risk assessments. Technical Report YCS-92-183, University of York, 1992.

[BO92]   Don Batory and Sean O'Malley. The design and implementation of hierarchical software systems with reusable components. *ACM Transactions on Software Engineering and Methodology*, 1(4):355–398, October 1992.

[Boe81]   Barry W. Boehm. *Software Engineering Economics*. Prentice Hall, 1981.

[Boe88]   Barry W. Boehm. A spiral model of software development and enhancement. *IEEE Software*, 25(5):61–72, May 1988.

242   References

[Boe91]   Barry W. Boehm. Software risk management: Principles and practice. *IEEE Software*, pages 32–41, January 1991.

[Boe96]   Barry W. Boehm. Software reuse economics. In Sitaraman [Sit96], page 20. 1996.

[Boo87]   Grady Booch. *Software Components with Ada: Structures, Tools, and Subsystems.* Benjamin/Cummings Publishing Company, Inc., Menlo Park, CA, 1987.

[BP89a]   Ted J. Biggerstaff and Alan J. Perlis, editors. *Software Reusability, Vol. I: Concepts and Models.* ACM Press, 1989.

[BP89b]   Ted J. Biggerstaff and Alan J. Perlis, editors. *Software Reusability, Vol. II: Applications and Experience.* ACM Press, 1989.

[BR88]   Victor R. Basili and Hans Dieter Rombach. Towards a comprehensive framework for reuse: A reuse-enabling software evolution environment. Technical Report CS-TR-2158, University of Maryland, December 1988.

[BR89]   Ted J. Biggerstaff and Charles Richter. Reusability framework, assessment, and directions. In Biggerstaff and Perlis [BP89a], pages 1–17. 1989.

[BR92]   F. Bott and M. Ratcliffe. Reuse and design. In Hall [Hal92], pages 35–51. 1992.

[Bra94a] Christine L. Braun. NATO standard for the development of reusable software components, volume 1 (of 3 documents), 1994.
          http://wuarchive.wustl.edu/languages/ada/docs/nato_ru/ (Public Ada Library).

[Bra94b] Christine L. Braun. NATO standard for management of a reusable software component library, volume 2 (of 3 documents), 1994.
          http://wuarchive.wustl.edu/languages/ada/docs/nato_ru/ (Public Ada Library).

[Bra94c] Christine L. Braun. NATO standard for software reuse procedures, volume 3 (of 3 documents), 1994.
          http://wuarchive.wustl.edu/languages/ada/docs/nato_ru/ (Public Ada Library).

[Bra94d] Christine L. Braun. Reuse. In Marciniak [Mar94], pages 1055–1069. 1994.

[Bro75]   F. P. Brooks, Jr. *The Mythical Man-Month.* Addison-Wesley, 1975.

[BST89]   Henri E. Bal, Jennifer G. Steiner, and Andrew S. Tanenbaum. Programming languages for distributed computing systems. *ACM Computing Surveys*, 21(3):261–322, September 1989.

[BST+94] Don Batory, V. Singhal, J. Thomas, S. Dasari, B. Geraci, and M. Sirkin. The GenVoca model of software-system generators. *IEEE Software*, 11(5):89–94, September 1994.

[CC94]   Dave Card and Ed Comer. Why do so many reuse programs fail? *IEEE Software*, 11(5):114(2), September 1994.

[Che89]   Thomas E. Cheatham, Jr. Reusability through program transformations. In Biggerstaff and Perlis [BP89a], pages 321–335. 1989.

[Chi91]   Bart Childs. Literate programming, a practitioner's view. *TUGboat, Proceedings of the 1991 Annual Meeting*, 12(3):1001–1008, 1991.

[CL95]   Marhall P. Cline and Greg A. Lomow. *C++ FAQs: Frequently Asked Questions.* Addison-Wesley, 1995.

[Cle88]   J. Cleaveland. Building application generators. *IEEE Software*, 5(6):25–33, July 1988.

[Coa92]   Peter Coad. Object-oriented patterns. *Communications of the ACM*, 35(9):152–159, 1992.

[Coo94]   Jack Cooper. Reuse-the business implications. In Marciniak [Mar94], pages 1071–1077. 1994.

[CS96a]   Bart Childs and Johannes Sametinger. Literate programming and documentation reuse. In Sitaraman [Sit96], pages 205–214. 1996.

[CS96b]   Bart Childs and Johannes Sametinger. Reuse measurement with line and word runs. *TOOLS Pacific '96*, November 1996.

[CS97]   Bart Childs and Johannes Sametinger. Analysis of literate programs from the viewpoint of reuse. *Software—Concepts & Tools*, 18(1), 1997.

[CSPK92] S. Cohen, J. Stanley, Jr, A. Peterson, and R. Krut, Jr. Application of feature-oriented domain analysis to the army movement control domain. Technical Report CMU/SEI-91-TR-28, Software Engineering Institute, Carnegie Mellon University, June 1992.

[Dew79]   M. Dewey. *Decimal Classification and Relative Index*. Forest Press Inc., 19th edition, 1979.

[DF93]   Paolino Di Felice. Reusability of mathematical software: A contribution. *IEEE Transactions on Software Engineering*, 19(8):835–843, August 1993.

[DFSS89] Ed Dubinsky, Stefan Freudenberger, Edith Schonberg, and J. T. Schwartz. Reusability of design for large software systems: An experiment with the SETL optimizer. In Biggerstaff and Perlis [BP89a], pages 275–293. 1989.

[DJ95]   Herbert L. Dershem and Michael J. Jipping. *Programming Languages: Structures and Models*. PWS Publishing Company, 2nd edition, 1995.

[DK93]   Michael F. Dunn and John C. Knight. Certification of reusable software parts. Technical Report CS-93-41, University of Virginia, August 31,, 1993.

[dM95]   Vicki de Mey. Visual composition of software applications. In Nierstrasz and Tsichritzis [NT95], pages 275–303. 1995.

[DS94]   Gail Dutton and Dave Sims. Patterns in oo design and code could improve reuse. *IEEE Software*, 11:101, May 1994.

[DvK87]   E.M. Dusink and J. van Katwijk. Reflections on reusable software and software components. In Tafvelin [Taf87], pages 113–126. 1987.

[DW92]   Ted Davis and Roger Williams. Toward a reuse maturity model. In *WISR 5* [WIS92]. 1992.

[Ell96]   Michael Elliot. Implementing o-o design concepts with literate programming. In Mitchell et al. [MNM96], pages 29–43. 1996.

[Faf94]   Danielle Fafchamps. Organizational factors and reuse. *IEEE Software*, 11(5):31–41, September 1994.

[FI94]   William B. Frakes and Sadahiro Isoda. Success factors of systematic reuse. *IEEE Software*, 11(5):15(5), September 1994.

[FP94]   William B. Frakes and Thomas P. Pole. An empirical study of representation methods for reusable software components. *IEEE Transactions on Software Engineering*, 20(8):617–630, August 1994.

[Fra94a] William B. Frakes, editor. *3rd International Conference on Software Reuse*, Rio de Janeiro, Brazil, November 1–4, 1994. IEEE Computer Society Press.

[Fra94b] William B. Frakes. Systematic software reuse: A paradigm shift. In *3rd International Conference on Software Reuse* [Fra94a], pages 2–3. 1994.

[Fra95a] Frame. *Frame Developer's Kit: Programmer's Guide*. Frame Technology, Release 5, 1995.

[Fra95b] Frame. *Using FrameMaker*. Frame Technology, Release 5, 1995.

[Fre87a] Peter Freeman. Reusable software engineering concepts and research directions. In *Tutorial: Software Reusability* [Fre87b], pages 10–23. 1983.

[Fre87b] Peter Freeman, editor. *Tutorial: Software Reusability*. IEEE Computer Society Press, 1987.

244   References

[GAO95]   David Garlan, R. Allen, and J. Ockerbloom. Architectural mismatch or why it's hard to build systems out of existing parts. In *ICSE 17*, pages 179–185. Seattle, WA, April 23–30, 1995. 1995.

[Gar95]   David Garlan. Research directions in software architecture. *ACM Computing Surveys*, 27(2):257–261, June 1995.

[Ge93]   Erich Gamma and et al. Design patterns: Abstraction and reuse of object-oriented design. In *European Conference on Object-Oriented Programming (ECOOP)*. Kaiserslautern, Germany, 1993.

[GFW94]   Martin L. Griss, John Favaro, and Paul Walton. Managerial and organizational issues— starting and running a software reuse program. In Schäfer et al. [SPM94], chapter 3, pages 51–78. 1994.

[GHJV95] Erich Gamma, Richard Helm, Ralph Johnson, and John Vlissides. *Design Patterns: Elements of Reusable Object-Oriented Software*. Addison-Wesley, 1995.

[GM95]   James Gosling and Henry McGilton. The Java programming language, 1995. OOPSLA '95 Tutorial Notes, Austin, TX.

[GR95]   Adele Goldberg and Kenneth S. Rubin. *Succeeding with Objects: Decision Frameworks for Project Management*. Addison-Wesley, 1995.

[Gri93]   Martin L. Griss. Software reuse: from library to factory. *IBM Systems Journal*, 32(4):548–566, 1993.

[GS94]   David Garlan and Mary Shaw. An introduction to software architecture. Technical Report CMU/SEI-94-TR-21, Software Engineering Institute, Carnegie Mellon University, 1994.

[Hal92]   P.A.V. Hall, editor. *Software Reuse and Reverse Engineering in Practice*. Chapman & Hall, 1992.

[HC91]   James W. Hooper and Rowena O. Chester. *Software reuse: Guidelines and Methods*. Plenum Press, New York, 1991.

[HCK+90] James A. Hess, Sholom G. Cohen, Kyo C. Kang, A. Spencer Peterson, and William E. Novak. Feature-oriented domain analysis (FODA) feasibility study. Technical Report CMU/EI-90-TR-21, Software Engineering Institute, Carnegie Mellon University, 1990.

[HKN85]   E. Horowitz, A. Kemper, and B. Narasimhan. A survey of application generators. *IEEE Software*, 2(1):40–54, January 1985.

[Hol92]   Joseph Eugene Hollingsworth. *Software Component Design-for-Reuse: A Language-Independent Discipline Applied to Ada*. PhD thesis, Ohio State University, 1992.

[Hor93]   Ken Horner. More to reuse than objects. *Software Magazine*, 13(7):6(2), May 1993.

[HP88]   Robert Holibaugh and J. Perry. Phase I testbed description: Requirements and selection guidelines. Technical Report CMU/SEI-88-TR-13, Software Engineering Institute, Carnegie Mellon University, September 1988.

[HS93]   Brian Henderson-Sellers. The economics of reusing library classes. *Journal of Object-Oriented Programming*, 6(4):43–50, July-August 1993.

[Hub94]   Theresa R. Huber. Reducing business and legal risks in software reuse libraries. In Frakes [Fra94a], pages 110–117. 1994.

[ICS94]   *ICSE 16: 16th International Conference on Software Engineering*, Sorrento, Italy, May 16–21, 1994.

[Jal94]   Pankaj Jalote. *Fault Tolerance in Distributed Systems*. Prentice Hall, 1994.

[Joc95]   Alan Joch. How software doesn't work. *Byte*, 20(12):49–60, December 1995.

[Jon84]   Capers T. Jones. Reusability in programming: A survey of the state of the art. *IEEE Transactions on Software Engineering*, 10(5):488–494, September 1984.

[Jon94]   Capers Jones. Economics of software reuse. *Computer*, 27:106–107, July 1994.

[Joo94]   Rebecca Joos. Software reuse at Motorola. *IEEE Software*, 11(5):42(6), September 1994.

[Kai96]   J. Bradford Kain. Components: The basics: Enabling an application or system to be the sum of its parts. *Object Magazine*, 6(2):64–69, April 1996.

[Kan87]   Kyo C. Kang. A reuse-based software development methodology. In *Workshop on Software Reuse*. Boulder, CO, October 1987.

[Kan89]   Kyo C. Kang. Features analysis: An approach to domain analysis. In J. Baldo and Christine L. Braun, editors, *Reuse in Practice Workshop*. Pittsburgh, Penn., July 1989.

[Kar95]   Even-André Karlsson, editor. *Software Reuse: A Holistic Approach*. John Wiley & Sons, 1995.

[Ker84]   Brian Kernighan. The Unix system and software reusability. *IEEE Transactions on Software Engineering*, SE-10(5):513–, 1984.

[KH91]   Philip Koltun and Anita Hudson. A reuse maturity model. In *WISR 4* [WIS91]. 1991.

[Kic94]   Gregor Kiczales. Why are black boxes so hard to reuse? Towards a new model of abstraction in the engineering of software. In *Invited Talk at OOPSLA'94 (Portland, OR) and ICSE-17 (Seattle, WA)*, 1994.

[KL93]   Donald E. Knuth and Silvio Levy. *The CWeb System of Structured Documentation, Version 3.0*. Addison-Wesley, 1993.

[Knu73a]   Donald E. Knuth. *The Art of Computer Programming, Vol. I: Fundamental Algorithms*. Addison-Wesley, 1973.

[Knu73b]   Donald E. Knuth. *The Art of Computer Programming, Vol. II: Seminumerical Algorithms*. Addison-Wesley, 1973.

[Knu73c]   Donald E. Knuth. *The Art of Computer Programming, Vol. III: Sorting and Searching*. Addison-Wesley, 1973.

[Knu84]   Donald E. Knuth. Literate programming. *IEEE Computer Journal*, 27(2):97–111, 1984.

[Knu86a]   Donald E. Knuth. *The TEX Book*, volume A of Computers & Typesetting. Addison-Wesley, 1986.

[Knu86b]   Donald E. Knuth. *TEX: The Program*, volume B of Computers & Typesetting. Addison-Wesley, 1986.

[Knu86c]   Donald E. Knuth. *The MetaFont Book*, volume C of Computers & Typesetting. Addison-Wesley, 1986.

[Knu86d]   Donald E. Knuth. *MetaFont: The Program*, volume D of Computers & Typesetting. Addison-Wesley, 1986.

[Knu92]   Donald E. Knuth. *Literate Programming*. Leland Stanford Junior University, 1992.

[Kon95]   Dimitri Konstantas. Interoperation of object-oriented applications. In Nierstrasz and Tsichritzis [NT95], pages 69–95. 1995.

[Kro90]   John Krommes. FWeb (Krommes) vs. FWeb (Avenarius and Oppermann). *TEXhax*, 90(19), 1990.

[Kru92]   Charles W. Krueger. Software reuse. *ACM Computing Surveys*, 24:131–83, June 1992.

[Kuh70]   Thomas S. Kuhn. *The Structure of Scientific Revolutions*. Chicago University Press, 2nd edition, 1970.

[Lev86] L. S. Levy. A metaprogramming method and its economic justification. *IEEE Transactions on Software Engineering*, 12(2):272–277, February 1986.

[Lev93] Silvio Levy. Literate programming and CWeb. *Journal on Computer Language*, 10(1):67–70, January 1993.

[LI93]   Mitchell D. Lubars and Neil Iscoe. Frameworks versus libraries: A dichotomy of reuse strategies. In *WISR 6* [WIS93]. 1993.

[Lib90] Don Libes. expect: Curing those uncontrollable fits of interaction. In *Summer 1990 USENIX Conference*. Anaheim, CA, June 1990.

[Lim94] Wayne C. Lim. Effects of reuse on quality, productivity, and economics. *IEEE Software*, 11(5):23(8), September 1994.

[Lim95] Wayne C. Lim. *Managing Software Reuse*. Prentice Hall, 1995.

[Mal93] Ruth A. Malan. Motivating software reuse. In *WISR 6* [WIS93]. 1993.

[Mar90] J. Martin. *Information Enginnering Book III: Design and Construction*. Prentice Hall, 1990.

[Mar94] John J. Marciniak, editor. *Encyclopedia of Software Engineering*. John Wiley & Sons, 1994.

[MB87]   J. Margono and E.V. Berard. A modified Booch's taxonomy for Ada generic data-structure components and their implementation. In Tafvelin [Taf87], pages 61–74. 1987.

[McI76] M. D. McIlroy. Mass produced software components. In J.M. Buxton, P. Naur, and B. Randell, editors, *Software Engineering Concepts and Techniques*, pages 88–98, 1968 NATO Conference on Software Engineering, 1976. 1968.

[MDK96] John D. McGregor, Jim Doble, and Asha Keddy. A pattern for reuse: Let architectural reuse guide component reuse. *Object Magazine*, 6(2):38–47, April 1996.

[Mer94] Steven Merrit. Reuse library. In Marciniak [Mar94], pages 1069–1071. 1994.

[Met94] Meta Group. *Component Software*. Meta Group, Inc., December 5 1994. White Paper.

[Mey88] Bertrand Meyer. *Object-Oriented Software Construction*. Prentice Hall, 1988.

[Mey92] Bertrand Meyer. *Eiffel: The Language*. Prentice Hall, second printing edition, 1992.

[Mey94] Bertrand Meyer. *Reusable Software: The Base object-oriented component libraries*. Prentice Hall, 1994.

[Mic93a] Microsoft. *VisualBasic: Professional Features, Book 1, V3.0*. Microsoft Corporation, 1993.

[Mic93b] Microsoft. *VisualBasic: Professional Features, Book 2, V3.0*. Microsoft Corporation, 1993.

[Mic93c] Microsoft. *VisualBasic: Programmer's Guide, V3.0*. Microsoft Corporation, 1993.

[Min85] Marvin Minsky. *The Society of Mind*. Simon and Schuster, 1985.

[MMM95] Hafedh Mili, Fatma Mili, and Ali Mili. Reusing software: Issues and research directions. *IEEE Transactions on Software Engineering*, 21(6):528–562, June 1995.

[MNM96] Richard Mitchell, Jean-Marc Nerson, and Bertrand Meyer, editors. *TOOLS 19: Technology of Object-Oriented Languages and Systems*, Paris, France, 1996. Prentice Hall.

[Moo89] Walter Moore. *Schrödinger: Life and Thought*. Cambridge University Press, 1989.

[Moo94] James W. Moore. Debate on software reuse libraries. In Frakes [Fra94a], pages 203–204. 1994.

[Mor91] John S. Morrison. The emerging market in adaptable and reusable software components—impact on system engineering and enterprise integration. In WISR 4 [WIS91]. 1991.

[MR90] Roland T. Mittermeir and Wilhelm Rossak. Reusability. In Ng and Yeh [NY90], chapter 7, pages 205–235. 1990.

[Mye86] Brad A. Myers. Visual programming, programming by example, and program visualization: A taxonomy. In CHI '86, Human Factors in Computing Systems, pages 59–66. 1986.

[MZ95] J. Thomas Mowbray and Ron Zahavi. The Essential Corba: Systems Integration Using Distributed Objects. John Wiley & Sons, 1995.

[Nav92] James J. Navarro. Organization design for software reuse. In WISR 5 [WIS92]. 1992.

[Nav93] James J. Navarro. Organization design-based software reuse adoption strategy. In WISR 6 [WIS93]. 1993.

[ND95] Oscar Nierstrasz and Laurent Dami. Component-oriented software technology. In Nierstrasz and Tsichritzis [NT95], pages 3–28. 1995.

[Nei89] James M. Neighbors. Draco: A method for engineering reusable software systems. In Biggerstaff and Perlis [BP89a], pages 295–319. 1989.

[Nie95] Oscar Nierstrasz. Research topics in software composition. In A. Napoli, editor, LMO '95: Langages et Modèles à Objets, pages 193–204. Nancy, France, October 12–13 1995.

[NM95] Oscar Nierstrasz and Theo Dirk Meijler. Research directions in software composition. ACM Computing Surveys, 27(2):262–264, June 1995.

[NT95] Oscar Nierstrasz and Dennis Tsichritzis, editors. Object-Oriented Software Composition. Prentice Hall International, December 1995.

[NY90] Peter A. Ng and Raymond T. Yeh, editors. Modern Software Engineering: Foundations and Current Perspectives. Van Nostrand Reinhold, 1990.

[Ous90] John K. Ousterhout. Tcl: An embeddable command language. In Winter USENIX Conference, 1990.

[Ous94] John K. Ousterhout. Tcl and the Tk Toolkit. Addison-Wesley, 1994.

[PC91] A. Peterson and S. Cohen. A context analysis of the movement control domain for the army tactical command and control system (atccs). Technical Report CMU/SEI-91-SR-3, Software Engineering Institute, Carnegie Mellon University, 1991.

[Pet96] A. S. Peterson. Features–the heart of object integration. In Sitaraman [Sit96], pages 227–228. 1996.

[PF87] Rubén Prieto-Díaz and Peter Freeman. Classifying software for reusability. IEEE Software, pages 6–16, January 1987.

[PF93] Rubén Prieto-Díaz and William B. Frakes. Advances in Software reuse. IEEE Computer Society Press, 1993.

[Pit93] Matthew Pittman. Managing reuse: Exposing the hidden agenda. IEEE Software, 10(1):46–47, January 1993.

[Pom84] Gustav Pomberger. Software Engineering and Modula-2. Prentice Hall International, 1984.

[Pou92] Jeffrey S. Poulin. Measuring reuse. In WISR 5 [WIS92]. 1992.

[Pou95] Jeffrey S. Poulin. Populating software repositories: Incentives and domain-specific software. The Journal of Systems and Software, 30(3):187–199, September 1995.

[Pre92] Roger S. Pressman. Software Engineering: A Practitioner's Approach. McGraw-Hill, 3rd edition, 1992.

[Pre95]   Wolfgang Pree. *Design Patterns for Object-Oriented Software Development.* Addison-Wesley, 1995.

[Pri87]   Rubén Prieto-Díaz. Domain analysis for reusability. In *COMPSAC 87*, pages 225–234. Tokyo, Japan, 1987.

[Pri89]   Rubén Prieto-Díaz. Classification of reusable modules. In Biggerstaff and Perlis [BP89a], pages 99–123. 1989.

[Pri90]   Rubén Prieto-Díaz. Domain analysis: An introduction. *ACM SIGSOFT Software Engineering Notes*, 15(2):47–54, April 1990.

[Pri91a]   Rubén Prieto-Díaz. A domain analysis methodology. In *Workshop on Domain Modeling for Software Engineering (ICSE13)*, 1991. Position Abstract.

[Pri91b]   Rubén Prieto-Díaz. Implementing faceted classification for software reuse. *Communications of the ACM*, 34(5):88–97, May 1991.

[Pri91c]   Rubén Prieto-Díaz. Making software reuse work: An implementation model. *ACM SIGSOFT Software Engineering Notes*, 16(3):61–68, July 1991.

[Pri93a]   Rubén Prieto-Díaz. *Software Reuse: From Concepts to Implementation.* Tutorial: International Symposium on Applied Computing (ISAC), 1993.

[Pri93b]   Rubén Prieto-Díaz. Status report: Software reusability. *IEEE Software*, 10(3):61–66, May 1993.

[Pri94]   Rubén Prieto-Díaz. Historical overview. In Schäfer et al. [SPM94], chapter 1, pages 1–16. 1994.

[PSC+92]   Sukesh Patel, Alan Stein, Paul Cohen, Rich Baxter, and Steve Sherman. Certification of reusable software components. In *WISR 5* [WIS92]. 1992.

[PY93]   Jeffrey S. Poulin and Kathryn P. Yglesias. Experiences with a faceted classification scheme in a large reusable software library (RSL). In *Seventeenth Annual International Computer Software and Applications Conference*, pages 90–99. Phoenix, AZ, November 3–5 1993.

[QW93]   John S. Quarterman and Susanne Wilhelm. *UNIX, POSIX, and Open Systems.* Addison-Wesley, 1993.

[Ram94]   Norman Ramsey. Literate programming simplified. *IEEE Software*, 11(5):97–105, September 1994.

[Rei95a]   Steven P. Reiss. *The FIELD Programming Environment: A Friendly Integrated Environment for Learning and Development.* Kluwer Academic Publishers, 1995.

[Rei95b]   Steven P. Reiss. Fragments: A mechanism for low cost data integration. Technical report, Brown University, Dept. of Computer Science, 1995.

[Ren94]   John Rennie. OpenDoc, IBM and Apple's pitfall for mega-applications. *Scientific American*, pages 130–131, October 1994.

[RGI94]   Maria del Rosario Girardi and Bertrand Ibrahim. Automatic indexing of software artifacts. In Frakes [Fra94a], pages 24–32. 1994.

[RGI95]   Maria del Rosario Girardi and Bertrand Ibrahim. Using English to retrieve software. *The Journal of Systems and Software*, 30(3):249–270, September 1995.

[RGM94]   J. Rymer, M. Guttman, and J. Matthews. Microsoft OLE 2.0 and the road to Cairo; how object linking and embedding will lead to distributed object computing. *Distributed Computing Monitor*, 9(1):3(24), January 1994.

[RW92]   M. Reiser and N. Wirth. *Programming in Oberon: Steps beyond Pascal and Modula.* Addison-Wesley, 1992.

[Sam94]   Johannes Sametinger. Object-oriented documentation. *ACM Journal of Systems Documentation*, 18(1):3–14, January 1994.

[Sam96]   Johannes Sametinger. Reuse documentation and documentation reuse. In Mitchell et al. [MNM96], pages 17–28. 1996.

[SB93]   Vivek Singhal and Don Batory. P++: A language for large-scale reusable software components. In *WISR 6* [WIS93]. 1993.

[Sel89]   Richard W. Selby. Quantitative studies of software reuse. In Biggerstaff and Perlis [BP89b], pages 213–233. 1989.

[SG94]   Mary Shaw and David Garlan. Characteristics of higher-level languages for software architecture. Technical Report CMU-CS-94-210, CMU/SEI-94-TR-23, Software Engineering Institute, Carnegie Mellon University, December 1994.

[Sha94]   Mary Shaw. Procedure calls are the assembly language of software interconnection: Connectors deserve first-class status. Technical Report CMU/SEI-94-TR-2, ADA281026, Software Engineering Institute, Carnegie Mellon University, 1994.

[Sha95]   Mary Shaw. Architectural issues in software reuse: It's not just the functionality, it's the packaging. In Mansur Samadzadeh and Mansour Zand, editors, *SSR '95: ACM SIGSOFT Symposium on Software Reusability*, pages 3–6. ACM Press, Seattle, WA, April 28-30, 1995. 1995.

[Sit96]   Murali Sitaraman, editor. *4th International Conference on Software Reuse*, Orlando, Florida, April 23–26, 1996. IEEE Computer Society Press.

[Smo96]   Smolowe. Out-of-control tower. *TIME*, 147(8):52–53, February 19 1996.

[Som92]   Ian Sommerville. *Software Engineering*. Addison-Wesley, 4th edition, 1992.

[SPM94]   Wilhelm Schäfer, Rubén Prieto-Díaz, and Masao Matsumoto, editors. *Software Reusability*. Ellis Horwood, New York, 1994.

[SS92]   Johannes Sametinger and Alois Stritzinger. Exploratory software development with class libraries. In *Shifting Paradigms in Software Engineering*. Springer Verlag, Klagenfurt, Austria, 1992.

[Sta86]   R. Stallman. *GNU Emacs Manual*. 4th edition, February 1986. V17.

[STA93]   STARS. Application engineering with domain-specific reuse. Technical Report STARS-AC-04102B/001/00, Informal Technical Report for the STARS Program, (Course Description), June 1993.

[Str94]   Bjarne Stroustrup. *The Design and Evolution of C++*. Addison-Wesley, 1994.

[Sun96]   Sun Microsystems. Java Beans: A component architecture for Java. December 1996.
http://splash.javasoft.com/beans/WhitePaper.html.

[Szy95]   Clemens Szyperski. Component-oriented programming: A refined variation on object-oriented programming. *The Oberon Tribune*, 1(2):1, 4–6, December 1995.

[Taf87]   Sven Tafvelin, editor. *Ada Components: Libraries and Tools, Proceedings of the Ada-Europe International Conference*, Stockholm, May 26–28, 1987. Cambridge University Press.

[Tai93]   Antero Taivalsaari. *A Critical View of Inheritance and Reusability in Object-oriented Programming*. PhD thesis, University of Jyväskylä, Finland, 1993.

[TBSS93]   Jeff Thomas, Don Batory, Vivek Singhal, and Marty Sirkin. A scalable approach to software libraries. In *WISR 6* [WIS93]. 1993.

[TG93]   J. R. Tirso and H. Gregorius. Management of reuse at IBM. *IBM Systems Journal*, 32(4):612–615, 1993.

[Tra88a]   Will Tracz. Software reuse: Motivators and inhibitors. In *Tutorial: Software Reuse: Emerging Technology* [Tra88b], pages 62–67. 1987.

[Tra88b] Will Tracz, editor. *Tutorial: Software Reuse: Emerging Technology.* IEEE Computer Society Press, 1988.

[Tra94] Will Tracz. Software reuse myths revisited. In *ICSE 16* [ICS94], pages 271–272. 1994.

[Tra95] Will Tracz. *Confessions of a Used Program Salesman: Instituionalizing Software Reuse.* Addison-Wesley, 1995.

[Uma93] Amjad Umar. *Distributed Computing: A Practical Synthesis.* Prentice Hall, 1993.

[VB96] Vijay K. Vaishnavi and Rajendra K. Bandi. Measuring reuse. *Object Magazine*, 6(2):53–57, April 1996.

[VK89] Dennis M. Volpano and Richard B. Kieburtz. The template approach to software reuse. In Biggerstaff and Perlis [BP89a], pages 247–255. 1989.

[Wan94] Paul S. Wang. *C++ with Object-Oriented Programming.* POWs Publishing Company, 1994.

[Was94] Michael Wasmund. Reuse facts and myths. In *ICSE 16* [ICS94], page 273. 1994.

[Weg83] Peter Wegner. Varieties of reusability. In Freeman [Fre87b], pages 30–44.

[Weg89] Peter Wegner. Capital-intensive software technology. In Biggerstaff and Perlis [BP89a], pages 43–97. 1989.

[Weg93] Peter Wegner. Towards component-based software technology. Technical Report No. CS-93-11, Brown University, 1993.

[Weg95] Peter Wegner. Interoperability. December 1995. Short Article.

[Weg96] Peter Wegner. Foundations of interactive computing. Technical Report CS-96-01, Brown University, 1996.

[WG82] Anthony Wasserman and S. Gutz. The future of programming. *Communications of the ACM*, 25(3):201, March 1982.

[WIS91] *WISR 4: 4th Workshop on Institutionalizing Software Reuse*, Reston, VA, November 18–22, 1991.
ftp://gandalf.umcs.maine.edu/pub/WISR/wisr4/.

[WIS92] *WISR 5: 5th Workshop on Institutionalizing Software Reuse*, California, October 1992.
ftp://gandalf.umcs.maine.edu/pub/WISR/wisr5/.

[WIS93] *WISR 6: 6th Workshop on Institutionalizing Software Reuse*, New York, November 1993.
ftp://gandalf.umcs.maine.edu/pub/WISR/wisr6/.

[WIS95] *WISR 7: 7th Workshop on Institutionalizing Software Reuse*, Illinois, August 1995.
ftp://gandalf.umcs.maine.edu/pub/WISR/wisr7/.

[WR94] Claes Wohlin and Per Runeson. Certification of software components. *IEEE Transactions on Software Engineering*, 20(6):494–499, June 1994.

[Yoc89] E. R. Yoches. Legal protection for computer software. *Communications of the ACM*, 32(2):169–171, February 1989.

[YR95] Aarne H. Ylä-Rotiala. How to convince the management? In *WISR 7* [WIS95]. 1995.

[Zal96] N.S. Zalman. Making the method fit: An industrial experience in adopting feature-oriented domain analysis (FODA). In Sitaraman [Sit96], pages 233–235. 1996.

[ZS95] Mansour Zand and Mansur Samadzadeh. Software reuse: Current status and trends (guest editor's corner). *The Journal of Systems and Software*, 30(3):167–170, September 1995.

Glossary

Ad-hoc reuse
  practice of *reuse* in an informal way without a *reuse* strategy and without organizational support for *reuse*
  – also called *individual reuse, opportunistic reuse*
  – contrast to *institutionalized reuse, planned reuse, systematic reuse*
  – compare with *centralized reuse, domain-based reuse, repository-based reuse*
  – see Section 4.3.1 (page 41), Section 4.3 (page 40)

Application engineering
  software engineering with *systematic reuse* of *components* and *domain* knowledge
  – compare with *component engineering, domain engineering*
  – see Chapter 15 (page 185)

Application group
  organizational unit responsible for the creation of *applications* (mainly *component consumers* performing *application engineering* tasks)
  – compare with *component group, domain group*
  – see Section 4.3.2 (page 41)

As-is reuse
  reusing *components* without modifying them
  – contrast to *reuse by adaptation*
  – compare with *black-box reuse, white-box reuse*
  – see Section 3.5 (page 28)

Black-box reuse
  reusing *components* without seeing, knowing or modifying any of their internals
  – contrast to *white-box reuse*
  – compare with *glass-box reuse, grey-box reuse*
  – see Section 3.5 (page 28)

Centralized reuse
  reuse with a *repository* that is accessed by various *application groups* and is administered by a *component group*

    — compare with *ad-hoc reuse, domain-based reuse, repository-based reuse*

    — see Section 4.3 (page 40)

Coarse-grained components

large-size *components* like subsystems and applications, e.g., databases

    — contrast to *fine-grained components*

    — see Section 9.2.2 (page 123)

Coarse-grained reuse

reuse of *coarse-grained components*

    — contrast to *fine-grained reuse*

Code scavenging

copying and modifying blocks of source code from an existing system

    — compare with *design scavenging*

    — see Section 3.4.2 (page 24)

Component

see *reusable software component*

Component adaptation

modifications as planned by *component* developers (e.g., parameterization) and/or as supported by *component* technology (e.g., inheritance)

    — compare with *component modification*

    — see Section 15.1.2 (page 187)

Component certification

ensuring that a *component* adheres to a specific set of quality guidelines

    — see Section 14.3 (page 174)

Component classification

grouping of similar *components* and attaching search information which can be used for *component* retrieval

    — compare with *component taxonomy*

    — see Section 14.5 (page 179)

Component composition

the process of constructing software systems by interconnecting *components* through well-defined ways of interaction and communication

    — compare with *component interoperation*

    — see Section 7.1 (page 83)

Component consumer

individual or group with a primary responsibility to *reuse* available *components*

    — contrast to *component producer*

    — see Section 4.3.3 (page 45)

Component granularity
the size of *components*, mainly classified in *fine-grained components* and *coarse-grained components*
– see Section 9.2.2 (page 123)

Component engineering
software development for *reuse*
– compare with *application engineering, domain engineering*
– see Chapter 14 (page 171)

Component group
organizational unit responsible for a *repository* of *components* (mainly *component producers* performing *component engineering* tasks)
– compare with *application group, domain group*
– see Section 4.3.2 (page 41)

Component interoperation
communication and cooperation of *components* despite differences in language, interfaces and platforms
– compare with *component composition*
– see Section 7.2 (page 98)

Component library
see *repository*

Component modification
modifications not planned by *component* developers or supported by *component* technology
– compare with *component adaptation*
– see Section 15.1.2 (page 187)

Component platform
additional software a *component* requires for its *reuse* (e.g., operating system, windows system, compiler, function library)
– see Section 6.3 (page 76)

Component producer
individual or group with a primary responsibility to create reusable *components*
– contrast to *component consumer*
– compare with *lone producer, nested producer, pool producer, team producer*
– see Section 4.3.3 (page 45)

Component repository
see *repository*

Component taxonomy
  a general classification of *components* (as opposed to the classification of particular *components*)
  - compare with *component classification*
  - see Chapter 9 (page 117)

Compositional reuse
  reuse of *components* which ideally remain unmodified and become part of the system to be composed
  - compare with *generative reuse*
  - see Section 3.4.2 (page 24)

Copyright protection
  protection of software itself, but not any underlying ideas and principles (most common form of software protection)
  - compare with *patent protection, trade secret protection*
  - see Section 4.1 (page 38)

Design pattern
  systematic naming, motivation and explanation of a general design that addresses a recurring design problem in object-oriented systems
  - see Section 3.6.6 (page 34)

Design scavenging
  copying large blocks of code, deleting many of the internal details, but retaining the global template of the design
  - compare with *Code scavenging*
  - see Section 3.4.2 (page 24)

Domain
  area of activity or knowledge containing applications that share common capabilities and data
  - see Chapter 13 (page 159)

Domain analysis
  identifying, collecting, organizing and representing relevant information in a *domain*
  - see Section 13.1 (page 160)

Domain-based reuse
  reuse with *repositories* for different *domains* that are accessed by various *application groups* and administered by *domain groups*
  - compare with *ad-hoc reuse, centralized reuse, repository-based reuse*
  - see Section 4.3 (page 40)

Domain boundary
defines a *domain*'s scope, i.e., what components, features and relationships belong to a *domain*
− see Section 13.2 (page 163)

Domain engineering
identifying candidate *domains* and performing *domain analysis* and *domain implementation*
− compare with *application engineering, component engineering*
− see Chapter 13 (page 159)

Domain expert
experienced person working and/or developing software in a certain *domain* (source of knowledge for *domain analysis*)
− see page 164 (Section 13.2.1)

Domain group
component group responsible for *components* in a certain *domain* (mainly *component producers* for a specific *domain* performing *domain engineering* and *component engineering* tasks)
− compare with *application group, component group*
− see Section 4.3.2 (page 41)

Domain implementation
building *components* using *domain analysis* products (*domain models*, domain languages, domain taxonomies, etc.)
− see Section 13.5 (page 168)

Domain model
identification of objects, operations and relationships that are likely to occur in more than one application and characterize applications in a *domain*
− see Section 13.1.2 (page 161)

Domain-specific reuse
see *vertical reuse*

External reuse
reuse of *components* which were originally written for other software systems
− contrast to *internal reuse*
− see Section 3.3 (page 23)

Fine-grained components
small-size *components* like functions, modules and classes, e.g., input/output functions, file access modules, etc.
− contrast to *coarse-grained components*

— see Section 9.2.2 (page 123)

Fine-grained reuse
   reuse of *fine-grained components*
   — contrast to *coarse-grained reuse*

General-purpose reuse, general reuse
   see *horizontal reuse*

Generative reuse
   reuse of a tool or generator that takes specifications as input and generates programs as output
   — compare with *compositional reuse*
   — see Section 3.4.3 (page 26)

Glass-box reuse
   reusing *components* by examination of both their internal structures and external interfaces, but not changing internals
   — compare with *black-box reuse, grey-box reuse, white-box reuse*
   — see Section 3.5 (page 28)

Grey-box reuse
   reuse of *components* by applying only minor changes to them
   — compare with *black-box reuse, glass-box reuse, white-box reuse*
   — see Section 3.5 (page 28)

Horizontal domain
   a *domain* addressing particular features across applications
   — compare with *vertical domain*
   — see page 160 (Section 13.1)

Horizontal reuse
   reuse of *components* across different *domains*
   — also called *general-purpose reuse, general reuse*
   — compare with *vertical reuse, domain-specific reuse*
   — see Section 3.3 (page 23)

Individual reuse
   see *ad-hoc reuse*

Initial investments
   investments needed in order to install a *reuse* program, including costs that do not directly support the completion of primary development goals but to make *components* of this development effort more reusable
   — see Section 4.2.1 (page 40)

Institutionalized reuse
   see *systematic reuse*

Internal reuse
multiple *reuse* of *components* within the software system for which they were originally written

- contrast to *external reuse*
- see Section 3.3 (page 23)

Large-scale reuse
systematic reuse of *coarse-grained components*

- contrast to *small-scale reuse*
- see Section 3.3 (page 23)

Lone producer
a single individual that handles the *reuse* needs of several *component consumers* (*application groups*)

- compare with *component producer, nested producer, pool producer, team producer*
- see Section 4.3 (page 40)

Nested producer
individual members of *application groups* that handle *reuse* needs and produce *components*

- compare with *component producer, lone producer, pool producer, team producer*
- see Section 4.3 (page 40)

Open component
component that has dependencies on *open platforms* only

- see Section 6.3.3 (page 80)

Open platform
see *open system*

Open system
vendor-transparent *platforms* in which users can mix and match hardware, software and networks from various vendors

- see Section 6.3.3 (page 80)

Opportunistic reuse
see *ad-hoc reuse*

Organized reuse
see *systematic reuse*

Patent protection
protection of technical inventions that are new and involve inventive steps

- compare with *copyright protection, trade secret protection*
- see Section 4.1 (page 38)

Planned reuse
see *systematic reuse*

Pool producer
two or more collaborating groups that handle *reuse* needs and produce *components*
— compare with *component producer, lone producer, nested producer, team producer*
— see Section 4.3 (page 40)

Portability
ease with which a *component* can be transferred from one computer system or environment to another
— see Section 6.3.3 (page 80)

Repository
a database for the storage and retrieval of *components*, including their documentation and classification information
— see Section 14.4 (page 178)

Repository-based reuse
a *repository* is accessed by various *application groups*; any *components* can be put into the *repository*; there is no control over their quality and usefulness
— compare with *ad-hoc reuse, centralized reuse, domain-based reuse*
— see Section 4.3 (page 40)

Return on investment
ratio of *reuse* savings to generalization costs
— see page 50 (Section 4.4.3)

Reusability
the extent to which a *component* can be reused in multiple systems

Reusable software component
self-contained, clearly identifiable piece that describes and/or performs specific functions and has clear interfaces, appropriate documentation and a defined *reuse* status
— see Section 6.1 (page 68)

Reuse
process of creating software systems from existing software *components* rather than building them from scratch
— see Section 2.1 (page 9)

Reuse by adaptation
reusing *components* by first adapting them

— contrast to *as-is reuse*
— compare with *black-box reuse, white-box reuse*
— see Section 3.5 (page 28)

Reuse effectiveness
ratio of *reuse* benefits to *reuse* costs

— compare with *reuse maturity*
— see page 52 (Section 4.4.4)

Reuse efficiency
ratio of the percentage of exploited *reuse* opportunities to the percentage
of intended *reuse* opportunities

— compare with *reuse maturity*
— see page 51 (Section 4.4.4)

Reuse intention
defines how *components* are used, e.g., *black-box reuse/white-box reuse,
as-is reuse/reuse by adaptation*

— see Section 3.5 (page 28)

Reuse level
ratio of reused *components* (their lines of code) to the total *components*
of a software system (total amount of code)

— see page 48 (Section 4.4.1)

Reuse library
see *repository*

Reuse maturity
indication of how effective and systematic an organization is at *reuse*

— compare with *reuse effectiveness, reuse efficiency, reuse proficiency*
— see Section 4.3.4 (page 47)

Reuse maturity model
model to assess *reuse maturity*

— see Section 4.3.4 (page 47)

Reuse mode
defines how *reuse* is conducted, e.g., *ad-hoc reuse/planned reuse, opportunistic reuse/systematic reuse*

— see Section 4.3.1 (page 41)

Reuse proficiency
ratio of actual *reuse* to potential *reuse*, i.e., ratio of the percentage of
exploited *reuse* opportunities to the percentage of potential *reuse* opportunities

— compare with *reuse maturity*

– see page 51 (Section 4.4.4)

Reuse product
product to be reused, e.g., specification, design, architectures, source code, documentation
– see Section 3.6 (page 31)

Reuse scope
form and extent of *reuse*, e.g., *vertical reuse/horizontal reuse*, *internal reuse/external reuse*, *small-scale reuse/large-scale reuse*
– see Section 3.3 (page 23)

Reuse substance
the essence of reused items, e.g., ideas, concepts, *components*, procedures, skills
– see Section 3.2 (page 22)

Reuse technique
the approach to implement *reuse*, e.g., *compositional reuse/generative reuse*
– see Section 3.4 (page 24)

Search effectiveness
effectiveness of *component* search, measured by *search recall* and *search precision*
– compare with *search precision, search recall*
– see Section 14.5.7 (page 183)

Search precision
ratio of relevant *components* retrieved to the total number of *components* retrieved
– compare with *search effectiveness, search recall*
– see Section 14.5.7 (page 183)

Search recall
ratio of the number of relevant *components* retrieved to the number of relevant *components* in the *repository*
– compare with *search effectiveness, search precision*
– see Section 14.5.7 (page 183)

Small-scale reuse
ad-hoc reuse of *fine-grained components*
– contrast to *large-scale reuse*
– see Section 3.3 (page 23)

Software component
see *reusable software component*

Software engineering
the cost-effective production of high-quality software systems
- compare with *application engineering*
- see Chapter 11 (page 143)

Software repository
see *repository*

Software reuse
see *reuse*

Systematic reuse
reuse based on a formal process model
- also called *institutionalized reuse, organized reuse, planned reuse*
- contrast to *ad-hoc reuse, individual reuse, opportunistic reuse*
- see Section 4.3.1 (page 41)

Team producer
groups of *component producers* interacting with groups of *component consumers*
- compare with *component producer, lone producer, nested producer, pool producer*
- see Section 4.3 (page 40)

Trade secret protection
protection of the know-how that is embodied in software
- compare with *copyright protection, patent protection*
- see Section 4.1 (page 38)

Vertical domain
a *domain* addressing all levels of a single application area
- compare with *horizontal domain*
- see page 160 (Section 13.1)

Vertical reuse
reuse of *components* in a specific *domain*
- also called *domain-specific reuse*
- compare with *horizontal reuse, general-purpose reuse*
- see Section 3.3 (page 23)

White-box reuse
reusing *components* through examination and use of both their external interfaces and their internal structures
- contrast to *black-box reuse*
- compare with *glass-box reuse, grey-box reuse*
- see Section 3.5 (page 28)

Index